# GENDER & SEXUALITY
## FOR BEGINNERS

# GENDER & SEXUALITY
## FOR BEGINNERS®

### BY JAIMEE GARBACIK
### ILLUSTRATED BY JEFFREY LEWIS

FOR BEGINNERS®

For Beginners LLC
155 Main Street, Suite 211
Danbury, CT 06810 USA
www.forbeginnersbooks.com

A For Beginners® Documentary Comic Book
Copyright © 2013

Cataloging-in-Publication information is available from the Library of Congress.

ISBN # 978-1-934389-69-0 Trade

Manufactured in the United States of America

For Beginners® and Beginners Documentary Comic Books® are published by For Beginners LLC.

First Edition

10  9  8  7  6  5  4  3  2

# CONTENTS

# WHO SAID THAT?

Hate flipping to the back of the book every time you want to know where a quote came from or who performed a particular study? For Beginners has created the **Gender & Sexuality For Beginners Supplemental Reference Guide** for an easier reading and teaching experience!

The guide includes the author's end notes, bibliography, and additional resources and is downloadable at:

**http://www.forbeginnersbooks.com/genderandsexualityfb.html**

By the way, the above quote is from feminist scholar Elizabeth Grosz's essay, "Experimental Desire: Rethinking Queer Subjectivity." *

---

*Grosz, Elizabeth. "Experimental Desire: Rethinking Queer Subjectivity."
In Joan Copjec, ed. *Supposing the Subject*. London: Verso, 1994, 133–157.
As quoted in Annamarie Jagose. *Queer Theory: An Introduction*,
Melbourne: Melbourne University Press, 1996, 89.

# INTRODUCTION

Emerging in the turbulent 1960s, and growing considerable strength during the 90s, sexual orientation is now one of the most divisive topics in any political debate. Between ending "Don't Ask, Don't Tell," the push for gay marriage, and numerous gay teen suicides in the news, LGBT issues can no longer be ignored. And so, understandably, many believe that sexual orientation is the American civil liberties issue of our time. But while seeking some very specific (and no doubt important) freedoms, I worry that we are ignoring an even larger problem.

If you ask young people what the most pressing issue of our time is, you will receive a myriad of answers, from racism or sexism to transphobia and homophobia, poverty and classism—even climate change or the economy. It is all too easy to attribute the diversity of answers to a difference in opinion or priority. I think it is subtler than that. I think that the majority of these concerns, so many of which have a suffix attached to indicate hatred or fear, are so interwoven, so connected in their essential nature, that they are inextricable, and to some degree, to name one is to name them all.

To me, and to many other LGBTQIA (lesbian, gay, genderqueer, bisexual, transgender, transsexual, questioning, queer, intersex, ally, and asexual) people, feminists, activists, educators, and allies, much of the disparity is rooted in gender. Equality cannot truly be attained on the basis of sexual orientation or even the righteous call for feminism—which, in its most essential construction, asserts a need for consciousness raising about gender equality. Because what does sexual orientation even mean if the very categories of gender are in question? How do we measure gender equality when our society's definitions of "male" and "female" leave out much of the population? There is no consensus on what a "real" man or woman is, where one's sex begins and ends, or what purpose the categories of masculine and feminine traits serve. To me, it is simplest to say that these categories are inadequate, that they fail to describe us, and leave many people not just in the margins, but in the cold.

My concern is first and foremost for young people. I often find myself wanting to yell out that intersex teens are always falling through the cracks, that transgender kids are dying left and right—but as seventeen-year-old femme educator Hanna King once told me, "Queer kids have been killing themselves as long as I've known them. This is nothing new. It's just that some upwardly mobile suburban white kids tried it, so now people are paying attention."

To be fair, no one really knows exactly how many queer kids of any race, social class, or economic background have committed suicide. Many queer youths try to avoid being bullied by keeping their orientation and gender identity a secret. Some queer young people are not accepted by their families, and face the dour options of abuse or homelessness. Few grieving parents publicize their kid's LGBTQIA status, and deaths on the street do not always get properly attributed.

In other words, many queer suicides stay out of the statistics. What we do know is that "out" queer teens are attempting suicide at more than four times the rate of their heterosexual identified peers. In fact, 30 percent of lesbian, gay, and bisexual youths attempt suicide between the age of fifteen and twenty-four. That's more than one in four. While suicide is already the third most common cause of adolescent deaths in the United States, it is likely that the leading cause of death for queer teens in America is suicide.

So yes, I'm glad people are finally paying attention, but sorrowful that more young lives were lost before the public began to take notice. I'm grateful that there are tens of thousands of It Gets Better Project videos and that some kids will see them and know what queer looks like when they grow up. I'm even happier to see young people making their own videos, educating others, and advocating for themselves. After all, no one should have to wait until they grow up to live safely and visibly or to seek happiness. Nor should LGBTQIA people of any age be frequently faced with discrimination, poverty, or abuse so devastating that survival becomes the only goal.

But like I said, this is what's simplest for me to say. What's more complicated and frustrating and utterly, unmistakably true is that even in LGBTQIA communities or among feminists, inclusivity is difficult to attain. Though our struggles are overlapping, we are oppressed as individuals, one by one. It is unfortunate, but not surprising, that in our desire to form alliances under one label or issue, we often silence others and exclude potential allies. As soon as you call it "a war on ___," and fill in that blank with "the gender binary," "heteronormativity," "racism," "classism," "sexism," or any other classification—inevitably other people who face related oppressions get left out.

Early feminist groups alienated lesbians and people of color because they were afraid of social stigma derailing their primary goal of equality for women. Gay and lesbian communities have long marginalized bisexuals and transgender people. Intersex people are frequently left out of LGBT issues and forums, despite facing many of the same concerns about gender archetypes. Asexuality is seldom included in discussions of sexual orientation. Youth voices are almost universally undervalued. And accessibility for disabled, poor, or illiterate people is generally treated as an afterthought, even by some of the most intentional and accountable organizations. We keep leaving people behind in favor of the simplest, most easily digested vision of an empowered future.

We look for someone charismatic to ignite the rallying cry, and in our search for valiant leadership we forget many of the most necessary participants. We fail to include people who, on the ground level, have to lead the day-to-day battles that effect real, measurable change.

Progressive educators understand this: how class is connected to education, and how access to education and opportunities for success are related to discrimination on the basis of race, sex, disability, and so on. But education is overseen and overruled by public policy. Legislators and politicians tackle the issues individually. Even most activists settle on one primary issue so that they can air their grievances concisely and reach more people. I am often afraid that oppression is a war with too many fronts to identify a primary battle; we only know that it needs discussing. Just as surely as in the early days of the AIDS epidemic, we know that silence is death—this has always been true.

The people most motivated to stand up and demand better solutions are those who have the most at stake and the most to lose: the youth. I find that young people are less afraid to hold one another and their politicians, educators, parents, and community accountable. Their voices make all the difference. They tell new, more complicated stories than the ones replicated in our current textbooks and media. Young people are loathe to reduce complicated humans to genitals, hormones, and chromosomes that do not adequately explain or represent anyone's strengths, weaknesses, personalities, or identities. They assert how getting married works against many disabled people's access to aid and health care. How ethnicity, race, and creed often fall by the wayside in gay and lesbian activism. How we are defeating ourselves with labels that divide the oppressed into smaller categories. Such categories can never be as strong as the sum total of everyone who struggles for accountable policies and visibility.

It is the responsibility of all adults to educate ourselves and each other, and to align with the youth. Young people must be empowered to inform policy. They often have a much better idea of what they need than adults do. The more adults trust and listen to young people, the more visibility and access they attain, the better we will all become at articulating how labels are barriers. It is my position that despite many diverse battles, this is ultimately one fight. Young people understand intuitively the limited rhetoric of "us vs. them." They find it ridiculous that in America a gold standard of white, heterosexual, cisgender, male, middle class, and adult has emerged. America is championed as a veritable melting pot of all of the excluded, marginalized people from everywhere else. Our variety makes us strong, equipped with diverse ideas and innovations. If we forget this, it will be our undoing. Young people believe, as I do, that it is possible to make alignments without deleting personal histories. By being more inclusive, we will surely have fewer apologies to make later.

In the process of writing this book, I interviewed service providers and academics, activists, and many queer young people. It was a life-altering experience to hear their stories, and perhaps even more so to hear young people's expectations for the future. In some cases, they weren't expecting much, which was heartbreaking and unfair, and to them, utterly realistic. But this almost never reflected a flagging in their will to effect change and to bring it about by pushing for awareness about the interconnected nature of these issues. They were not daunted by the difficulty of interdisciplinary work. They thought it a lazy concession to compartmentalize gay and lesbian, bisexual, transgender, queer, intersex, and asexual issues, or to separate them from class, disability, age, race, and citizenship concerns. They consider it a blatant lie to rely solely on these rather nondescript labels that do not include everyone. They find it indefensible to sell out their friends, who may not fit any of the categories we've come up with yet. Young people are not content to wait for adults' rules, policies, curricula, and media to catch up with them.

I know this book is an inadequate discussion of some really complicated issues, none of which I am a scholar of. I did my best to provide a balanced, accessible, and on-the-ground account of gender and sexuality in this country. I am sure I left some people and many ideas out; this book is part of a series, and it's necessarily a "starting point," I tried only to cover some basics with which to build a lexicon to catapult further exploration, and to illuminate some of the discrimination in our society that limits every citizen's aptitude and personal expression. I hope it furthers the conversation about gender, sexuality, feminism, LGBTQIA concerns, and interconnected oppression—human issues. I hope at least one or two readers become more conscious of the impact of their actions and assumptions. And I especially hope it arms some young people with the courage to seek more information. I want to hear them raise their voices against the idea that this world is not yet theirs to claim and improve.

To the communities whose lives and identities this book addresses: Thank you for the opportunity to be heard, to bring attention to your messages and concerns as best I can, but never, ever to speak for you.

This book is in utter and total dedication to the young people that power The Vera Project and Reteaching Gender and Sexuality; two organizations that truly embody the ideas and principles of which I am writing. *Veri et recti amici.* True and sincere friends.

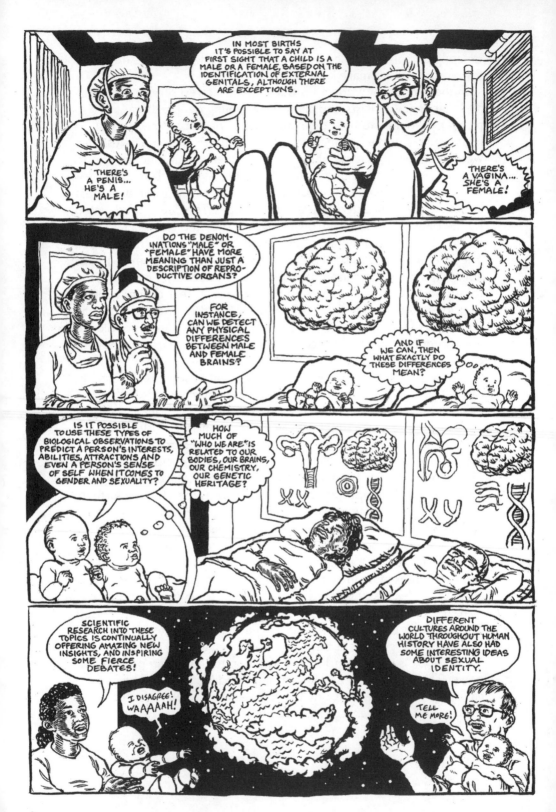

# CHAPTER 1

# THE BIOLOGY OF SEX AND GENDER

When do we first become aware of gender? Is it when certain clothing or toys are given to us to match a culturally specific model of how a child should look and play? Is it when we see genitals other than our own and are forced to compare and contrast? Or maybe the first time we truly process the idea of gender occurs when checking off a box to identify ourselves, almost invariably as either "male" or "female."

Neurobiologists often suggest that the formation of gender identity starts much earlier than any of these events. Some say that gender is simply embedded in our genes. Others believe that the introduction of particular hormones in the womb shape how we will emerge. It is commonly held that the number of X vs. Y chromosomes an individual has in their cells provides the basic determination of an individual's sex. And yet, few contest that chromosomes fall quite shy of explaining the roles and patterns of behavior that are associated in our society with being a man or a woman. What's more, there are plenty of individuals who don't fall neatly into either of these categories, either biologically speaking or with regards to their personality and sense of identity. And, of course, being a man or a woman (as well as combinations thereof and other identity classifications entirely) has meant different things to different cultures throughout the

---

## SEX VS. GENDER: A BASIC GLOSSARY

One's "sex" refers to the physical attributes that distinguish between typical male, female, and intersex people. "Gender," on the other hand, refers to the behaviors, activities, roles, and actions that are socially attributed to boys, girls, men, women, and transgender people in a given society. Descriptions of genders and gender roles differ in each culture, and many people's gender (or genders) do not match the socially-designated attributes of the sex that they are assigned at birth. The term "gender identity" describes the gender that a person inhabits, experiences, and expresses in their daily life.

"Sexuality" refers to desire and attraction. One's "sexual orientation" indicates who one is generally attracted to, emotionally, romantically, and/or sexually. People can be attracted to members of their own sex or a different sex, to more than one sex or gender, or not experience attraction at all. Some people also have emotional and romantic feelings for people they are not sexually attracted to (or sexual attraction to someone they do not have romantic or emotional feelings for); this also falls under one's sexual orientation. A "sexual identity" describes how someone feels about or relates to their sex, gender(s), and sexual orientation.

course of history. These categories continue to evolve as economics, politics, popular culture, art, science, and other factors shift society's perception of itself, and alter the roles which comprise our collective and individual sense of identity.

When examining gender as a category, one of the first distinctions we explore is dividing people on the basis of their genitals, hormones, or chromosomes. Although, is this not as arbitrary as dividing the world up on the basis of left- and right-handedness or by eye color? Such logic may be valid in theory, but dividing people on the basis of handedness or eye color would ignore the historical and cultural meaning, weight, and power assigned to a man or a woman. On the other hand, separating people according to genitals, hormones, and chromosomes ignores the experience of transgender, intersex, androgynous, and genderqueer people (to name a few categories).

For this discussion, the categories of male and female will be overrepresented due to the amount of pertinent study that has strictly attended to those two identities. It should nevertheless be noted that on almost every continent throughout history, a variety of cultures have acknowledged more than two genders. Western society's currently rigid description of people as deterministically "one or the other" leaves little room for variation in one's experience of a mixed or changing gender identity, gender expression, or variance within what the words "men" and "women" signify. Even progressive terms like "transgender" are sometimes employed in ways that imply that there are

## SEX ASSIGNMENT AND GENDER DOCUMENTATION

It is telling that very few surveys, tests, or paperwork requiring someone to check a box noting their sex or gender provide alternative options to "male" or "female." In the majority of binding legal, medical, and governmental documentation it is assumed that gender is fixed, assigned at birth, and has no room to evolve, change, or fall outside those two boxes. When a doctor signs a legally binding birth certificate, they personally and permanently assign a child's sex, which can only be changed through complex legal proceedings that vary by state.

CHECK ONE:

FEMALE ☐

MALE ☐

## GENETICS 101

DNA contains the genetic instructions that manage the development of all living organisms. These molecules store information in a codelike fashion. The segments carrying this data are referred to as genes. Genes pass on traits between generations of organisms and determine what characteristics each individual organism will inherit. For example, there is a gene for eye color.

A chromosome is a structure of DNA and protein that is found in cells. Chromosomes organize DNA into a discrete package that regulates its genes' meaning and expression. In humans, there are two kinds of chromosomes: autosomes and sex chromosomes. The traits which are connected to someone's sex are transmitted through their sex chromosomes. All other hereditary information resides in autosomes. All human cells contain 23 pairs of nuclear chromosomes—1 pair of sex chromosomes and 22 pairs of autosomes.

Most people have one pair of sex chromosomes per cell; usually, females have two X chromosomes and males have one X and one Y. Both sexes retain one of their mother's X chromosomes, and females inherit a second X chromosome from their father. Males inherit their father's Y chromosome instead.

Although X chromosomes contain several thousand genes, almost none (if any) relate specifically to the determination of sex. As females develop in the womb, one of their X chromosomes is almost always deactivated in all cells (except for in egg cells). This process guarantees that both males and females have one working copy of the X chromosome in each cell. The Y chromosome contains the SRY gene which prompts testes to develop, distinguishing male organisms from females. Y chromosomes also house the genes that produce sperm.

"normally" two sexes (male and female) and two genders (man and woman). This leaves out equally legitimate identities such as "nádleehí," a designation in Navajo culture for an individual who considers themself both a boy and a girl. The Navajo are far from the only culture with a malleable concept of gender identity, but Western traditions have marginalized all but a binary notion of gender, and by extension, the sexuality of those genders.

MALE = OF OR DENOTING THE SEX THAT PRODUCES SMALL, TYPICALLY MOTILE GAMETES.

In the Oxford English Dictionary, a male is "of or denoting the sex that produces small, typically motile gametes, especially spermatozoa, with which a female may be fertilized or inseminated to produce offspring." This definition is strictly biological, and refers only to a male's ability to impregnate a fe-

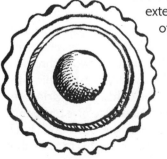

FEMALE = OF OR DENOTING THE SEX THAT CAN BEAR OFFSPRING OR PRODUCE EGGS.

male. To some biologists, this is the only characteristic which differentiates the male sex in an inarguable fashion. A female, by contrast, is "of or denoting the sex that can bear offspring or produce eggs, distinguished biologically by the production of gametes (ova) that can be fertilized by male gametes." By this account, an animal, plant, or human is a female if "she" can produce eggs and therefore bear children or offspring.

Doctors assign humans' sex at birth on the basis of genitalia, not the ability to reproduce. Likewise, doctors seldom check individuals to verify whether or not they have XX or XY chromosomes, but generally assume the presence of a penis or a vagina is indicative of these chromosome pairings.

This is not always the case, as with intersex people who may have both male and female genitalia, atypical genital and/or reproductive anatomy, or ambiguous sex characteristics. Being intersex is relatively common, occurring in 1.7 percent of the population. Intersex people sometimes have gonosomes (sex chromosomes) that are different from the most typical XX-female or XY-male presentations. According to the Intersex Society of North America, intersex genitals "may signal an underlying metabolic concern, but they themselves are not diseased; they just look different. Metabolic concerns should be treated medically, but [intersex] genitals are not in need of medical treatment."

CHROMOSOME

> ## VIRILITY AND FERTILITY
> Legally-speaking, a woman who cannot conceive or a man who cannot inseminate a female is not considered any less representative of their sex. Still, there are definitely social connotations surrounding women's infertility and men's virility. For example, men who are impotent (or assumed to be on the basis of exhibiting fewer masculine traits) are sometimes mocked by their peers. Likewise, women who are unable to bear children or choose not to sometimes experience stigmatization.

Despite the fact that intersex genitals do not require treatment, there is a history of medical practitioners stepping in and performing surgeries that carry significant risk to intersex infants which has had a pathologizing effect on intersex people and their families. As biologist, historian, and feminist Anne Fausto-Sterling explains, "If a child is born with two X chromosomes, oviducts, ovaries, and a uterus on the inside, but a penis and scrotum on the outside ... is the child a boy or a girl? Most doctors declare the child a girl, despite the penis, because of her potential to give birth, and intervene using surgery and hormones to carry out the decisions. [But] choosing which criteria to use in determining sex, and choosing to make the determination at all, are social decisions for which scientists can offer no absolute guidelines." Because these "normalizing" surgeries are generally irreversible, if they are performed at birth or in infancy without the individual's consent, they also run a serious risk of assigning a sex that may not fit the child's identification when they grow up.

## INTERSEX SURGERIES TODAY

While "normalizing" surgeries are now less commonly advised at birth by medical professionals, some parents of intersex infants still request them. Individuals with intersex characteristics may more safely opt for a surgery later in life to more clearly distinguish their sex. Such a surgery is not automatically necessary or desirable for life or health. It is usually performed mainly to ease social and sexual interactions, or to help an intersex person achieve a lack of ambiguity about their gender. These surgeries can sometimes result in difficulty with sexual functioning later in life, in problems with fertility, continence, or sensation; they can also be life-threatening.

Aside from chromosomes and genitals, there are other physical characteristics that are commonly used to distinguish between males and females, but they are far from foolproof and do not indicate one's gender identity. Secondary sex characteristics are physical features that occur more frequently in either male or female members of a species, which do not relate to reproduction or sex organs. In humans, most secondary sex characteristics are fairly similar in male and female children until puberty, when hormone levels increase and result in both similar and different changes to the body.

In males, once puberty hits, facial and body hair growth occurs (abdominal, chest, underarm, and pubic), as well as a possible loss of scalp hair, enlargement of the larynx, and a deepened voice. Their shoulders and chest will broaden as they gain more muscle mass, a heavier skull and bone structure, and larger stature in general (males, on average, are taller than females). A male's face will also become more square, and their waist will narrow (though it typically remains wider than in females).

Females, by contrast, experience breast growth and nipple erection during puberty, as well as widening of their hips, and a rounder face. Females generally develop smaller hands and feet than males. They grow some body hair during puberty as well, but it is mostly limited to the underarm and pubic areas. Their upper arms are generally a bit longer than men's, proportionately, and their weight distribution will change, distributing more fat into the thighs, hips, and buttocks. There are also a variety of other changes occurring in puberty to male and female sex organs, but these are not considered secondary sex characteristics.

Sometimes individual or several secondary male sex characteristics may be present in a female-identified person, or the reverse, complicating a "common sense" definition of what makes a "man" or "woman." For example, some males retain erect nipples or develop tissue in their pectoral muscles, resulting in a chest similar in appearance to female breasts. Many females grow some facial hair on their chin or upper lip, or have square jaw lines. People of both sexes often have larger or smaller feet, hands, thighs, or buttocks than is typical of their assigned sex. Plenty of males are short or have high voices; lots of females are tall or have low voices. Suffice to say, while secondary sex characteristics describe the "average" male and female traits, very few real people fit neatly into that "average" box.

It is possible to use gonads (gametes that make ova or sperm; i.e., ovaries and testicles) and chromosomes as the basis for differentiating females from males, but this leaves a lot of gray area regarding many people's more ambiguous primary or secondary sex characteristics. While the vast majority of babies' genitalia may be clearly regarded as biologically male or female, their chromosomes may not reflect that assigned sex. They may develop secondary sex characteristics later that complicate that definition. Furthermore, once one's sex is assigned, the way in which an infant is treated by its parents, caretakers, and everyone they meet will be profoundly shaped by assumptions about the child's sex. Being raised as a boy, girl, a combination of the two, or identifying as neither is in many respects an entirely separate concern from one's sex.

## ONLY TWO SEXES?

Recently, the "general reducibility" of the biological sexes to male and female has been called into serious question by various biological researchers and feminists who posit that beliefs about gender may "affect what kinds of knowledge scientists produce about sex." For example, grouping and sampling methods may reflect and reinforce ideas of "hardwired" sex-specific intelligence and behaviors in studies that seek to examine sex differences in the brain. Without these preconceptions, it's possible that we might find several distinct sexes, or at least a blurrier boundary between males and females.

Gender differs from one's assigned sex in that it can be self-defined. Doctors may look at a baby's genitals and say that it is a male, but the baby itself, in tandem with their parents' rearing and social experiences, will ultimately define what gender it is identified as. The distinction between a biological sex and a gender "role" was first introduced by the work of sexologist John Money in 1955. Before that, "gender" was strictly a grammatical term that referred to words with masculine or feminine connotations within a given culture. For example, in most languages derived from Latin ("romance languages," which are part of the Indo-European language family, and include French, Catalan, Italian, Portuguese, Romanian, Spanish, and others), many nouns are assigned a gender and corresponding pronoun. In Spanish, chairs, cities, and radios are a few random nouns which are considered feminine, while plates, hearts, and days of the week are deemed masculine.

One's "sex," on the other hand, was formerly used all-inclusively to describe someone's body and identity without any consideration of a possible distinction. Money's definition of the word "gender" spread to popular culture and usage in the 1970s when feminists began to debate the rigid categories of social roles for men and women. Today, cultural models of male and female roles greatly influence the opportunities, behaviors, and personality profiles that are assumed to correspond to one's gender. The impact gender has on a person's experience necessitates analyzing whether (or to what degree) gender is biological as opposed to culturally imposed, or shaped by one's environment and raising.

JOHN MONEY (1921-2006)

## CISGENDER

As defined by sociologists Kristen Schilt and Laurel Westbrook, "cisgender" is a label that describes all "individuals who have a match between the gender they were assigned at birth, their bodies, and their personal identity." A cisgender woman, for example, is someone whose body fits into our society's description of a female body, who was called a "girl" at birth, and who sees herself as female or a woman. Most of the test subjects used in the studies in this chapter to examine brain structure and hormone levels were cisgender people, which, it may be argued, make the studies more narrow and less inclusive. From the viewpoint of the scientists, though, the subjects were likely selected that way in order to keep the results as clear and uncomplicated as possible.

## SEXOLOGY

Sexology is the scientific study of human sexuality, including sexual interests, behavior, and function. Sexologists primarily study puberty, sexual orientation, sexual relationships, sexual intercourse, and sexual disorders or dysfunctions.

From a neurological standpoint, scientists have been debating for some time about the differences between men and women's brains, and by extension, their abilities, personalities, and tendencies. It was once believed that male and female brains developed differently in utero in nonhuman animals, and that mating and bearing children was, for them, a hardwired instinct. Scientists thought that sex differences in humans, by contrast, came purely from how children were raised. Today, some studies show neurological differences between typical male and female brains prior to birth, but again, many scientists question the methods by which these differences are ascertained. If it turns out to be true that male and female infants have measurable brain differences, the way in which a child is socialized and treated by its parents and peers would still have tremendous impact, perhaps equal to or even surpassing any biological hardwiring. What's more, the alleged brain distinctions in no way appear to be predictive of behavior, gender-specific interests, or cognitive strengths and weaknesses.

According to Louann Brizendine, a prominent neuropsychiatrist, all brains begin as female, until eight weeks after conception, when testosterone present in males shrinks the communication center of their brains, reduces the hearing cortex, and makes the part of the brain that processes thoughts about sexual activity twice as large. She believes that male and female infants do not enter the world with the same brain structure, that the communication and emotional memory center is larger in the female brain, and that male brains have more cells which correspond to aggression.

Contrary to arguments for the importance of socialization, Brizendine contends that hormones triggered at different stages in women's lives relate to their capacity to cope with stress, the desire to pursue one's own interests, concern for others' emotions, and even to the desire to be attractive. Brizendine thinks these hormones stimulate an interest in procreating, childbirth, and nursing at different stages of a woman's life, and affect their behavior and emotions. She essentially says that if you give a female child a toy truck, she will invariably cuddle it.

Moods are certainly affected by hormones, and over time they can help to shape our sense of how we see the world. Just as ingesting chocolate (which contains theobromine, a stimulant similar to caffeine) or wine (which acts as a depressant, slowing down one's heart rate and breathing) can shift one's attitude by altering the chemicals in our brains, Brizendine believes that hormones cause male and female brains to form entirely different structures that stimulate, explain, and categorize our impulses and desires. For example, the pituitary gland produces fertility hormones, affects milk production, and, in Brizendine's opinion, turns on the "nurturing behavior" switch in women. The anterior cingulate cortex (or ACC), on the other hand, helps people to weigh options, make decisions, and is the "worrying center" of the brain; according to Brizendine's interpretation of the studies she cites, the ACC is larger in women.

Her conclusions have struck a common sense chord in many readers, as they reinforce archetypal behavior for men and women in our society, but Brizendine's sex-specific structures do not have a reputable basis in scientific research. She pointedly mentions her dismay at learning that many neurological studies are based on males alone, yet several of the studies Brizendine cites to demonstrate sex-based differences used only male or female participants. Brizendine nevertheless calls on these studies to make sexed contrasts that are necessarily speculative. In fact, numerous reviews of her book, *The Female Brain* (2006), found that "despite the author's extensive academic credentials … [t]he text is rife with 'facts' that do not exist in the supporting references."

Even when researchers are meticulous, there are a number of drawbacks to considering the size and function of brain regions as direct proof that gender is rooted in brain structure. Likewise, there are concerns when assuming that "gender-specific" behavior and strengths can be understood by examining male and female brains. For starters, human brains definitely cannot be as easily "sexed" as Brizendine describes (that is, consistently sorted into "male" and "female"), and in many researchers' opinions, they can't be sexed at all. In *Brain Storm* (2010), sociomedical scientist Rebecca M. Jordan-Young asserts, "In spite of much trumpeting that there exist 'female brains' and 'male brains,' the extent and nature of physical differences in the brains of human females and males is highly controversial, with some scientists claiming there are no clear-cut differences, others claiming that there are some subtle average differences, and still others claiming that the differences are dramatic." Jordan-Young rebukes the notion that there are sex-related centers in the brain at all, much less that men's are much larger. She explains that while there is a small cell group in the hypothalamus that is generally larger in men (the $INAH_3$), and it *may* be related to some aspect of sexual function (or something "as nonpsychological as menstruation"), no one knows yet what it does. There's no evidence at all that it's related to "processing thoughts about sex," as Brizendine claims. Jordan-Young goes on to say that literally no reported sex differences in other areas of the brain have "held up to independent replication." In other words, when researchers attempt to retry one another's experiments on brain structure differences to check the conclusions, not a single one has been able to yield the same results.

A perfect example of this is the corpus callosum. A large bundle of nerve fibers that connect the two hemispheres of the brain, the corpus callosum's varying size and structure has been credited as explaining almost every strength and ability that has been attributed at one point or another to sex. From affirming the holistic thinking of women or men's visuospatial skills, to the female intuition and superior communication skills that Brizendine describes, this "slice" of the brain is given a lot of weight.

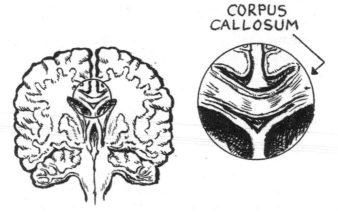

CORPUS CALLOSUM

Unfortunately, the corpus callosum is a nearly impossible region of the brain to partition off. The fibers aren't really separable from other brain portions, and the fibers themselves are tangled and do not lay flat. Methods for actually examining parts of the corpus callosum are disparate and highly debated. What's more, in Anne Fausto-Sterling's examination of numerous scientific papers based on the corpus callosum, all of which used the newest and greatest technology, no one found absolute size differences. The only differences found were in adults, offering no conclusive evidence about children or fetuses' structure before conditioning.

Moreover, as science journalist Sharon Begley pointed out in a 1995 *Newsweek* cover story, even if the studies alleging that the corpus callosum is larger in females are correct, there is another problem: "A bigger corpus callosum matters only if it has more neurons, the cells that carry communications. After all, fat phone cables carry more conversations only if they contain more wires. But despite years of searching, scientists cannot say for sure that women's corpus callosum has more neurons." Add to this the obvious preference in the approach and analysis of sex and gender research for finding differences instead of similarities, which Jordan-Young thinks encourages scientists to overstate even very modest findings. Pretty soon, it starts to almost seem strange that we don't see *more* sex differences in the brain, if only because of differing male and female reproductive abilities.

99 percent of male and female DNA coding is the same. That said, a one percent difference influences every cell in our bodies. Studies show that mothers respond more to the facial expressions of female children, particularly with regards to their happiness. So it may be true that infant girls' skill with eye contact and face gazing improves 400 percent in the first few months, while boy babies' skills in this area remain stagnant, but how can we be sure that this is not simply an adaption to the habits of the mother? Perhaps brains simply develop in response to the way that we stimulate them. In other words, assuming scientists could eliminate all the problems in conducting brain studies, how would we know that any neurological differences they may find are innate?

While one can hotly debate Brizendine's analysis of the hormones at play in a female brain and their corresponding relationship to women's behavior, her assertion that a surge in testosterone typically occurs in utero for males and not females appears fairly incontrovertible. The impact that testosterone has on development and any developmental differentiation between the sexes, however, warrants some closer examination.

Let's take a look at how hormones first came to be associated with gender and sex: For starters, farmers have known for centuries that castration (or removing the gonads) changes the body and demeanor of animals. Yet it was not until British gynecologist William Blair-Bell declared that social sex differences and hormones were related, that gonads stopped being regarded as the fundamental sex distinction. Anne Fausto-Sterling notes in her research that once scientists began to measure male and female hormones, all of the changes those hormones produced gained a sexed connotation.

Despite the fact that testosterone and estrogen affect nerves, blood, the heart, bones, and kidneys, these non-reproductive areas are considered secondary to what is viewed as hormones' main function—the differentiation of the male and female.

DNA

## EMBRYOLOGY
Embryologists study embryos from fertilization to the fetus stage. Embryology is "the branch of biology that deals with the formation, early growth, and development of living organisms."

As early as 1915, scientists were at an impasse about whether chromosomes or hormones defined sex development, until an embryologist named Frank Rattray Lillie demonstrated how the two could work hand-in-hand. Lillie conducted a series of experiments with calves where "a genetic female whose development [was] altered by hormones from her twin brother" produced a "masculinized" female. Essentially, he laid the foundation work for the view that genes determine the basis for sex distinction, and hormones continue to shape masculine or feminine characteristics afterward.

Male levels of testosterone prompt growth of the penis and testicles, as well as affecting the prostrate, while estradiol (one form of estrogen) works with other hormones to develop female breasts, induce uterine growth, and regulate menstruation. That said, estrogen is necessary in men for normal bone growth and fertility, and is used by the brain, lungs, bones, intestines, liver, and blood vessels for growth and development. Today, both estrogen and testosterone are taken by both males and females for a number of medical reasons. Testosterone treatments, for example, can promote more energy, sexual interest, and youthful virility in both men and women. It is, indeed, fascinating that hormones which affect so many areas of the body are so commonly reduced to being called "sex" hormones, instead of signifying growth in general.

Male and female fetuses have the same gonads until the sixth week of gestation in the womb, when the male Y chromosome forms testes. Without a Y chromosome, the fetus will instead begin to form female ovaries. Between the eighth to sixteenth week of pregnancy, a male fetus produces testosterone in large quantities. Its testosterone surge abates

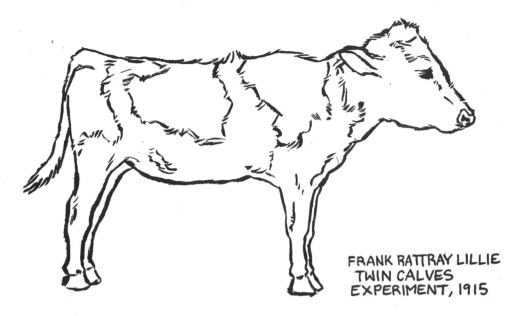

after the sixteenth week, and by the twenty-sixth week is on par with a female fetus again. A genetic male who does not produce adequate testosterone between the eighth and sixteenth week of gestation will be born with feminized external genitalia, such as a phallus (penis) that appears rather like an enlarged clitoris. Such a "feminized male" may retain internal gonad structures for functional testicles. Likewise, genetic females who produce large amounts of testosterone during that period often grow external genitalia with masculine characteristics and may be assigned as a male upon birth.

Does this testosterone bath "organize" the brain in a masculine way, though? Concerned about how socialization might affect an infant brain, developmental psychobiologist Celia Moore set out to study how early hormones bring about sex-specific behavior in rats' postnatal life. Among other discoveries, she found that young rats' brain stems developed relative to the amount of genital licking they received from their mother. The amount of licking was in turn greatly influenced by the level of testosterone the mother smelled in their urine. Yes, rats brains developed differently on the basis of their sex (or at least on the basis of their testosterone level), but the maternal treatment they received had everything to do with this divergence in development.

Behavioral neurologist Norman Geschwind famously argued that the male surge in fetal testosterone causes a smaller left hemisphere in the brain. He believed that this gave males an advantage for artistic, musical, and mathematical talent, which are often associated with the brain's right hemisphere. Yet, postmortem studies of fetal brains do not demonstrate a reduced or "cramped" left hemisphere in males, nor does neuroimaging of newborns.

So, are boys with more fetal testosterone more masculine than boys (or girls) with lower levels? Are their brains more likely to develop aptitudes that correspond to gender stereotypes for men? As Cordelia Fine points out in *Delusions of Gender* (2010), blood is only very rarely sampled from an unborn baby, making it impossible for doctors to quantify the testosterone in their blood. Instead, researchers look at the testosterone in the pregnant mother's blood or in the amniotic fluid in the sac surrounding the fetus.

This all leads to a pretty surprising truth: "Researchers don't actually know for sure whether what they are measuring correlates well, or even at all, with the level of testosterone acting on the fetal brain." So then, on the basis of the testosterone level in the amniotic fluid, do scientists find that eye contact for one-year-olds or social relationships for four-year-olds corresponds to gendered stereotypes for male and female children? Do they find that male- or female-assigned children describe their experiences using more emotional language, or that they score differently on an empathy test? Apparently, the differences are negligible between the sexes.

Examining how prenatal hormones "organize" the brain is further complicated by another aspect of testing methods. Jordan-Young's *Brain Storm* draws on a close analysis of over three hundred studies exploring the hypothetical connection between prenatal hormone exposures, gender and sexuality. She concludes that studies on prenatal hormones are not "true experiments." Unlike the normal academically accepted format for an experiment, these test subjects are not randomly assigned to receive hormone exposures, their development is not consistently watched, nor can it generally be followed throughout a test subject's entire life span. Their environments and experiences cannot be controlled or kept constant at all. Instead, scientists glean information from animal studies and partial, relatively uncontrolled human studies. Thus, their results clearly cannot be considered verified.

In addition, many of the assumptions about the very character of testosterone have also been called into question in the last twenty years. In *Gender Shock: Exploding the Myths of Male & Female* (1996), Phyllis Burke cites the case of endocrinologist Dr. Christina Wang, who treated men who produce too little testosterone. Apparently, when Dr. Wang gave those men testosterone replacement therapy, "they became optimistic and friendly." If aggression and testosterone's link doesn't turn out to be valid after all, what does that say about some of the "hypermasculine" traits that testosterone is associated with?

## ENDOCRINOLOGY

Endocrinologists are doctors specially trained to diagnose diseases that affect glands. They diagnose and treat hormone imbalances and related problems.

As far back as 1983, psychologists Nancy Eisenberg and Randy Lennon discovered that the so-called female empathetic advantage diminishes when it isn't obvious that empathy is the focus of a study or assessment. It turns out that the difference previously observed was probably related to how empathetic the test subjects wanted to appear to others. In Eisenberg and Lennon's study, and many others, a trend has emerged implying that aptitude (male, female, or otherwise) may be shifted by associations that people link to abilities. Since society places positive and negative connotations on different supposedly gender-related abilities and behaviors, test subjects often strive (consciously or subconsciously) to meet those expectations. This may be mirrored in our everyday lives. What we know for sure is that gender differences in aptitude show up at astonishingly higher rates in self-reported studies than when measures are more objective. In fact, Begley states that in most studies with large sample pools, men and women's scores on most psychological tests overlap so much that "any randomly chosen woman might do better at a 'male' skill than a man and vice versa."

ENDOCRINOLOGIST DR. CHRISTINA WANG

We also know that hormonal shifts can cause growth or shrinkage in parts of the brain, even in adulthood. Ironically, instead of reinforcing the idea of biological determinism, this information may actually support the hypothesis that experience plays a role in adult nervous system changes, potentially affecting both gender identity and behavior. After puberty, the hormone levels that result from any genetic predisposition tend to become relatively constant for most of one's adult life, with the exception of a drop in testosterone levels in men later in life and a drop in estrogen levels in women after menopause. But nutrition, stress, sex, and other day-to-day experiences continue to shift adult hormone levels, sometimes dramatically. As such, it is more than plausible to suggest that experience plays a significant role in our hormone levels and the way our brains develop, including after puberty.

"Myelinization" is when fat covers the nerve fibers of a neural connection like a sheath. This process is what causes the brain to slowly harden,

**BIOLOGICAL DETERMINISM**

Biological determinism is a theory hypothesizing that genes and early biology shape humans absolutely, including our abilities and personalities.

and stop growing and shifting as easily. Myelinization has not finished at birth, and continues throughout the course of one's life, increasing by twofold between one's first and second decade, and 60 percent between one's fourth and sixth decade, leaving the door open for experience shifting one's neural patterns and connections. This could explain why some people's gender identities change over the course of their life, or simply provide evidence that our brains continue to change as a result of our environment and life experiences. Either way, if one is still at all inclined to reduce aptitudes and behavior to hormones and gendered brain structure, then one must also concede that these structures and hormones are mutable and affected by conditioning.

Why then, do we have gender-specific expectations for male and female children's behavior patterns, interests, tendencies, and aptitudes? Regardless of whether one actively buys into stereotypes of pink and blue, the brain has stored associations from representations of people, feelings, behavior, and motives. Our brains draw parallels between experiences when one has paired concepts together. So when you see ads where men do heavy lifting outside their home as women fix dinner, regardless of what your conscious mind thinks about these roles, there is a lasting impression stored in the brain. Patterns in media and society are registered in our minds and are difficult to fully dismiss, at least on a subconscious level. For example, if asked to categorize personality traits by gender, your first impulse might be to pair emotion-oriented terms like "compassionate" or "sensitive" with women, and active or task-focused terms like "analytical" or "dominant" with men.

Many people might reject the idea that they would make such gross generalizations, but keep in mind how flexible your self-image is relative to social context. Do you act differently when you're around family members, work colleagues, classmates, friends, or potential romantic partners? In *Delusions of Gender*, Cordelia Fine points to a study where French high school students were asked to rate the legitimacy of gender stereotypes relative to aptitude in math and the arts, and then to rank their own talent. Afterwards, they were asked their scores on a standardized test they had taken two years prior. They almost invariably inflated or downgraded their scores relative to the stereotype that boys excel in math while girls have artistic sensibilities. If a male and female child have the same ability at a given subject, but the female thinks that she's less talented, which one is more likely to succeed?

Author Barbara J. Berg expands on this principle in *Sexism in America* (2009). Berg cites the high numbers of women working in technology in many parts of the world, (especially Eastern Europe), and asserts that there is no biological basis for differences in subject aptitudes. She states quite simply that in the U.S., "the culture has convinced girls they don't belong in [the fields of science, math, and computer science]." She cites instances of teachers telling girls not to take certain courses, favoring boys in the classroom (or simply giving them more opportunities to speak), and off-color jokes and comments in classrooms that discourage female participation. Berg acknowledges Janet Shibley Hyde, who conducted a meta-analysis of forty-six research studies by different psychologists, and found tremendous similarity between the sexes, rather than differences. "One's sex has little or no bearing on personality, cognition, and leadership," according to Hyde and her colleagues.

Another argument questioning the validity of sex differences goes like this: Scientists' experiments and medical practices create "truths" about human sexuality and gender. Then the media and education institutions reinforce those ideas through constant reiteration until, in various ways, we change to conform to these "norms." Sometimes these changes are overt—like changing one's breast size or dieting to fit a cultural ideal of beauty. Other times, it's less obvious or even subconscious, like not being able to concentrate on an aptitude test because of the expectation that you will fail. Eventually, small shifts due to a scientist's manner of study (such as a geneticist looking at things on a submolecular level or a sociologist examining economic statistics) can result in a changed culture.

Of course, there are some indisputable biological differences between most representatives of the sexes, including pelvic bones, females' ability to give birth, and average height differentiation. But the differences, according to scientists like Janet Shibley Hyde, are far less dramatic than we have been led to believe. It is also possible that most of the supposed "biological differences" that some scientists link to abilities or capacities (like amygdala size in girls enhancing communication skills) are not innate biological differences, but rather ways that males and females develop as the result of social conditioning. Again, no brain structure besides the INAH$_3$ is consistently found to be sex-specific, or to have a consistent size difference between male and female subjects.

So is hardwiring anything to write home about? Are there any demonstrable differences in male and female aptitude that suggest inherent variation in perception, behavior, strengths, and weaknesses? Keep in mind that male and female brains are so similar that many scientists say they cannot be differentiated on an individual basis. If viewed through a lens acknowledging that psychology and neurobiology tend to look for differences rather than similarities, and if we take into account that socialization makes gender study participants perform relative to what they believe is expected of them, then there is only one area in which scientists have consistently found a disparity in ability: mental rotation tests.

In a mental rotation test, one performs a kind of three-dimensional Tetris. You are given a figure of connected blocks to examine, and then shown several pictures where that block or a strikingly similar block has been turned to another angle. It is the task of the participant to determine which blocks match the original. In these tests, male participants outperform females from three to four months of age upwards. That said, it should be noted that mental rotation is a skill that can be honed through practice. And when an Italian researcher, Angelica Moè, gave a mental rotation test to some high school students, she obtained very different results. After breaking up the class into three sections, she informed one portion that "men perform better than women in this test, probably for genetic reasons," then told an-

**MENTAL ROTATION TEST**

other portion that women performed better (using the same language); the last portion was given no disclaimer at all. The females who had been told that women outperform men matched the skill level of the males in their group. This example suggests that even this one supposed "male advantage" has more to do with practice and expectation around their ability than genuine aptitude.

Furthermore, it can be gleaned from numerous studies that the brain works to suppress stereotypes in situations that call for an ability with a social gender association. For example, Dr. Christine Logel's research found that women who are interrupted in the midst of a difficult math test will be delayed in responding to terms that have been used to stereotype women as having poor math aptitude, such as "illogical" or "intuitive." It appears that the need to ignore negative messages uses up concentration that makes it more difficult to perform the task at hand. As Cordelia Fine says, "These jittery, self-defeating mechanisms are not characteristic of the *female* mind—they're characteristic of the mind *under threat*."

If male and female brains (and bodies in general) don't clearly account for gender differences, then why do we perpetuate them? Why are gonads, chromosomes, hormones, and brain structures the factors that we use to define sex or gender, particularly when we know that there is variance in all three? If experience can shift our hormones and brains, then is any biological distinction that we *do* find between the sexes truly innate? Phyllis Burke makes a strong case when she states that, "The single most important fact in the biological comparisons of the sexes is that there are greater differences between men *as a group* and between women *as a group*, than there are between men and women." But if that's true, what purpose does the category of gender serve? Why has a dual category for men and women been so pervasive in Western society? And what about everyone who is left out of that binary classification? By examining some of the history behind gender roles, and male and female socialization, perhaps it will become clearer where our ideas about gender come from.

# HISTORICAL CONSTRUCTION OF GENDER ROLES

Whatever one believes about the science surrounding biological differences, both men and women have incredibly varied personality traits and abilities—as divergent within each sex as between the two. So can gender-specific labeling really be reduced to female bodies' sex-specific function in bearing children or the average male's slightly larger frame? For most of recorded history (and with some cross-cultural exceptions), women's access to various types of work and expression have been limited, and yet the sexes demonstrate primarily overlapping competencies in child rearing, math, science, the arts and humanities, not to mention communication skills. What accounts for how differently men and women are treated and described? From family roles and romantic relationships to legal rights, politics, the media, and the workplace, gender roles and behaviors are certainly ever present . . . but do we know why?

Let's start at the beginning: In prehistoric times, early Homo habilis men hunted and initiated young warriors through elaborate rites of passage in dark caves while women sat around twiddling their thumbs or tending to young children...or so goes dozens of stories about our ancestors. Actually, there's no evidence whatsoever about who performed what gender role in prehistoric times. Although some information about our ancestors can be inferred from contemporary behavior among tribal societies, the accuracy of anthropologists' assumptions cannot be assessed using any raw data because of poorly preserved archaeological artifacts. Quite simply, scientists can't be sure who was doing the hunting or child rearing from fossils and the few impartial skeletons preserved from our earliest ancestors.

Furthermore, the long-standing notion that prehistoric people hunted their food at *all* is being called into question by new data and interpretations. It was previously assumed that humans came from trees and first walked on the ground to obtain more prey and hunt in the savanna, which was expanding in East Africa at the time of our earliest "human" ancestors. Ecologically speaking, however, the location of most of our earliest ancestors' bones implies that they lived in a tropical environment. The current hypothesis is supported by the tropical adaptation traits that both humans and apes exhibit, such as slow reproduction, large parental investment in their offspring, and social behavior, all of which contrast sharply from savanna animals. Archaeologist and human ecologist Anna Roosevelt has written significantly that despite animal and ancestral "human" remains being found in close proximity, it is likely that they were killed by mutual predators. In fact, prehistoric men's teeth indicate mainly plant consumption.

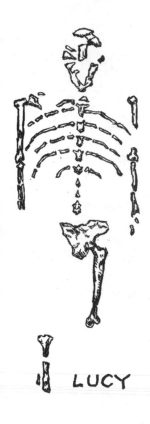

As for whether we can look to the biological differences between sexes in prehistoric days to explain later societies' division along gender lines, we know only that overall body size differences were more dramatic in australopithecines than in any species of homo. Teeth or other characteristics that might distinguish between the two sexes lack discernible variation in these prehistoric remains, possibly due to the very few samples on which archaeologists can draw. The pelvic region's bones— which are not always preserved—show the sole definitive difference: females have a cavity there where they can bring offspring to term. Unfortunately, in the case of many of our ancestors' remains, we cannot determine the sex other than by assuming how large an individual was on the basis of a few skull fragments, bones, or teeth. For example, scientists have debated for years over whether the famous australopith find, Lucy, was actually a female. Discovered somewhat intact, "her" feet showed that "she" was the earliest known human ancestor to walk upright that had yet been unearthed. But Lucy's sex was assigned purely on the basis of her size. She could just as likely have been a juvenile male.

LUCY

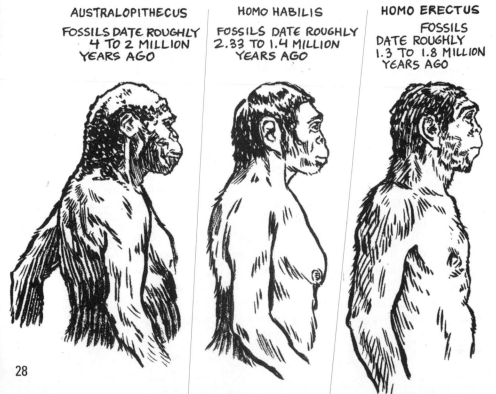

AUSTRALOPITHECUS
FOSSILS DATE ROUGHLY 4 TO 2 MILLION YEARS AGO

HOMO HABILIS
FOSSILS DATE ROUGHLY 2.33 TO 1.4 MILLION YEARS AGO

HOMO ERECTUS
FOSSILS DATE ROUGHLY 1.3 TO 1.8 MILLION YEARS AGO

## SEXUAL SELECTION AND HUMANS

Females giving preference to size during selection of a mate is less common with one-to-one pairings than in harem situations. On the other hand, anthropologist Joan Silk notes that the current size disparity between male and female humans suggests monogamous (or possibly some polygamous) arrangements, with very rare instances of polyandry or harems. Since we know that in the past the size disparity between males and females was more pronounced, it is likely that at some point other forms of competition may have superceded size for impressing mates, such as the ability to obtain goods or to create and use weapons.

When considering sexual selection, it's important to remember that natural selection occurs between individuals, not at the level of a group or species, nor by selecting an individual trait or actual DNA. Occasionally, an environmental effect, such as a massive drought, will cause an entire group to develop a survival mechanism specific to that situation. Still, individuals generally adapt diverse strategies and those that survive continue. Traits can become amplified due to consistent selection by mates, but what benefits a particular female to survive might not work for a male or another female. Each individual surviving and reproducing is what results in evolution over time.

And why are average males larger than females? There are several potential reasons, but according to anthropologist Joan Silk, sexual selection probably accounts for this difference. Many other species demonstrate an analogous situation, where larger males are typically preferred by females and have more opportunities to pass on their genes, gradually increasing their size differentiation from females. Whether or not prehistoric human males' larger size resulted in dominance over females is debatable

NEANDERTHAL

FOSSILS DATE ROUGHLY 500,000 - 24,000 YEARS AGO

HOMO SAPIEN

FOSSILS DATE ROUGHLY 200,000 YEARS AGO TO PRESENT

## LIMITS TO PRIMATOLOGY
Readers should take into account that chimpanzee behavior today may not reflect our common ancestor, as chimpanzees have undergone five to seven million years of their own distinct evolution.

**BONOBO**

though, especially since modern male and female humans are much closer in size than our ancestors. In modern humans (where the average male to female height and weight ratios are 1: 0.93 and 1: 0.84, respectively), our size difference is not pronounced enough to predict broad physical capabilities.

By looking at primates, some scientists have made hypotheses about our common ancestors and early human socialization. Among primates, males spend more time and energy in achieving higher status than females do, but some studies have also shown that females are aggressively competitive amongst one another (and often with males as well). Violence seems to occur with equal initiation by male and female primates; bonobo groups, for example, are dominated by females, while chimpanzees have more male antagonists.

Furthermore, though some scientists once hypothesized that caring for children would make it difficult for prehistoric females to forage for themselves, both chimpanzee behavior and ethnographic research on surviving hunter-gatherer tribes imply that prehistoric mothers resumed gathering food directly after giving birth. In primates, sex-specific hunting behaviors and social groupings vary by region, and tools used for foraging are created and used even more often by females than by males. Among human foraging cultures, in many instances, women farm, gather, and carry more than

**CHIMPANZEE**

men, producing more of the food, which they distribute. As a result, one can conclude that among both primates and our prehistoric ancestors, there was not overwhelming male or female dominance.

So when did gender roles or social division between the sexes begin to take root? Cross-cultural differences are simply too numerous to pinpoint any universal marking point, but in Western civilization, there have been a few key turning points, including the myth of the "fall," the development of a two-sex model for anatomy, and the Industrial Revolution.

Many early hunter-gatherer cultures shared both economic and religious tasks across sex lines. There were also ruling queens in Ancient Egypt and female emperors in Ancient Japan. Among Seneca American Indians, women controlled the food supply and had to be consulted with before waging war. Ancient Sumerian women could hold religious leadership posts and were active in the marketplace, in addition to owning property. In Celtic and Mesopotamian origin stories, there was no mention of an "inferior" sex. What's more, a number of early societies celebrated both male and female gods or spirits.

*"It is hard to define when gender appears...obviously animals understand sex, but the cultural definition of gender? The expectation that an individual will perform actions not biologically related to their sex because of what type of genitals they have? It's really hard to say...[Even in instances of significant biological differences between sexes] cultural practices can mitigate these factors...*
*I don't know if Lucy had gender as we define it. Did s/he have tasks unrelated to reproduction that were required of her because s/he was a male or female? It would be impossible to prove one way or the other...*
*I would say as a rule of thumb, definitive statements about gender before historical or iconographic representations are debatable."*
*– Scott Johnson, archaeologist*

Then, about five thousand years ago, Western monotheistic religions were born in the Middle East, rife with myths that encouraged male leadership and dominance. Almost immediately, female deities disappeared from popular belief. The Old Testament of the Bible mainly portrayed women as either pure and sexless virgins placed on a pedestal, or as manipulative seductresses whose wiles defiled man. In either case, the stories dehumanized women and placed a horrible taboo on their sexuality. These new religions were headed by male priests and prophets, who were the only ones to hear God's decrees.

# MISOGYNY AND PATRIARCHY

Misogyny is a cultural ideology prominent in some societies that suggests that women—just by being female—are worthy of contempt, hatred, or else are simply inferior. Irish author and journalist Jack Holland makes the point in his book *Misogyny* that, for many men, long before conflicts of race or class, women were the original "other" that could never be truly avoided. The discrimination found in some societies that deprivilege women are based on ideas that they are not full citizens or human beings; they are excluded from rituals, sports, certain kinds of paid work, and other supposedly "male" roles. This exclusivity becomes part of laws, religious rites, and the institutions which reinforce those roles, such as education and the media.

"Patriarchy" is a natural extension of misogyny. The term refers to the Old Testament of the Bible, meaning "the rule of the fathers." In the Bible, it meant that power belonged to male elders; when used today, "patriarchy" describes a society in which men dominate the major institutions. Many believe that since there are more men in government positions, religious appointments, writing (and represented in) educational curriculum, the military, high-paying jobs, and both owning and appearing in the media, American society is a patriarchy.

One clear example of misogyny and patriarchy at work is the seemingly innocent use of a single word attached to a person's name. In most Western societies, women are legally referred to as "Miss," "Mrs.," or "Ms.," whereas men's names are simply preceded by "Mr.," regardless of their marital status. Note that both Miss and Mrs. define women strictly through their relationships to men.

## MISANDRY

Part of the backlash against women's fight for equality has popularized the term "misandry," which is the notion that men are now undervalued in our society. Most scholars agree that this argument has little basis and makes an unfair comparison to misogyny, since women continue to hold less powerful positions and have been discriminated against for centuries.

In Ancient Greece and in Judaea (part of ancient Palestine), the parallel myths of Pandora's box and the story of Adam and Eve were popularly accepted depictions of a woman's curiosity leading to man's downfall and the beginning of death and human suffering. Celibacy or marriage as a refuge from unconstrained lust became the idealized ways to live a moral life. Plato and other Greek theorists declared that women's "weaker" nature was dangerous to the state, which was becoming increasingly associated with male rationality. Women were summarily divorced from politics and pushed into the private sphere. In fact, women in Ancient Greece were commonly sequestered to separate women's quarters within a household—a far cry from ruling over Egypt. Soon, no more temple priestesses were worshipped as men gained political power over Hebrew, Greek, and Roman civilizations.

## CELIBACY

Celibacy is a personal promise to abstain from sexual intercourse.

Between 3100 and 600 BCE, settled agriculture also developed, with more specific farming, bartering of extra goods, and a new class hierarchy where male children inherited property. In the midst of an already drastic shift in gender and class relations, women were suddenly relegated to the home. It would be nearly impossible to resolve the "chicken or egg" debate here. Did men's new ascent to economic and political dominance result in the creation of myths and doctrine that scorned women? Or did new myths offer the necessary justification for subjugating women? Either way, these were the circumstances in which women lost clout in the West.

## THE STATE

The term "the state" can be used to refer to any organized and governed community.

## ROMAN WOMEN FIGHT BACK

There are few records of individual Ancient Greek women's lives, but we do know that Ancient Roman women did not give up their status to new laws and decrees passively. Among them were a handful of ambitious individuals, such as Cleopatra and Agrippina who sought opportunities to overthrow the new status quo. They were therefore depicted by historians and poets as ruthless, bloodthirsty, and opportunistic; an interesting foreshadowing of the conservative media's handling of women with power today.

(69 B.C.E. – 30 B.C.E.)

AGRIPPINA
(15 C.E. – 59 C.E.)

Both Ancient Greek and Roman women were also regularly accused of arousing lust in men just by existing; they were held solely responsible for both consensual adultery and rape. One can't help but think of this as the very first instance of the "she asked for it" defense. Roman women bear the distinction of the first public protest on record in search of women's rights (in this case to dress as they pleased), which sparked a Senate debate wherein women's nature was debated. Despite being compared to animals who would trample men if treated equally, the women's side won.

## EDMUND BURKE (1729-1797)

Classical religious assertions about women helped lay the groundwork for other periods in history where men and women's roles were strictly divided as a result of culturally-bound distinctions between the sexes, such as the Renaissance. In Medieval Europe, women had been able to earn wages (supposedly half to two-thirds of a man's wage), and nuns performed charity work and cared for sick people. But around 1215 AD, the Catholic church began to restrict nuns' influence to their convents. After the Black Death plague killed 20 million people between 1347 and 1350 AD, a new era of religious hysteria arose and spurred pessimism, supernatural beliefs, persecution of Jewish people, and a resurgence in Catholic depictions of the devil (often embodied in human form).

## MORAL CONSERVATIVES AND THE NATURE OF THE SEXES

Today, moral conservatives carry on some of the traditional values and assertions about human nature that originated in early Christianity and among philosophers who refused to ascribe to the rational goals of the Enlightenment, such as Edmund Burke (1729–1797). Burke claimed that carrying on traditions from families and the church created a moral state and community. Moral conservatives typically assert that men and women have innately different natures, wherein men are more socially and politically powerful, and should be independent and work-focused. They think that society should encourage women to attract men, require monogamy, and avoid sex prior to or outside of marriage. In this world view, women's primary role is to keep men loyal and take care of their emotional and sexual needs so that men can channel their risk-taking and competitive natures into protecting and providing for the family.

In other words, moral conservatives believe that separate spheres create a "social order" that keeps men's otherwise brutish nature in check and ensures women and children are provided for through the institutions of marriage, the church, family, and community. This view contends that male dominance is natural, and masculinity serves a purpose. As such, they sometimes view feminist ideas as potentially damaging to the nuclear family and upsetting the "natural order" of civilization. For example, if a woman is given complete control over her body, and can have sex or reproduce if and when it suits her, they think men will no longer have incentive to settle down, and morality will cease. They may also claim that when men and women attempt to pursue more equal or interchangeable roles (which, in their views, don't suit our different natures), neither will be as proficient or as satisfied as in a more "traditional" model. But again, while "traditional" roles are often stressed by moral conservatives, we now know that these roles, as described, have only existed since the Industrial Revolution.

## THE ENLIGHTENMENT

The Enlightenment was a cultural movement in 18th century Europe that emphasized reason and science over myth and religion.

By the Renaissance, even as literature and the arts flourished, the Classical idea of irrational and "sexually uncontrollable" women had returned with an increased emphasis on women as the cause of original sin in the Bible. This ideology mixed with renewed endorsement of supernatural beliefs set the stage for witch hunts, between 1500 and 1800 AD, which resulted in somewhere between 100,000 and one million women's deaths. In the meantime, missionaries spread Christianity across the globe, converting cultures who still believed in more than one deity or in spiritualities grounded in nature.

So goes the legacy of Western religion's early effect on male and female roles. But many of the same changes in sex roles and beliefs about gender can also be interpreted through the developing theories of anatomy and evolution. Over the course of the Enlightenment and the 19th century, science began to exert greater authority and gain more widespread respect. Suddenly, religious doctrines were no longer the only popular view of human nature. One scientific development that altered views of males and females was the shift from a one- to two-sex model of anatomy.

BEFORE THE ENLIGHTENMENT ERA, ANATOMICAL STUDY WAS FOCUSED ON MALE BODIES; A "ONE-SEX" MODEL OF ANATOMY.

Sexologist Thomas Laqueur's *Making Sex* (1990) describes how, before the Enlightenment, a one-sex model of anatomy was used It was based on the male body. Female organs were considered a "lesser" version of the male model, and did not have separate terms to distinguish their parts; the vagina was considered an interior penis, ovaries were understood to be internal testicles, and the womb was deemed a kind of scrotum. When a two-sex model of anatomy became popularized in the 18th century, however, each sex was depicted with their own organs and respective functions. Before the 17th century, a person's gender identity was considered their "essence" or "real" self, and the body was simply thought to express or represent that self (though, of course, they didn't use the term "gender" then). With the invention of a two-sex model of anatomy, suddenly the body became the "solid" foundation for understanding differences between men and women. At that point, a bigger cultural division arose between one's "body" and "spirit" (or "soul"), with the body (or sex) as the basis for what we now call "gender."

## MALE OVERREPRESENTATION AS TEST SUBJECTS

When assessing the biases of the medical community, consider that, historically, scientists have overwhelmingly used primarily—and very often only—male test subjects in research studies. This is true both in terms of testing humans and when using animal test subjects. It seems fairly obvious how this could tend to limit scientific knowledge and skew their perception of females.

Charles Darwin's groundbreaking concept of natural selection and publication, *On the Origin of Species* (1859), further dramatized the culturally perceived differences between men and women. In theorizing about sexual selection, he suggested that male animals employed more varied and complex strategies to attract mates, and were generally superior. He saw human males as "more courageous, pugnacious, and energetic than women, and [as having] a more inventive genius." Having been shaped by Victorian views of men and women's behavior, Darwin blatantly ignored species without the dominating male and passive female characteristics that he expected (such as hyenas, anglerfish, ring-tailed lemurs, black widow spiders, meerkats, and praying mantis, to name a few). In this way, science began to reinforce ideas of female dependence and rationalize male privilege.

CHARLES DARWIN
(1809 - 1882)

Darwin's influence on gender roles was bolstered in the 19th century by a new concept of childhood as a malleable period where children were shaped by parenting. The qualitative differences Darwin had described between men and women were now assumed to account for their respective skills; man's "aggression" and "competitive" behavior therefore made him appropriate for the marketplace, while woman's "altruism" and "nurturing" ability made her a kind of shepherd for her children. This perception of separate male and female abilities contrasted sharply from prior notions of sex differences, which had been a matter of degree not quality (as a one-sex model of anatomy reflects). Although women had been held subordinate to men in Western culture, they were previously considered somewhat less strong or less intelligent, not fundamentally different from men, with each sex having their own specific abilities (as a two-sex model of anatomy implies). A group of theorists known as social Darwinists later drew on these concepts to suggest that society and politics also operated through a kind of "natural selection." They supposed that Europeans were more advanced and superior to nonindustrialized nations and hunter-gatherer tribes, where male and female tasks overlap more. They also considered themselves morally superior for designating men and women tasks which suited each "appropriately."

The legacy of Darwin's bearing on beliefs about sex differences can also be seen in modern conservative sociobiologists, who often argue that human behaviors and social roles are tied directly to their biological differences. They think that because society is comprised of individuals who have survived evolution, whatever archetypes can be found in society represent strategies that were selected in evolution. In *Contemporary Perspectives on Masculinity* (1990), philosopher Kenneth Clatterbaugh describes the conservative sociobiologist mindset thusly: "If men tend to be traditionally masculine and women traditionally feminine, it is because these behaviors have allowed them to be biologically successful. These behaviors have become innate to men and women precisely because those who tended to behave differently did not survive." Opponents of conservative sociobiologists' views contend that this oversimplifies human nature, leaves out studies of primates and extant hunter-gatherer tribes who are not male dominant, and falsely gives human attributes to animals. For instance, generalizations about terms like "war," "altruism," and "rape" are sometimes applied by sociobiologists to animal activities in order to defend universal statements about the sexes. Obviously, this is misleading, as there is no objectively measurable moral content to animal behavior. After all, if a male monkey surprises a female monkey and begins to mate with her, scientists cannot exactly evaluate their intercourse on the basis of informed consent.

## HOW DO WE EVALUATE INFORMATION'S AUTHENTICITY?

Today's laboratories are often given more legitimacy as a concrete source of knowledge than social scientists' examination of environmental variables. This is a privileging of specific types of knowledge that affects our culture's views. Knowledge is produced and perpetuated by academics and educational curricula, the media, ideas' enactment into laws and policies, as well as through social interactions and religious institutions. But when one considers the extent to which an idea is considered "true" or "objective," the reputation of the person who produced it becomes key, even though it is not always an accurate or fair measurement of their expertise. Our society often values marks of prestige, such as education degrees, over other kinds of practical experience. The social relationship between different people interested in the same subject also influences what knowledge is produced about a given topic. Academics, for example, gain validation for their ideas through peer review—or evaluating one another's work.

In addition to religion and science, economic trends also played a considerable role on Western societies' evolving roles for the sexes. Social scientist and political philosopher Friedrich Engels argued that women's oppression originated in the beginning of private property, when families replaced larger clans and communal living groups. His book, *The Origin of the Family, Private Property, and the State* (1884), questioned whether women's roles had always been inferior to men's. He concluded that women were primarily oppressed by economics, and that monogamy, private property, and excluding women from "social production" is at the root of male dominion.

In *The Creation of Patriarchy* (1986), feminist historian Gerda Lerner agrees that the transition to settled agriculture was the lynchpin in male privilege. She describes how the domestication of farm animals and beginning of private land in the Middle East coincided with the beginning of a state governed by male elders and the military. She also adds that reproduction in and of itself is key to women's subjugation. Since women "produced" workers by giving birth, Lerner believes they were viewed in early history as a commodity that was purchased with the dowry given to a woman's family when she was married. Lerner uses this view of women as commodities to account for why women are often kidnapped during war raids, and to explain the historic prizing of chastity as a method of ensuring who a woman's offspring "belonged" to.

Despite the fact that the beginning of settled agriculture coincided with the formation of several male-governed states, it's worth noting that in many agricultural societies, women also do a lot of the physical labor and often have commensurate power and prestige.

The rise of capitalism in the 1600s significantly shifted the Western European economy. This new system focused on investments, expanding markets, and the potential for immense wealth earned within a single lifetime. Before capitalism, an individual's wealth was mainly inherited or based on a family's stature over many generations. Capitalism's early success was partially due to colonialist expansion and the cheap labor of slavery, both of which affected gender and class relations in the United States and in Africa. Capitalism also encouraged wage labor, production, and merchants, which soon ended women's production of goods in the household and decreased their work's perceived importance. New apprenticeships for specialized labor were only open to men; while some working class wage options remained, the only real "profession" open to women outside of the house between the 1500s and 1600s was midwifery.

## IT'S NOT ALL ABOUT SEX

Feminist historian Estelle B. Freedman calls attention to how other factors figured equally into men and women's status besides sex, such as class, age, and family, particularly before the 18th century. In Hindu caste systems, for example, men and women within a caste had more similar privileges and rank than women of different castes.

She also describes how, as women's domestic production of goods lost value in the West to new wage labor, missionaries and colonial officials spread both capitalism and Christianity to the majority of the world. They justified their overthrow of tradition and previous governments by saying they were bringing civilization and progress to "primitive" people. But many of the cultures they invaded—Arabs, Chinese, Maya, and Inca people, for example—had complicated technology, political hierarchy, and social order long before Europeans arrived.

The English, French, Germans, Belgians, and Americans brought their ideas about the sexes with them, assuming that their system of the division of labor was preferential to whatever the cultures they colonized had in place. Any political positions that women had previously held in colonialized territories were ignored (such as in Nigerian, Incan, and Native American traditions), as were female agricultural laborers (in Africa, Asia, and elsewhere) who often had considerable social currency. In North America, for instance, protestants encouraged Native American women to stop performing agricultural work and make textiles instead.

Ironically, this new model of separate spheres in colonialized territories did not even reflect the most progressive gender roles in England and America: those of the working class. Working class women's options may have been limited by the new "domestic ideal" to seamstress and servant positions, but their wages' importance in their families ensured that they had more equal footing than many women in the middle and upper classes.

As industry increased, women were initially called upon to spin fabric for textiles, but soon shops and factories took over, and childrearing kept most middle class women at home. Protestantism reinforced this new, more domestic role by encouraging women to be the pious moral guardians of their households and children. Those who didn't marry or have children became quickly vulnerable, both economically and socially. In fact, spinsters and widows were the women most commonly accused of being witches in the 1700s.

In addition to considering economic reasons for gender inequality, some social scientists and psychologists have also had a tremendous impact on the formation of gender roles in the West, particularly in the 20th century. While he was most significant for inventing psychoanalysis and shifting public perception of sexuality, Austrian neurologist Sigmund

Freud's model of developmental psychology was also extremely popular in Europe and America, beginning around 1900. Freud's theories of child development centered on a child's erotic relationship to stimuli, and their ability to transition successfully between appropriate methods for acting out their impulses. For example, he classically configured all children as having a sexual attraction to their mother, which most eventually realize should not be fulfilled and instead seek other subjects of infatuation.

A sexual attraction to one's mother is called an Oedipus complex, after the Greek mythological character Oedipus, who unknowingly kills his father and marries his mother.

Freud focused much more heavily on studying boys and men than on girls or women, but he made particular note of what he considered the most important event in a young girl's life: the moment she discovers she does not have a penis. Freud speculated that at this moment, females became aware that they are incomplete, and remain so until they marry and have children. He considered men the basis for civilization and the more fundamental sex. By contrast, he characterized women as secondary, resentful, and less rational.

Erik Erikson, a psychologist who was influenced by Freud and known for his theories on the social development of humans, wrote extensively on the stages of maturity throughout a human life. He expanded Freud's stages of early life and sexuality to include adult life changes in personality, ego and social interaction. Like Freud, Erikson considered a woman's identity incomplete until marriage. His work has been widely taught in American universities from the 1950s to the present. Both Freud and Erikson have been heavily critiqued, but their legacy in the field of child development and on psychoanalysis can still be seen in the language and method of modern psychology. Their impact is also evident in many "common sense" assumptions made about child development in self-help books—which often fail to cite Freud or Erikson as a somewhat obvious influence on the author's thinking.

Some social scientists and cultural anthropologists have also had mitigating effects on generalizations about gender roles. One important example was Margaret Mead, a cultural anthropologist whose studies of men and women in Samoa and New Guinea shocked the American public in the 1930s. Mead found that adolescence in Samoa had little of the malaise and emotional distress of a "typical" American adolescence; she also observed that young Samoan women often engaged in casual sex for several years before choosing a life partner and raising children. In New Guinea, Mead's personal interviews and participant observation of three different tribal groups revealed three vastly different gender norms. Both men and women Mundugumor were equally aggressive and dominating; among the Arapesh people both sexes exhibited very passive and equally maternal behaviors; and Tchambuli women appeared quite businesslike, while the men were flamboyant and very socially oriented. When Mead's studies were released, they met with both academic and public praise, but were also controversial due to the public's surprise at the varied gender roles she observed (as well as the frequency and normalization of incest in Samoan society). Margaret Mead's conclusions provide a powerful counterpoint to universalized theories of gender roles.

IN NEW GUINEA AND ELSEWHERE, MARGARET MEAD'S PERSONAL STUDIES OF TRIBAL GROUPS REVEALED SIGNIFICANTLY VARIED GENDER ROLES FROM GROUP TO GROUP.

While we have no proof that women's roles in prehistory were subservient, from the beginning of written history they have generally performed somewhat different tasks than men in the Western world. Women's value and nature have been called into question repeatedly in the West, by both theological and biological explanations of male dominance. Women's work, though its scope has varied over different periods in history, was nevertheless considered essential until the Industrial Revolution. Many theorists pose that women's work was devalued in the shift to a wage economy, the advent of private property, and the spread of colonialism and capitalism. But when women gained access to education, new ideas about personal freedoms and rights became popular, and feminist politics began to take shape.

ESTELLE B. FREEDMAN (B. 1947), AMERICAN HISTORIAN, EXPLAINS...

FEMINISM!!!

FEMINISM IS A BELIEF THAT WOMEN AND MEN ARE INHERENTLY OF EQUAL WORTH.

MOST SOCIETIES PRIVILEGE MEN AS A GROUP...

BECAUSE OF THIS, SOCIAL MOVEMENTS ARE NECESSARY TO ACHIEVE EQUALITY BETWEEN WOMEN AND MEN!

CHAPTER 3

# FEMINISM

ACCORDING TO THE 2010 CATALYST CENSUS, WOMEN FILL 14.4% OF EXECUTIVE OFFICER POSITIONS AT FORTUNE 500 COMPANIES AND 7.6% OF TOP EARNER POSITIONS.

Imagine an America where more than half of the population isn't allowed to vote, seek higher education, hold public office, find gainful employment at almost anything besides manual labor, open a bank account, or even own property. In the U.S. today, women have claimed these essential rights and many more, but it was not always this way; in fact, only a little more than a century ago, American women were legally treated as the property of their husbands or fathers.

### WHERE DOES THE WORD "FEMINISM" COME FROM?

The term "feminism" came from the French "féminisme," used in the 1880s to combine the ideas of "women" and "political ideology" into one word. Its use swept across Europe in the 1890s and arrived in North and South America sometime before 1910, where it was initially associated with controversy and radicalism. Some women who were fighting to obtain decent wages for working women did not adopt the term to describe themselves because they interpreted "feminism" as referring primarily to middle-class women's demands for property and voting.

According to Estelle B. Freedman, "feminism" is "a belief that women and men are inherently of equal worth." She explains its significance thusly: "Because most societies privilege men as a group, social movements are necessary to achieve equality between women and men, with the understanding that gender always intersects with other social hierarchies."

After the philosophy of "separate spheres" justified dividing men and women's work on the basis of their differing biology, capitalism and the Industrial Revolution rendered much of women's domestic labor obsolete. But when women gained access to education and found the means to a public voice, they began to seek autonomy, rights, and eventually, new methods to articulate their identities. Despite narrow constructions of gender that called women's agency into constant question, a series of movements known as "feminism" resulted in social and political upheaval across the world, opening up new opportunities for all genders.

Estelle B. Freedman asserts that the very first feminist movements came from places where critiques of industrial growth, democratic theory, and the change in the division of labor all "converged," such as in Europe and North America shortly after 1800.

When printing presses extended literacy beyond the church and the ruling class in Europe in the 15th to 17th century, broader education offered only to men increased the disparity between men and women's power and knowledge. As factory-produced goods replaced homemade clothes and homegrown food, formerly crucial "women's work" became less essential. Suddenly, women found themselves dependent on men's wages which now purchased all the needs of a household.

By the late 1700s, however, under the guise of preparing themselves to raise sons, upper class women were gaining more opportunities for learning. Literacy expanded slowly to encompass more middle class women over the course of the next century. Educated women began to read about citizenship—a value given much merit within the new capitalist system. As they studied the new democratic social contracts that hailed "universal rights," the recent shift in gender and power relations was likely contextualized for many women in a new way. Some wealthy and educated English women, such as Mary Wollstonecraft, started to write about how the new theories of representation and independent rights were only being applied to men. In *A Vindication of the Rights of Woman* (1792), Wollstonecraft laments how decisions in women's lives were being made by men despite many women's fierce intellects. She argued that if women had equal access to education, it would lead to a better social order.

As upper class women produced literature to inform others about the new oppressive division of labor, middle class women started

MARY
WOLLSTONECRAFT
(1759-1797)

advocating at the ground level for property rights, education, and the vote for women in England. Assisting them, philosopher and political economist John Stuart Mill made an unlikely contribution as one of the first male allies to feminists. After being arrested at age seventeen for passing out birth control information, Mill was later elected to parliament, where he became a very active voice for the newly formed English woman's suffrage movement, in which his wife, Harriet Taylor, was a key figure.

## "SUFFRAGE" MEANS THE RIGHT TO VOTE.

In John Stuart Mill's essay "The Subjection of Women" (1869), he espouses his belief that not only should the legal subordination of women be ended and replaced by gender equality, but also that women's situation was worse than slavery, as each "individual [woman]...is in a chronic state of bribery and intimidation combined." He goes on to say that because men want women to like them as well as serve them, they try to indoctrinate women from a young age to think that they're most attractive when meek. Mill thought that this conditioning resulted in society incorrectly perceiving a gentle, weak personality as women's "nature." Journalist Margaret Fuller caused a similar stir in the U.S. with *Woman and the Nineteenth Century* (1845). Instructing women to be independent, withdraw into the self, and get ready for change, Fuller believed women's barriers would soon fall away. Though it was not critically well-received, Fuller's book was very popular, and greatly influenced American middle class women.

During the same period, white American women of all classes were becoming increasingly involved in political organizing against slavery. They formed new Female Anti-

> EACH INDIVIDUAL WOMAN IS IN A CHRONIC STATE OF BRIBERY AND INTIMIDATION COMBINED.

### RULING CLASS

The term "ruling class" refers to a portion of the upper economic class in some societies which has strong political and cultural influence, generally in addition to enormous wealth.

Slavery Societies to address the rape of black female slaves and the dispersion of slaves' families. Women in the North marked safe houses with special quilts on their clotheslines, and gathered signatures to persuade legislators to end slavery.

A few brave women who spoke publicly against slavery also mentioned women's rights, sparking terrific controversy. Sarah M. Grimké and her sister Angelina, for example, toured the country to discuss abolitionism and their experiences growing up in a slaveholding family, and included side remarks about women's equality to men. Although their actions were condemned by churches who said their public speaking was "unwomanly," Sarah often quoted biblical scripture to reinforce her stance that women have "an equal moral responsibility to act for the common good of all people."

With limited rights to speak in public or vote on the temperance and antislavery issues they supported, women abolitionists became fed up with their work being ignored. Finally, in July 1848, men and women organizers gathered in Seneca Falls, New York, at the behest of Elizabeth Cady-Stanton and Lucretia Mott, a charter member of the Female Anti-Slavery Society, in an open forum convention to discuss "the civil and political rights of women." At the conference, Elizabeth Cady Stanton read from a document mirroring the Declaration of Independence that included women's grievances against men in place of the colonists' complaints about the King of England. Sixty-eight women and thirty-two men signed the document, which outlined women's equal right to education, property, jobs, and an active role in politics. As a result of the meeting at Seneca

**ELIZABETH CADY STANTON (1815 – 1902)**

"DECLARATION OF SENTIMENTS AND RESOLUTIONS" 1848

"The history of mankind is a history of repeated injuries and usurpations on the part of man toward woman, having in direct object the establishment of an absolute tyranny over her... He has compelled her to submit to laws, in the formation of which she had no voice...He has made her, if married, in the eye of the law, civilly dead. He has taken from her all right in property, even to the wages she earns... He closes against her all the avenues to wealth and distinction which he considers most honorable to himself. As a teacher of theology, medicine, or law, she is not known."

Falls, another conference just a few weeks later adopted suffrage as the first primary goal of the new women's rights movement, and the "first wave" of feminism in the United States was born.

Throughout the 1850s, women's rights conventions met locally in the Northern states where they gave speeches, petitioned legislature, developed pamphlets, and wrote to newspapers. Although journalists portrayed them as cigar-smoking, masculine, and shrill, the new feminists obtained more educational opportunities and chipped away at state laws in order to control their own wages. But perhaps the most significant gain in the early years of the women's movement was New York's Married Women's Property Act of 1848.

At the time, the United States had more or less co-opted English common law, based on Sir William Blackstone's book, *Commentaries on the Laws of England* (1765), which was the standard textbook of law students in the U.S. at the time. Blackstone's interpretation of common law stated that the legal existence of a woman was suspended when married. This practice effectively gave all women's property to their husbands, and disallowed wives from speaking on their own behalf in court. But when a new property law was proposed in the New York state legislature, Ernestine Rose, a Polish immigrant who had arrived in New York that very year, began a door-to-door petition to support its passage. The bill stated that married women should retain their personal property and be able to obtain new property which no husband could assume as his own. When the Married Women's Property Act came into effect, it reflected a real advance in economic power for women in the U.S.; it also marked the first time American women were engaged in political activity for themselves, specifically as women.

> **DID YOU KNOW?**
> Women weren't allowed on American juries until 1975.

As women's movement organizations grew in size and number, African-American women attempted to join them; but in spite of the women's movement having been founded on anti-slavery activism, black women were largely barred from entry in first wave groups, even after slavery was abolished in 1865. The Young Women's Christian Association did, however, invite four distinguished African-American women to speak at a conference in Memphis in 1920. Among them, educator Charlotte Hawkins Brown discussed the daily attacks and insults inflicted upon black people, and used her own experiences to entreat feminists to expand their agenda to include black women.

Since white women organizers were not including black women in the new feminist groups, African-American feminists started some of their own organizations. They established day care centers, hospitals, and women's groups. They also organized to eliminate black lynching, spoke

## LYNCHING

"Lynching" is when a mob of people executes someone for an alleged crime without a trial or permission from a legal authority or court. The practice of lynching is often tied to the desire to control or intimidate a group of people through fear and violent coercion.

up about the race barrier, and advocated for women's rights. By 1909, the National Association of Colored Women (NACW) had twenty state branches, but Jim Crow laws and the Ku Klux Klan continued to enforce segregation. Black women marched at the back of suffrage parades and rallies—and sometimes physically fought their way to the front. Many African-American women found themselves torn between prioritizing women's and black rights, though some considered race and gender to be inseparable barriers.

Sojourner Truth was one of the first black American women to speak publicly and widely about women's rights. Born into slavery, Sojourner escaped to the North with her daughter in 1826 and became an ardent abolitionist and a prominent figure in women's rights movements due to her powerful speaking abilities. She ardently believed that black women deserved the same rights as white women, and that if black men were poised to receive the vote, it was time for all women to reach for it as well. Her speech at the 1851 Ohio Woman's Rights Convention has been recorded from a handful of attendee's memories, in which she declared,

SOJOURNER TRUTH (1797-1883)

"I can carry as much as any man, and can eat as much too, if I can get it. I am as strong as any man that is now. As for intellect, all I can say is, if woman have a pint and a quart—why can't she have her little pint full? You need not be afraid to give us our rights for fear we will take too much, for we can't take more than our pint'll hold."

At the same time that middle-class white women began to organize for property rights and education and join with upper class women to seek suffrage, working-class white women were joining labor movements and asking for decent wages, fair hours, and more job security. As capitalism gained steam, individualism was regarded as the source of innovation and middle class success. Even so, craftsmen, artists, and unskilled workers who were accustomed to setting their own hours and fees found clocked hours and streamlined wages oppressive. Agricultural and manufacturing jobs suffered from increasingly poor work conditions in the 1800s, and women and children were forced to work long days in nasty environments where they feared illness and injury. Some workers viewed collective ownership as a way out, and when the Karl Marx and Friedrich Engels' *Communist Manifesto* was published in 1848, the ideas of a worker-run government and cooperative family roles were attractive to working-class men and women alike.

---

**LUCY STONE: THE EXCEPTION TO EVERY RULE**
Lucy Stone was of the few white supporters of African-American women's involvement in the first wave of feminism. She fought all her life for women's liberation, and lectured for the Anti-Slavery Societies while invoking women's rights in most of her speeches. Lucy Stone was also the publisher of *Woman's Journal*, the longest lasting first wave periodical.

---

IN EDUCATION, IN MARRIAGE, IN RELIGION, IN EVERYTHING, DISAPPOINTMENT IS THE LOT OF WOMAN. IT SHALL BE THE BUSINESS OF MY LIFE TO DEEPEN THIS DISAPPOINTMENT IN EVERY WOMAN'S HEART UNTIL SHE BOWS DOWN TO IT NO LONGER.

LUCY STONE
(1818-1893)

Most working-class men did not take up women's plight, perhaps fearing competition for their jobs, but women increasingly entered the paid workforce anyway. A socialist feminist division of the women's movement publicized working women's specific needs in books and speeches. Working class women who had emigrated to the U.S. began to organize garment workers on New York's Lower East Side, including Clara Lemlich, who encouraged shirt makers in New York to walk off the job and incited 20,000 women to strike for better pay in 1901.

Another immigrant garment factory worker, Emma Goldman, was both a feminist and anarchist who gained notoriety for her speeches and essays advocating for free speech and contraception. Emma thought that the woman's movement was being limited by seeking only property rights and education. She demanded sexual and reproductive freedom as well; an idea that would greatly influence second wave feminists in the late 1960s and 70s. Before Goldman was deported in WWI for being an anarchist, her essays captured her displeasure with the occupations that were becoming available to American women. She worried that the need to compete voraciously for unrewarding jobs would soon make marriage seem more inviting to women than work.

THE TRAGEDY OF WOMAN'S EMANCIPATION -1906-

EMMA GOLDMAN (1869 - 1940)

"...emancipation has brought woman economic equality with man; that is, she can choose her own profession and trade, but as her past and present physical training have not equipped her with the necessary strength to compete with man, she is often compelled to exhaust all her energy, use up her vitality and strain every nerve in order to reach the market value. Very few ever succeed, for it is a fact that women doctors, lawyers, architects and engineers are neither met with the same confidence, nor do they receive the same remuneration. And those that do reach that enticing equality generally do so at the expense of their physical and psychical well-being."

While socialist feminists sought fair wages and better working conditions, from the 1870s to the early 1900s, millions of middle-class American mothers organized around protecting women from drunken abuse and prostitution. At first, many "maternalist" temperance organizers were focused on the sexual exploitation of women and ignored the socialist feminist cause. Eventually, though, these moral reformers used the mantra of protecting the health of future mothers to seek laws to help working women gain better hours and wages.

## THE LEGACY OF MATERNALIST FEMINISM

First wave feminists had long cited universal rights as justification for ending inherited status, male dominion, and domestic servitude. But maternalist feminists simultaneously endorsed biologically-specific claims to power and morality as mothers. It was only gradually that many of these advocates began to take on suffrage as a means to achieving their goals. They suggested that if women could vote, their moral "superiority" would result in a healthier and more upright society. This "separate but equal" argument is similar to the ideology that enabled feminists to ignore class issues and leave black women out of the first wave. It nevertheless shifted the notion of "separate spheres" from a justification for keeping women in the home into a source of wholesome power for women that promoted their need for suffrage.

World War II overshadowed feminism, and prompted maternalists to reallocate their efforts toward supporting the men in battle. Later, however, in the 1960s, radical feminists reconsidered the "biological superiority" of women. They compared hierarchy in the home to colonialism and violence in international affairs. Such ideas mainly appealed to white, middle class women, but radical feminists also assumed that working class women and women of color would inherently benefit if male dominance was defeated.

Charlotte Perkins Stetson Gilman was an important feminist theorist at the turn of the 20th century, and a major figure for these moral reformers. Gilman thought economic independence was even more crucial than suffrage, and envisioned centralized community nurseries where people would co-raise children. Gilman critiqued what she saw as an aggressive man's world full of competition that directly opposed the "female" value of peace. Taking Darwin's theories of natural law and spinning them in her favor, she said that "life-giving women" were superior. Her arguments described the home as a sanctuary from increasing urban poverty and crime. Along with encouraging careers for women, she also offered them a new authority as mothers in charge of the domestic realm.

Susan B. Anthony was another crucial woman in the first wave who invoked moral codes and temperance to achieve better conditions for women. Anthony's lifelong feminist collaboration with Elizabeth Cady Stanton resulted in their formation of the National American Woman Suffrage Association (NAWSA). NAWSA's primary goal was a federal constitutional amendment to give

SUSAN B. ANTHONY (1820 - 1906)

women the vote. In the meantime, Anthony campaigned for women's property rights and suffrage at the state level, organized women factory workers, and spoke across the country about the necessity of a single moral standard for both sexes. Anthony agreed with maternalists that drunkenness led to the sexual abuse of women, and asked American men to follow the same standard of "purity" that they required of any "respectable" woman. She also blamed the existence of prostitution on job discrimination and on women's economic dependence, saying, "Whoever controls work and wages, controls morals. Therefore we must have women employers, superintendents…[et al.]"

Not everyone who contributed to the fight for suffrage took a moralistic or moderate approach like Susan B. Anthony. Alice Paul joined NAWSA, and as the chairwoman of their congressional committee in 1913, attempted to gain more backing for suffrage in Washington, D.C. But amidst organizing parades and garnering attention for the cause, Paul realized that NAWSA would continue to seek suffrage on a state-by-state basis, cautiously approaching a constitutional amendment. Instead, Paul formed the National Woman's Party with her close friend Lucy Burns and a handful of other radical suffragists. They immediately staged more drastic campaigns to force the government's hand, including picketing the White House and chaining themselves to the gate. Upon Alice Paul and Lucy Burns' arrest for "obstructing traffic" when protesting, both went on hunger strike in jail. Ultimately, the efforts of the National Woman's Party and a public outcry against the poor treatment of the activists in prison resulted in President Wilson's endorsement of suffrage. The 19th constitutional amendment, called the "Anthony Amendment" for Susan B. Anthony, went into effect in 1920, giving women the right to vote.

After suffrage was won, feminist interests divided into a flurry of different advocacy concerns. Many women of the 1920s were interested in gaining more freedom of sexual expression. A new generation refuted maternalist constructions of women's "superiority"; many stated bluntly that they were humans, period, and ought to have equal rights to men. The National Woman's Party introduced an additional Equal Rights Amendment in 1923, citing the need for a discrimination clause to accompany their right to vote, lest their ability to fully participate be restricted, but the amendment was never ratified.

## WHAT IS THE ERA?

The ERA, or Equal Rights Amendment, states that "equality of rights under the law shall not be denied or abridged by the United States or any state on account of sex." First introduced in 1923, it eventually passed Congress in 1972, but was not able to acquire the endorsement of enough states (38) to make it part of the Constitution. It has been reintroduced in Congress every year since, but still has not been adopted.

## ELEANOR ROOSEVELT, RACISM AND WOMEN'S RIGHTS

As civil rights debates became increasingly heated, feminists were faced with the question of whether their so-called "universal" womanhood encapsulated other races. After all, their own privileges and rights were being denied on the basis of supposed biological differences. In some respects, white women and women of color shared the similar plight of being told they were innately lesser.

Eleanor Roosevelt's rejection of racism and anti-Semitism had a profound impact on feminists who saw the first lady as a leader and pioneer for women's rights. After her husband, Franklin D. Roosevelt, was no longer the President of the United States, Eleanor continued to engage in public work and policy reform. She served on the UN's Commission on Human Rights, and co-wrote their Universal Declaration of Human Rights. In her essay "UN Deliberations on the Draft Convention on Political Rights of Women" (1953), Roosevelt argued that the United Nations must advocate for equal rights for women across the world and make sure that women are also directly involved in developing government policies.

Middle-class and working women assisted the war effort during the 1940s, taking on all sorts of jobs that were left behind by men sent away to WWII. After the war ended, more women than ever had become union members, and laborers revived the socialist feminist goals, seeking equal pay and more job opportunities. But despite various efforts, from the 1930s to 1950s feminist movements receded somewhat into the backdrop of Americans' focus as civil rights struggles came to center stage.

By the end of public school segregation in 1954, race relations were being completely overhauled, and black women activists were at the very center. African-American women in the South fed, clothed, and housed both black and white civil rights workers while continuing to organize. From 1955–56 they led a bus boycott in support of civil rights activist Rosa Parks, who refused to give up her bus seat to a white man. According to Estelle B. Freedman, "a movement for racial justice insisted that white supremacy had no place in the postwar democratic world."

With feminism sidelined by the Civil Rights movement, a handful of women in the late 1940s through the early 1960s wrote crucial books that raised women's awareness of their marginalization. The French prize-winning novelist Simone de Beauvoir and liberal feminist Betty Friedan drew on academic, socialist, and labor ideologies to make many women rethink where sex categories and women's roles come from.

Simone de Beauvoir's *The Second Sex* (1949) skewered biological arguments for women's reduced status. In it, she expounds on the diversity of female experiences, and describes how women's lack of birth control, child care, and economic independence have held them hostage. Beauvoir redefined the idea of "woman" as a myth that was constructed mainly in contrast with men, always relegating women to the status of an "other." She maintains that "...the relation of the two sexes is not quite like that of two electrical poles, for man represents both the positive and the neutral, as is indicated by the common use of *man* to designate human beings in general; whereas woman represents only the negative, defined by limiting criteria, without reciprocity."

## SIMONE DE BEAUVOIR (1908-1986)

"HE IS THE SUBJECT, HE IS THE ABSOLUTE— SHE IS THE OTHER."

This quote from Simone de Beauvoir's *The Second Sex* refers to how, even just linguistically speaking, history is generally conveyed with an over-emphasis on masculine pronouns, marginalizing women to the point of invisibility.

*The Second Sex* also illustrates how, throughout history, hierarchies which denied freedom to groups of people either occurred as the result of a defined power struggle (such as a war), or because the subjugated group was a minority. But women are neither a minority, nor is there any documentation of a time before women were treated as the secondary or lesser sex; thus, Beauvoir wonders how discrimination against women has continued so long. Beauvoir supposes that without much recorded history of our own, perhaps women are more easily deemed inessential. She also contends that descriptions of femininity and its varying degrees weakens the case made by men that women are, by nature, inferior (or even different). Women are asked "to be women, remain women, become women. It would appear, then, that every female human being is not necessarily a woman; to be so considered she must share in that mysterious and threatened reality known as femininity."

Following World War II, several media outlets launched campaigns to raise the appeal of the domestic sphere, in hopes that women would hand back the jobs they had filled for absent soldiers during the war. Articles in women's magazines focused on how to "catch" (or keep) a man, handling children's sibling rivalry, and cooking; women with careers or academic aspirations were portrayed as unhappy and masculine. The effects of this campaign were quite startling; though a century earlier women were fighting tooth and nail for higher education, 60 percent of women who attended college in the 1950s dropped out to get married, and the U.S. birthrate soon skyrocketed.

In reality, throughout the supposedly "idyllic" 1950s and early 1960s, many middle class women privately found that the return to managing their household was not as fulfilling as the media had portrayed. Because of the rampant media idealization of at-home motherhood and easier domesticity aided by new appliances, many women assumed any frustration was theirs alone. Right before the second wave of feminism was prompted by the radicalism of the late 1960s, the publication of Betty Friedan's *The Feminine Mystique* (1963) provided a liaison between many middle class housewives by articulating their discontent:

"The problem lay buried, unspoken, for many years in the minds of American women. It was a strange stirring, a sense of dissatisfaction, a yearning that women suffered in the middle of the twentieth century in the United States. Each suburban wife struggled with it alone. As she made the beds, shopped for groceries, matched slipcover material, ate peanut butter sandwiches with her children, chauffeured Cub Scouts and Brownies, lay beside her husband at night—she was afraid to ask even of herself the silent question—'Is this all?'"

## FEMINIST SCIENCE FICTION OF THE 1960s

Several feminist writers in the 1960s used the typically male-dominated science fiction genre to covertly comment on social and political concerns. Setting their novels in dystopian landscapes and futuristic societies, the writers were free to invent new social morays, gender roles, and forms of sexuality. A few of the most crucial feminist writers from the 1960s—some of whom are still writing groundbreaking fiction today—were Ursula K. Le Guin, Margaret Atwood, Joanna Russ, Octavia Butler, and Alice Sheldon (the latter of whom used the pen name James Tiptree, Jr.).

*The Feminine Mystique* used personal testimonies to show that affluence hadn't made suburban households the golden ticket that educated women were expecting when abandoning their ambitions. A newspaperwoman and journalist in the labor movement who had also married and raised her kids in a suburb, Friedan cast doubt on the prevailing stereotype of a neurotic career woman. She called out popular psychology, educators, and the media that had constructed an unrewarding feminine ideal. Friedan also encouraged women to seek creative work outside the home and championed the importance of individuality.

In the late 1960s, as political fervor grew around the Vietnam War and dissenters held demonstrations calling both for revolution and a movement for peace, feminism resurged with a whole new set of concerns. Many middle class women who had heard Betty Friedan's call to arms became interested in talking about women's lives and aspirations in special women-only spaces to see what concerns and experiences they shared. These "consciousness raising" groups met across the country and soon recognized a great deal of overlap in the ways that women's autonomy and strength were being subverted. Women began asserting their desire to earn equal wages *and* raise children as a new "women's liberation" movement questioned power dynamics in love relationships, fair treatment in the workplace, and their own stake in reproductive politics.

Like first wave feminists, second wave feminists critiqued men's exploitation of women. But while first wave feminists advocated for temperance and illegally circulated information about birth control, by the second wave, sex and abuse were addressed more frankly. Citing the failure of the justice system to address rape, domestic violence, and sexual harassment—issues that had long been deemed "private" and ignored by both law enforcement and legal statutes—feminists claimed that a misogynistic societal hierarchy was reinforced in American family life and sexual relationships. They also sought better access to contraception and reproductive rights, including abortion. With the new battle cry, "The personal is political!", second wave feminists printed pamphlets declaring how public and private spheres could no longer be kept separate. Consciousness raising groups pointed to the media's inaccurate and objectifying portrayal of women; they demanded equal pay, and attempted to place women into more political positions and trade unions.

A famous declaration from the Women's Liberation movement's "second wave" of feminism

## MARGARET SANGER, BIRTH CONTROL AND THE FIRST WAVE

Margaret Sanger was a first wave feminist and nurse involved in the socialist and labor movements in the U.S. Sanger saw a connection between overpopulation and poverty resulting from unwanted pregnancies, and believed that women should have a choice about when they bear children. She coined the term "birth control," and ignored the U.S. law banning information on contraceptives, which she published and circulated in both pamphlets and the newspaper, *The Woman Rebel.* She also advocated for access to contraceptives, and opened the first birth control clinic in 1916, serving jail time when it was raided by police.

Up to that point, contraception had only been used to permanently end fertility, not as a "barrier" method to prevent pregnancy (or specific pregnancies) during a woman's fertile years. Sanger encouraged women to learn about their bodies, and in 1921, with the assistance of other medical professionals and middle class allies, she founded the American Birth Control League, which later became Planned Parenthood.

Most forms of birth control are no longer illegal, but some conservative and religious groups say that using it is immoral. They believe that by lessening the risks of intercourse outside of marriage, birth control endorses casual sex. Some also object to married couples preventing pregnancy. These conservatives would prefer that people who do not wish to have children simply abstain from having sex. Health care professionals, on the other hand, generally endorse contraceptive use as a way to protect women's health, and to offer both men and women more choices about if and when they decide to have children. Some contraceptives, including condoms, also protect against sexually transmitted infections (STIs), such as HIV, the virus that causes AIDS.

MARGARET SANGER
(1879-1966)

### MARIE STOPES

Marie Stopes, a British palaeobotanist and advocate for women's rights, was another key pioneer in the field of birth control. As of 2010, a nonprofit bearing her name, Marie Stopes International, had 619 centers in 40 countries where they provide family planning, abortions, STI screenings, and health care for mothers and children.

During the 1970s, birth control and reproductive rights came into focus as a national policy issue when the Supreme Court decision on the court case *Roe v. Wade* made abortion legal. The judges found that the right to privacy in the 14th Amendment to the Constitution includes a woman's right to choose whether or not to abort a pregnancy. They also stipulated that this right needed to be weighed against protecting women's health and prenatal life, which are considered state concerns. Currently, the U.S. right to abortion ends with viability; that is, once a fetus becomes developed enough that it could live outside the mother's womb (usually 28 weeks into pregnancy, although six states draw the line at 20 weeks), it can no longer be terminated, except in the case of an emergency procedure to save the mother's life. Generally speaking, only first-trimester abortions are allowed for reasons unrelated to the mother's health.

ROE V. WADE
THE SUPREME COURT

### DID YOU KNOW?

Federal funding cuts for women's health care do not only limit access to abortions, but leave women without access to breast exams, cervical cancer screenings, and other crucial preventative care. In Texas, federal funding for women's health care was cut by two-thirds in early 2012.

In recent years, federal Medicaid funding for preventative and reproductive health care serving low-income or uninsured women has been drastically reduced in some states. Thirteen have placed bans on insurance coverage for abortions, limiting access to abortions and contraception for many women. Other states have policies that force pregnant women to view an ultrasound before terminating a pregnancy (North Carolina, Virginia, Texas, and proposed in Idaho and Pennsylvania). In many other countries, however, women do not have any legal right to say "no" to having a baby they do not want or cannot provide for, even if it was conceived as result of rape or incest.

A culture of violence against women is a feminist issue, a human rights issue, and a major concern in our society today. According to a 2005 study, globally, women and girls ages 15 to 44 are more likely to be maimed or killed by men than by malaria, cancer, war and traffic accidents combined.

Abortion is still a contested issue in America. Those who oppose abortion on moral or religious principles generally argue that ending a potential life is not a mother's right; they believe that a baby has its own consciousness and rights. Proponents of the woman's right to choose, by contrast, have various reasons for their stance. Some contend that at conception an embryo is simply a cluster of cells with the potential for life, not yet a "baby" with its own autonomy or consciousness. Others cite poverty and many women's lack of access to health care or preventative contraception as reasons that abortion should be an option. Still others simply think that a woman should have total control over her own health and body.

Discrimination against women costs many female lives. Globally, at least one in three women and girls has been beaten or sexually abused in her lifetime.

Second wave feminists made great strides in establishing women's shelters and resources for domestic abuse, but many assaults and violent crimes against women are committed by strangers or acquaintances. Domestic violence statistics are likely unreliable, given the fear of retribution and stigma attached to women in abusive relationships. Underreporting notwithstanding, incidents are still high, and 61 percent of female homicide victims are wives or intimate acquaintances of their killers. Studies further suggest that most domestic battering and intimate partner homicide results from an abusive partner's overwhelming desire for control. In other words, it's about power.

Rape was a particular concern of second wave feminists. Rape can occur in domestic situations, dating scenarios, or be inflicted by total strangers. Historically, rape has also occurred in the course of war,

## GENITAL MUTILATION

One form of ongoing violence against women is genital mutilation, a forced practice in some parts of sub-Saharan Africa and the Middle East where the clitoris and part or all of the labia is sliced off. Amnesty International reports that 135 million women have endured genital cutting or mutilation—ostensibly performed in order to prevent young women from having sex prior to marriage. In some variations of this practice, the vaginal opening may be sewn closed so that only urine can pass through. Even when performed by doctors, genital cutting can lead to copious bleeding, serious illness, or death from infections. It often results in very painful intercourse and ongoing urinary tract infections for the rest of a woman's life, as well as loss of pleasure or sensation, and complications when giving birth. The UN and many governments are attempting to stop this practice, deeming it an inhumane human rights violation.

wherein soldiers have raped women from the opposing territory or territories—a violation that is seldom brought before any court of law. Marital rape was not considered a crime in the United States until the 1970s, and as recently as the 1990s, only 44 of the 50 states had made it against the law. That means that until quite recently, marriage gave a husband access to his wife's body whenever he wanted it, regardless of whether his partner offered consent (or a wife access to her husband's body, though rape initiated by a woman statistically occurs far less frequently). U.S. laws also leave the burden of proving rape largely on the victim, who may be traumatized by the assault or afraid to confront the incident.

In *Against Our Will: Men, Women and Rape* (1975), second wave feminist Susan Brownmiller articulates how sexual relations reinforce men's control over women, making sex both a personal and a political concern. *Against Our Will* details the long history of rape in conquest, slavery, war, and within families, dispelling with inaccurate racial stereotypes and myths about rapists' demographics. Brownmiller argues that women who fear violence and rape will remain dependent on men's protection, and that this cycle reinforces male domination:

"Once we accept as basic truth that rape is not a crime of irrational, impulsive, uncontrollable lust, but is a deliberate, hostile, violent act of degradation and possession on the part of a would-be conqueror, designed to intimidate and inspire fear, we must look toward those elements in our culture that promote and propagandize these attitudes, which offer men, and in particular, impressionable, adolescent males, who form the potential raping population, the ideology and psychologic [sic] encouragement to commit their acts of aggression *without awareness, for the most part, that they have committed a punishable crime*, let alone a moral wrong."

Brownmiller's book and other second wave feminists' conferences and teach-ins about rape led to the creation of rape crisis centers, monitored rape trials (to assess sexism in the proceedings), self-defense classes, and legal reform. Nevertheless, there is still considerable stigmatization of rape victims, and some people continue to falsely claim that women "seduce" a man into rape, or that a woman's clothing can automatically imply interest or consent in sexual activity. The defense that "she was asking for it" is an obvious example of discrimination against women, wherein society deflects a violent act's cause onto its victim. The validity of rape rests on whether or not both parties consented to having sex; no article of clothing, flirting, or intimate behavior is a valid substitute for consent.

**FACTS ON RAPE AND SEXUAL ASSAULT**

In the United States, every two minutes someone is sexually assaulted, and every six minutes a woman is raped. One out of every six American women has been the victim of an attempted or completed rape in her lifetime.

Publicity around women's liberation peaked when demonstrators picketed a Miss America pageant, occupied *Ladies Home Journal* offices, and created public forums to discuss rape, prostitution, and abortion rights. Some of the demonstrations that won the most attention to feminism's second wave also gave the media ammunition to portray women activists as fierce and militant, making some people more cautious about adopting women's causes or the label "feminist."

**TEACH-INS**

Popularized during the Vietnam War protests, a "teach-in" is a public participatory forum on an issue (usually political) geared toward taking action. Aimed at inclusivity, not all speakers at a typical teach-in are academics or even "experts" on the topic of the forum.

Perhaps because the radical movement of the second wave was largely comprised of civil rights activists and student organizers, white feminists of the 1960s began to collaborate more frequently with black women activists. And although the integration was limited, a handful of feminist theorists acknowledged the possibility that racial categories might be as socially constructed as they considered gender. In 1964, African-American feminist Fannie Lou Hamer demanded that black delegates be seated at the Democratic National Convention. The same year, the Civil Rights Act prohibiting both racial and sex discrimination was finally passed—a bill that the National Woman's Party had adamantly supported. An Equal Employment Opportunity Commission was also formed in order to address discrimination charges, but when it failed to respond to gender concerns, feminists (including co-founder Betty Friedan) formed a new lobbying group modeled after the NAACP's structure called the National Organization for Women (NOW). By 1966, NOW had 300 active members and started once again to gather support for passage of the ERA and other equal rights legislation.

## FEMINISM IS NOT A DIRTY WORD

You might have heard people say "feminism" with a look of unease—or heard someone defending women begin a sentence with the phrase, "I'm not a feminist, but...." Why does the word "feminism" so often inspire fear or distaste? Feminists have often been cast in a negative light over the years, especially in the conservative media. Some news outlets portray feminists as women who dislike men, or who are trying to seize their power. Others cast them as being unattractive, unfeminine, or simply angry. These same journalists and politicians have also proclaimed feminism "dead" many times, ignoring its ever-evolving movements across the world.

Some people who speak poorly of feminism likely fear a change in hierarchy, family, and sex relations, or do not wish to reexamine sex and gender categories. Lesbian history and literature scholar Lillian Faderman also asserts that European sexologists in the 1890s made a false connection between homosexuality and feminism. They blamed feminism for women becoming more independent and accused feminists of causing women to reject marriage and "become" lesbians. Some people involved with other social justice movements may also hold a grudge against feminist movements for their previous lack of inclusivity. Finally, in a country where it is implied that everyone has the same chance to succeed, feminists who testify otherwise prompt people to face the uncomfortable question of whether everyone with power deserves their success.

NOW advocated on behalf of the liberal agenda of the second wave, publicizing the need for antidiscrimination laws regarding equal pay and the promotion of women workers. *Ms.* magazine, started and run by feminist journalist Gloria Steinem, also helped to promote these goals. These liberal feminists included some women of color, like Aileen Hernandez, who became NOW's second president. NOW continued to push for women in public office, and for the Equal Credit Opportunity Act (ECOA), which was eventually enacted in 1974 and helps to protect workers who experience racial or sexual discrimination in hiring, promo-

THE CONVENTION ON THE ELIMINATION OF ALL FORMS OF DISCRIMINATION AGAINST WOMEN (CEDAW), DRAFTED AND ADOPTED BY THE UNITED NATIONS GENERAL ASSEMBLY IN 1979, RATIFIED BY 185 COUNTRIES (BUT NOT BY THE UNITED STATES).

workers who experience racial or sexual discrimination in hiring, promotion, or in their general work environment. The ECOA also includes the Women's Education Equity Act, which bans sex discrimination in schools.

Even though second wave feminism was more racially integrated than the women's movements before them, feminist concerns retained a stereotype of being primarily white, middle class women's interests. Black feminist author and scholar Bell Hooks contends that numerous African-American women (and some African-American men) feared that the second wave would result in white women taking jobs currently held by qualified black men. Affirmative action campaigns (which place quotas on the percentage of minority applicants that need to be included when hiring for a company or in admissions to colleges) did not have multiple categories, so a white woman could fill the same quota "slot" as a black man. Further-

## AN INTERNATIONAL BILL OF RIGHTS FOR WOMEN: CEDAW

NOW additionally advocated for the United Nations Convention on the Elimination of all forms of Discrimination Against Women (CEDAW). Drafted and adopted by the United Nations General Assembly in 1979, CEDAW is essentially an international bill of rights for women. It simultaneously defines what counts as discrimination and outlines actions that need to be taken to address that treatment, including laws and institutions to protect women more effectively. Although the U.S. was involved in the document's writing, we have not yet joined the 185 countries who have ratified CEDAW.

more, Hooks thinks that feminists who advocated for "career women" failed to consider who would maintain homes or take care of children in their absence. Hooks believes that second wave feminists forgot the interests of women without access to education, as well as single women and women without children. For the working poor white or black woman, Hooks explains, many of Betty Friedan's concerns were moot. In her opinion, most maids, factory workers, and prostitutes would gladly take the place of a leisure-class housewife. She illustrated the situation thusly:

"If improving conditions in the workplace for women had been a central agenda for feminist movement [sic] in conjunction with efforts to obtain better-paying jobs for women and finding jobs for unemployed women of all classes, feminism would have been seen as a movement addressing the concerns of all women. [The f]eminist focus on careerism, getting women employed in high-paying professions, not only alienated masses of women from feminist movement [sic]; it also allowed feminist activists to ignore the fact that increased entry of bourgeois women into the work force was not a sign that women as a group were gaining economic power. Had they looked at the economic situation of poor and working-class women, they would have seen the growing problem of unemployment and increased entry of women from all classes into the ranks of the poor."

Despite moderate division over goals, after the Civil Rights movement and consciousness raising groups swept the nation, more people felt free to publicly identify more adamantly with their varied cultural backgrounds, sexual orientations, and personal experiences. Mexican-American, Native American, Asian-American, lesbian, and disabled women began to tentatively add their experiences to the second wave. Women's resistance movements outside of Europe and North America likely predated our own, but they became more organized and far-reaching as technology developed. Global feminisms gained increasing visibility during the 1970s, in both industrial countries and in places with agriculturally-based economies.

Because the second wave aimed to cut across race, religion, and sexual identity, the primary goal of gender equality became slightly less emphatic. Between the 1970s and 80s, more feminists contextualized their identity within international conflicts and cross-cultural differences. Others rejected labels of gender and race altogether—an act of resistance meant to demonstrate that people's complex, hybrid selves could not fit neatly into simple labels. Many people claimed new interracial titles, asserting legitimacy for both their American status and their family's country of origin, however long ago or recently they emigrated.

Alongside the feminists (and other advocates for social justice) who rejected simplistic racial categorization, those who questioned narrow gender categories sought alternatives to heterosexual relationships and archetypal gender roles. A new exploration of sexuality had begun in the 1960s, and its political focus expanded as radical and liberal feminists sought gender solidarity. Some women claimed lesbian identities not just as a sexual orientation, but as a statement of love for other women and a rejection of male dominance. Feminist theorist Monique Wittig, who co-founded of the Mouvement de Libération des Femmes in France in 1970, reasoned that lesbian society proves that there is no natural group called "women." Her essay "One Is Not Born a Woman" (1980) encourages women to explore lesbianism as a way to reconsider the limits of heterosexuality. Wittig felt that the distinctions between men and women, homosexual and heterosexual were the result of politics and socialization, not any preexisting natural category:

"The belief...in a prehistory when women created civilization (because of a biological predisposition) while the coarse and brutal men hunted (because of a biological predisposition) is symmetrical with the biologizing interpretation of history produced up to now by the class of men....not only is this conception still imprisoned in the categories of sex (woman and man), but it holds on to the idea that the capacity to give birth (biology) is what defines a woman....there are lesbians who affirm that 'women and men are different species or races...men are biologically inferior to women; male violence is a biological inevitability'... by doing this, by admitting that there is a 'natural' division between women and men, we naturalize history, we assume that men and women have always existed and will always exist."

Not all second wave feminists were such strong proponents of lesbians or gender nonconformity. In fact, for some second wave women, lesbians complicated the image of a feminist, and undermined their acceptance in mainstream society. The role of sexuality, sexual orientation, and trans women in feminism was also in question during the 1970s and 80s, both in mainstream politics and for feminists who were deciding whether lesbian and bisexual concerns were part of feminism, or a separate issue altogether.

In the 1980s, the former ideal of "safe [separate] space" for different minority groups to discuss experiences and address their concerns fell by the wayside of coalition politics. Feminists aligned with other social justice groups to address welfare reform, reproductive rights, and the AIDS crisis. In the face of a newly conservative government, Estelle B. Freedman says, "White women learned to protest racism, heterosexual women of color to support lesbian rights," and male allies who adopted the label "feminist" stepped forward to defend women's rights to abortions and birth control. Feminism became increasingly used as an umbrella term to describe anyone questioning gender relations; it was even applied to men and women who did not personally identify with the term. Likewise, a myriad of people asked for equal wages, parental leave from work, and pursued other social justice reforms that would previously have been described as feminist issues, all the while rejecting the term "feminist" to describe themselves.

Feminism largely fell out of fashion in America throughout the late 1980s, leaving continued disparity between male and female opportunities. As overt discrimination became less socially acceptable, mainstream society took a step aside from politicizing the personal, but inequality remained. Women could get into law school, but partners were almost exclusively male; then, as now, violence against women, abortion rights, and unequal pay remained prevalent. Many women and their allies continued to seek improved workplace rights, maternity leave, and protection from discrimination, but popular consensus said Americans no longer considered feminism necessary; it was commonly assumed that women had attained more or less equal options to men. This perception was likely based on a middle class white idea of "women," largely ignoring that many women of varying orientation, age, race, and class have far fewer options and experience discrimination daily. It also ignored continued disparity of pay and other ongoing concerns, such as access to reproductive health care.

Then, in 1992, African-American lawyer Anita Hill testified to the U.S. Senate Judiciary Committee that Supreme Court nominee Clarence Thomas had sexually harassed her. When Thomas was confirmed as a Supreme Court judge irrespective of Hill's testimony, Rebecca Walker, daughter of prominent feminist Alice Walker, was outraged. Overwhelmed by this compelling evidence that women's voices were still not as valued as men's, Rebecca refused to keep silent.

In an essay entitled "Becoming the Third Wave," she asked American women to create a third wave of feminism and address remaining obstacles particular to women. She wrote passionately, "To be a feminist is to integrate an ideology of equality and female empowerment into the very fiber of my life. It is to search for personal clarity in the midst of systemic destruction, to join in sisterhood with women when often we are divided, to understand power structures with the intention of challenging them." Walker launched a voter registration campaign to invigorate youth activists and created the Third Wave Foundation to finance young women's political projects. She also published an anthology called *To Be Real: Telling the Truth and Changing the Face of Feminism* (1994), which sparked new interest and enthusiasm among women for a more truly inclusive feminism.

REBECCA WALKER (B. 1969)

As the third wave progressed through the 1990s, the latest generation of feminist activists took on yet more new obstacles. Freedman lists sexual abuse, eating disorders, and low self-esteem among some of the more pressing third wave issues—problems that feminists generally consider symptomatic of a society that continues to systematically silence and dishearten women. Some third wave feminist activists in the punk rock music scene started a media campaign promoting "girl power," hoping to imbue young women with the confidence to assert themselves. They created "riot grrrl" fanzines, and musicians sang about female independence and sexuality. The overrepresentation of men in popular art and society continued to be critiqued by feminists like Kathleen Hanna of the female punk band Bikini Kill, whose "Riot Grrrl Manifesto" proclaims:

"...we are unwilling to let our real and valid anger be diffused and/or turned against us via the internalization of sexism as witnessed In girl/girl jealousy and self defeating girltype behaviors...[sic] BECAUSE doing/reading/seeing/hearing cool things that validate and challenge us can help us gain the strength and sense of community that we need in order to figure out how... racism, able-bodieism, ageism, speciesism, classism, thinism, sexism, anti-semitism and heterosexism figures in our own lives."

IN THE EARLY 1990s, ZINES LIKE KATHLEEN HANNA'S "RIOT GRRRL" (1991) WERE PART OF A YOUTHFUL AND PUNKY NEW ERA OF FEMINIST THOUGHT.

Finally, working class women, women of color, lesbians, and some non-industrialized nations found that new and drastically broader definitions of American feminism and third wave issues included them as well.

Since the year 2000, feminist movements across the world have developed diverse emphases, ranging from a concentration on specific women's issues to linked concerns of nationality, religion, race, and class. Local contexts play a large role in shaping gender relations, and so, today's feminists attempt to address issues, knowing that the term "woman" is not all-inclusive, nor universal; rather, "woman" means something very different depending on where and when you live. Feminists do not agree on all advocacy issues but they share a devotion to empowering women on their own terms, and within their specific cultures and contexts.

---

## THERE IS STILL A "GLASS CEILING"

In the U.S. Department of Labor and in economic terminology, "the glass ceiling" is a term used to refer to the invisible but undeniable barrier keeping women and other minorities from reaching the highest ranking positions in corporations and leadership regardless of their qualifications. Women hold many more leadership roles today than they did a century ago, and have better access to higher education, but many barricades remain for women in the workplace. Statistics show that employers are likely to promote less qualified men, endorse stereotypes about women that create a poor environment for female workers, and exclude women from informal networking opportunities. Among top earners, CEOs, and Fortune 500 companies, men are grossly overrepresented. According to the 2010 Catalyst Census, which calculates women's representation in large companies in the U.S., women fill only 14.4 percent of executive officer positions at Fortune 500 companies and 7.6 percent of top earner positions.

---

# Women's Representation in U.S. Politics

**Elected Positions held by Women**
- Percent of seats in congress     17%
- Percent of state legislative positions     35%
- Number of governors     6 (out of 50)

Although their views of an ideal society vary, and their negative portrayal in the media persists, feminists have helped to change the way that men and women relate over the last two centuries. They have gained significant rights, laws, and personal freedoms for women, improving their opportunities in the workplace, domestic life, and interpersonal relationships, as well as placing women in public office. But in a world where 70 percent of those living in poverty and two-thirds of those who cannot read are female, there is still much for feminists to work together on. Gender archetypes persist and the "glass ceiling" for women in the workplace is still present. It is time to deconstruct gender norms, and consider how they limit life options and opportunities for expression in our society.

# CHAPTER 4

# MODERN CONSTRUCTION OF GENDER ROLES

Following the Industrial Revolution, women in America began to seek rights, laws, and regulations to address sex discrimination in its various forms, hoping to eliminate the barriers to their aspirations and basic freedoms. Since then, women's history in America has consisted of a series of advances followed by steps backward for equal treatment. We know that religion, capitalism, myths about our prehistoric ancestors, and the development of scientific theories have all historically helped to shape the gender roles cultivated in our society. But with the rise of feminism and more empowered women in the workforce than ever before, how are gender roles evolving today? And why do old archetypes keep turning up again?

Parenting and early social interaction has a huge impact on the construction of identities for all genders. In *Delusions of Gender*, Cordelia Fine points out how different the early environment for male- and female-assigned children in our culture really is. For example, even six- to twelve-month-old infants have vastly "gendered" toys. As developmental psychologists Alison Nash and Rosemary Krawczyk confirm in their 2007 study on children's toys, boys are given more "toys of the world," while girls have more "toys of the home" (think: machines and trucks vs. dolls and tea sets). Mothers also talk and interact more with their girl infants, even though boys are just as attuned and attached to their words. Studies show

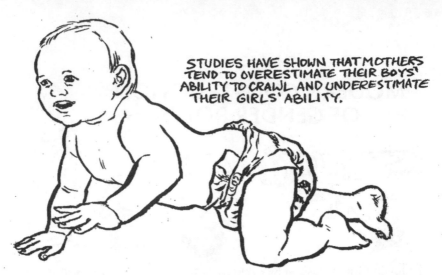

STUDIES HAVE SHOWN THAT MOTHERS TEND TO OVERESTIMATE THEIR BOYS' ABILITY TO CRAWL AND UNDERESTIMATE THEIR GIRLS' ABILITY.

that mothers tend to overestimate their boys' and underestimate their girls' ability to crawl. And by preschool age, female-assigned children are spoken to more often and in more detail about their emotions, which may lead to the so-called innate emotional proficiency of females that some scientists and psychologists advocate.

Many parents tell their children that they can grow up to pursue any career that they desire, but nevertheless demonstrate a partiality for "gender-typical" behavior. Fine claims that modern parents who attempt to raise their kids outside of gender stereotypes generally retain some gendered expectations for them. While parents may "sincerely believe that boys and girls deserve to be free to develop their own interests…they channel and craft their children's 'gender performances,' especially for boys." For example, parents may encourage domestic and nurturing skills in their sons, but continue to patrol the gender borderline (i.e., being unwilling to buy boys Barbie dolls, or mitigating a son's "feminine" interest in dance by suggesting that he play sports as well). One study initially found that parents generally agree that girls should play with blocks and trucks and that boys should develop equal social skills to girls. Ironically, when researchers talked to those parents' kids, they did not agree that their parents would want them playing with "opposite-gender" toys. It appears that children pick up on subtler cues than parents may realize they give off.

Still, there are plenty of studies that report children themselves demonstrating stereotypical gendered preferences in their interests prior to two years old. And since children of this age are unaware of their assigned sex, some scientists use such data to say their predispositions are biologically hardwired. But what if, even in their short lives, girl infants have simply seen "more pink and more dolls…paired with pleasurable experiences with caregivers?" Fine contends that infants don't need to know their own sex to respond to a parent's cues and behavior patterns.

And apparently, infants begin reacting differently to other people's expressed gender at three to four months of age. By ten months, babies appear to distinguish when objects are assigned a gender category or gendered association. For example, they will consistently look longer at a picture of men with an object that had previously been shown to them paired with women.

From noticing who inhabits which roles in a household, to pronoun usage, clothing, hairstyles, and gender-"appropriate" behavior, we begin to note the gender coding around us very early on. It therefore stands to reason that children would attempt to identify their "correct" path and seek approval by following the suggestions around them.

The gender distinction in apparel and toys for children was originally quite strategic. Sociologist Jo Paoletti asserts that until the late 1800s, children in the Western world were typically dressed in unisex white dresses from birth to roughly age five. At the close of the 19th century, as scientists, psychologists, and feminists raised new questions about whether or not masculinity and femininity are innate, dresses for boys two years or older swiftly became unfashionable. And once psychologists learned that infants were extremely sensitive to their surroundings, infants' clothing transformed as well. Color-specific fabrics for children's clothes were introduced (pink was originally a "male" color, due to its similarity to red, which symbolized "courage"). At the same time, child psychologists began to encourage gender distinctions to be actively taught, lest they not develop on their own. So while today people often think of color-coding and gender markers in clothing and toys as simply suiting boys' and girls' personalities and preferences, they were once a way of actively enforcing the gender archetypes that now are coming into question once again.

## RECOGNIZING GENDER ROLES

The question seems to hover in our peripheral vision: To what extent do we recognize the gender roles that have become so imbedded in our culture? How can we truly know what we are teaching kids, or whether any of our actions are really instinctual if we do not first identify those actions' origins?

"One mother who insisted on supplying her daughter with tools rather than dolls finally gave up when she discovered the child undressing a hammer and singing it to sleep. 'It must be hormonal,' was the mother's explanation. At least until someone asked who had been putting her daughter to bed."

—Deborah Rhode, legal scholar

In Gendered Spaces (1992), urban and environmental planning scholar Daphne Spain reveals how hierarchy can be reinforced in architecture... For instance, cubicles in the work place.

MIGHT THE VERY SPACES ONE LIVES AND WORKS IN HAVE AN IMPACT ON HOW WE SEE GENDER ROLES?

From infancy, we are encouraged to adopt different behaviors, interests, play patterns, and strategies for seeking attention in accordance with our assigned sex. Even so, most school-age children don't actually self-segregate along gender lines—except in the school yard, a highly structured environment where the majority of research on children takes place. In other environments, kids in small groups tend to play together with much less attention to gender, especially when adults aren't around to watch. Sociologist Barrie Thorne's book, *Gender Play*, describes how researchers pay the most attention to extreme examples of "dominant" boys and "passive" girls. Because such kids fit the expected archetypes, Thorne argues that most researchers ignore the vast majority of girls and boys whose behavior overlaps more than it differs. She stresses that gender-restricted play (such as "boys-only" games) only occurs among most kids when they're coerced by one or two strong personalities. Likewise, she offers case studies that demonstrate how so-called "gender-specific" behavior tends to blur when adults or bullies aren't present to tease or reinforce norms.

What changes occur in boys' and girls' behavior and treatment of one another when policies not only identify kids by gender, but actively segregate them? Clinical psychologist Mary Pipher's *Reviving Ophelia*, a critical examination of the development and relationships of adolescent girls, became a huge bestseller in the mid-1990s, evoking fear in school administrators and parents alike that girls were in terrible danger during their teenage years. Almost simultaneously, several studies were released suggesting that the media, sexism in schools, and other cultural pressures were destroying teen girls' self-esteem. Some studies said that teachers were calling more on boys, and that extracurricular programming for girls was underfunded; soon after, initiatives were raised for single-sex schools across America.

Proponents of single-sex schools suggested that both boys and girls should have access to an educational environment that catered to their unique ways of learning. The objective was to ensure that young girls' voices weren't lost, to help boys and girls to better socialize and be respectful of one another, and to design educational curricula around each gender's specific needs. Almost immediately, however, studies found that in new single-sex schools, boys were being taught in regimented ways and acquiring sexist behaviors, and girls were given a new nurturing environment where they were "applauded for being feminine and being concerned about their appearance."

What's more, there's no evidence to suggest that the sexes actually *do* learn differently, making gender-specific strategies for teaching an uncertain endeavor. Renown sociologist Cynthia Fuchs Epstein reports "no evidence of psychological or cognitive differences between the sexes that would make them learn differently." In fact, her research demonstrates that gender-specific teaching methods would serve no cognitive advantages whatsoever. Fine further attests, "It's simply not the case that people use one particular lobe, or a circumscribed area of the brain, to read a novel, or write an essay, or solve an equation, or calculate the angle of a triangle…even if we are happy to relate one part of the brain to complex cognition… this…is a very poor index of actual ability." Since the sexes' aptitudes are equal, and scientists cannot ascertain the complex relationships between the parts of the brain involved in learning any scholastic subject, gender-specific teaching strategies based on presumed brain structure differences set a dangerous precedent. But while many educators worry about the effectiveness of gender-specific teaching methods (or that limited socialization between genders will increase mutual stereotyping), others contest that single-sex schools can eliminate the marginalization girls sometimes experience in coed classrooms and counteract poor funding allocation for girl-specific programming in other public schools.

TITLE IX (AN EDUCATION CONSTITUTIONAL AMENDMENT ENACTED IN 1972) AIMED TO ELIMINATE SEX-BASED DISCRIMINATION IN ALL FEDERALLY-FUNDED EDUCATION PROGRAMS – INCLUDING, SIGNIFICANTLY, SPORTS.

Title IX, a constitutional amendment enacted in 1972, states plainly that, "No person in the United States shall, on the basis of sex, be excluded from participation in, be denied the benefits of, or be subjected to discrimination under any education program or activity receiving federal financial assistance." Disregarding reports that girls were still being discriminated against in the education system (or perhaps unaware of them), in 2002, 2003, and 2004, President George W. Bush attempted to cut Women's Educational Equity Act's funding ("which promotes equality in education for women and girls"). Then in 2006, the No Child Left Behind Act (NCLB) allowed public school districts to increase the number of single-sex classes and schools. Title IX makes equal coeducation opportunities required by law, but they are no longer uniformly enforced. Under the NCLB, schools only need to provide evidence that they are "substantially equal" to other public education programs—a vague qualification which in no way protects against stereotyped approaches, or even unequal allocation of funding.

## NO CHILD LEFT BEHIND

First signed into law in 2002, the NCLB makes federal funding for schools dependent on their employing standardized testing on a state-by-state basis to assess grade-level skills.

As the number of single-sex schools and gender-specific approaches to curricula grew, several more popular psychology and self-help books were released claiming that the new emphasis on elevating girls' self-esteem in the classroom was coming at the expense of the boys—even though boys' test scores were as high as ever. The books in question did not take race and class disparity into account in their studies, and used poor sampling guidelines—like taking their entire test group from boys in remedial classes. But they did manage to slow the media avalanche and public support for addressing girls' inequities in the classroom.

Why have recent books and studies that imply rigid sex differences been persuasive enough to impose policy changes? It is possible that their appearance is related to a cultural backlash against women gaining power. Shortly after feminist successes resulted in more women moving into the workforce, a number of neurobiological and psychology-based studies and books came out that found new avenues to dichotomize men and women. Alongside them, several self-help books such as *Men Are From Mars, Women Are From Venus* (1992) became bestsellers in the 1980s through the early 2000s, while effectively proclaiming that men and women's personalities and abilities were not as flexible as modern relationships had begun to dictate. (Other examples include Deborah Tannen's *You Just Don't Understand*, Michael Gurian's *The Wonder of Girls*, and Sylvia Ann Hewlett's *Creating a Life:*

*Professional Women and the Quest for Children).* Some of the books were written by conservatives aiming to reinvigorate more traditional and rigid ideas about gender roles. In a throwback to the theory of men and women's "separate spheres," sex difference advocates suggested that by acknowledging each sex's "unique strengths" in the workplace and at home, relationships would be more rewarding and work more fulfilling. Others were written by feminists and their allies who sought strategies for women to succeed without needing to abandon femininity.

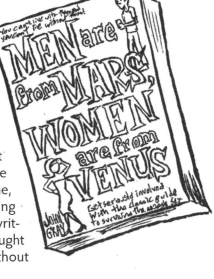

---

### MEN LEFT BEHIND

Our society's applauding of masculinity doesn't just hurt women. In many respects, men's "domination" has worked against them as well. Males in America are often socially ostracized if they exhibit "feminine" qualities. Stay-at-home dads, for example, are somewhat rare and are frequently stereotyped as lazy or unsuccessful, even though taking time off to raise their children may have been a calculated decision. Men's fiscal status is often used as a measure of their worth in a similar manner to the overvaluing of women's appearance, making the pressure for males to succeed tremendous. With masculine attributes associated with leadership and authority, young men are often taught to be tough and stifle their emotions. Statistically, American men live shorter lives, die younger, and have more stress-related health concerns than women.

---

One longstanding effect of promoting the dichotomy of men and women—from Ancient Greece to modern sex difference studies—is the elevated status of masculine qualities and the devaluing of femininity in both males and females. This privileging of masculinity can be better understood by considering the concept of heteronormativity. "Heteronormativity" is a term referring to "the practices and institutions that privilege heterosexuality, heterosexual relationships, and traditional gender roles as 'natural' within society. [It] implies that people fall into only one of two distinct sexes." A heteronormative perspective assumes that sex, gender identity, and gender roles should all conform to a binary system, wherein there are only two options and they are opposites. In our society, heteronormativity sets up men and women as opposites, wherein men are granted some kinds of superior power and status. Heterosexuality and homosexuality are also generally assumed to be opposites in America, as sexual and marital relationships between a man and a woman are often considered more "natural." Many people believe that heteronormativity results in the marginalization and mistreatment of LGBTQIA individuals as well as the underrepresentation and undervaluing of women and feminine qualities.

In addition to the ways in which play, gender segregation, and assumptions about strengths or abilities can shift young people's confidence or aptitude, heteronormativity is also a major factor. It figures prominently into what associations kids have with ideas of masculinity and femininity, and often discourages them from expressing any traits that don't perfectly conform to gender archetypes.

Masculinity's dominance can also have the effect of making femininity seem like a less preferable gender expression. Examples of this are prevalent in the media's disparagingly sexist discussion of women leaders as ineffectual, and in the limited and inaccurate representation of females in film and television. Furthermore, masculinity is sometimes employed as a strategy for women's success in our current society. Even some sex difference scientists concur that "tomboy" females' gender nonconformity can be advantageous. Physician and psychologist Leonard Sax, for instance, suggests in *Gender Matters* (2005) that masculine females who emulate "male" qualities will have the confidence to stand up for themselves, seek careers, and succeed both socially and academically. The case study Sax gives for his "anomalous" or irregular girl describes her (and other girls with masculine traits, by virtue of her being the only example of tomboys) as, "[knowing] what she wants—in school, from her friends, and from the boys in her life. She makes whatever arrangements are necessary to secure her objectives." He goes on to equate fearlessness and competitiveness with masculinity and success.

By contrast, Sax instructs feminine males to "[sign] up for the Boy Scouts or for an all-boys summer camp with lots of camping and hiking and sports. Avoid computer science camps, arts camps, music camps, and the like." He blames parents' overprotectiveness and permissiveness for these boys' traits, which he describes as being "geeky," sensitive, withdrawn, precocious (especially with language skills), more likely to have allergies, and opposed to new adventures or strangers. Of course, these traits could as easily describe an introverted intellectual of either sex as the "feminine male" that Sax attributes them to. Despite also acknowledging that they may have strengths in the arts *and* sciences, be highly articulate, well-behaved, and unlikely to get into trouble, Sax encourages parents to dissuade feminine males from their instinctual interests and abilities. He seems to believe that socializing boys with these supposedly "feminine" qualities to get along with other, more archetypal males, they may eventually become more masculine.

It seems somewhat ironic that Sax and other sex difference specialists say that gender variant children, if encouraged to do the opposite of their impulse, can adjust and will be better socialized. On some level, that seems to suggest that their gender identity is not hardwired after all (or is at least malleable). Regardless, Sax's suggestions clearly demonstrate how studies and publications in "sex difference" science don't just *perceive* some biological divergence between males and females. They can also actively *promote* the strict typecasting of how boys and girls should act, think, behave, and what areas of interest they should pursue. Such adamant delineation between genders also typically paints femininity as passive and weak—a stigma which has negative connotations for both men and women who embody feminine traits. For example, such thinking can position a mother as an almost automatically overbearing influence on her son —and as someone who he should avoid imitating. Furthermore, following the parenting or relationship advice of sex difference proponents will ultimately reinforce the notion that archetypal men and women have particular attributes that are "normal"—and that everyone else is, as Sax put it, "anomalous."

One of the most influential books on sex differences was written by feminist psychologist, Carol Gilligan. *In a Different Voice* (1982) acknowledged that the qualities which typically win respect in our society—independent thinking, decisiveness, and direct action—are often considered less desirable when embodied by a woman. Hoping to resolve this conundrum, Gilligan proposed a new take on child development. *In a Different Voice* suggested that because boys are "mainly"

brought up by an opposite-sex parent, they have to remain independent (or wean themselves away from their mother's influence early on) in order to develop a masculine identity. Therefore, Gilligan concluded, men are not as aware of others' feelings as women, who she believes spend their childhoods bonding and identifying with their mothers. Gilligan claims that due to this pattern, females may appear "undeveloped" if measured by masculine ideals. She states that, in reality, females simply have different strengths than males because females are primarily motivated by their connections to others. Fundamentally, Gilligan argues that caring and service are women's core principles, while men value justice and the rights of others.

Gilligan offers her theory of women's social motivation as context for why, in her opinion, men find relationships challenging, whereas women have difficulty asserting their autonomy. Although her theories recall arguments for the so-called "moral superiority" of women, Gilligan's framework gave women a desirable new edge on communication, and essentially let men off the hook for feeling clueless about what women want —making her theory attractive to many readers. Meanwhile, other scientists found evidence that it is not just women who value their connections to others; in fact, most research confirms that male- and female-assigned people depend equally on social approval. Furthermore, class, age, nationality, education, religion, and one's personal situation have just as much (and often more) weight as one's sex in determining behavior and self-image.

Gilligan's methods of conducting research have also been called into serious question; she mainly conducted interviews herself, taking no measure to ensure objectivity, and she included no men in her study. By this time, however, her theories had already impacted male-female relationships, and undermined equality in educational methods by reinstating sex difference assumptions. *In a Different Voice* was frequently cited as the justification behind changing social work practices and counseling methods to make different approaches for men and women, as well as for adopting gender-specific criteria for hiring, training, and promoting workers.

*In a Different Voice* was also used to decide precedent-setting legal cases of gender discrimination in the early 1990s. For example, when defending the right of Virginia Military Institute to exclude women, witnesses for VMI invoked Carol Gilligan's stance on female moral development, saying that girls are more emotional and less competitive than boys—and would not succeed there. She also prompted numerous studies to evaluate whether female judges are biased towards women in their decisions. These are only two of many similar consequences of Gilligan's work.

Carol Gilligan was far from the last psychologist to devise a new theory that reiterates unproven sex differences. In 2002, experimental psychologist and linguist Steven Pinker's *The Blank Slate* challenged the empiricist idea that the mind begins with no innate qualities. Starting from the premise that there is no separation between the body and one's conscious mind, Pinker asserts that all thoughts and behaviors have a biological root. He believes humans are born with predispositions, and are not primarily shaped by experiences, parenting, or conditioning. *The*

*Blank Slate* argues that instead of assuming that everyone is fundamentally "equal" (which, according to Pinker, is contradicted by evolutionary psychology and neurobiology), it would be better to create policies that treat all people as individuals with rights. This assessment lays Pinker's foundation for claiming that men and women are, by nature, suited to different roles. *The Blank Slate* describes men as biologically predisposed to become risk-takers and motivated achievers, whereas women would be more likely to pursue comfortable and less daunting administrative support-style jobs. While *The Blank Slate* is not principally focused on sex differences, the implications of those that Pinker asserts are far-reaching, and his book was a bestseller that appears on many college courses' curricula.

Psychologist Rosalind Barnett and media critic Caryl Rivers' book, *Same Difference: How Gender Myths Are Hurting Our Relationships, Our Children, and Our Jobs* (2004), by contrast, examines the flaws in sex difference theories that would situate men and women in different job tasks. Barnett and Rivers particularly take issue with research studies that lump groups of men or women together at work and compare behavioral traits, often failing to account for what position they are in. For example, if all of the women in a study have administrative support positions, the results may actually indicate traits of that position more than women broadly. Barnett and Rivers write that:

"It's easy to assume that the reason men and women were doing different kinds of work was biological. If you look around at a community and see only women weaving and only men tilling the soil, you are apt to conclude that the "cause" of this difference is that women are suited for weaving and men for tilling. But that conclusion would be wrong. Being female doesn't automatically give you a talent for weaving. Rigid cultural norms, not biology, are operating here. As gender roles loosen—as they have done in the developed world—women's and men's behavior reflects many forces: their gender, their individual talents and preferences, their personalities, and the situations in which they find themselves."

Although allowing that there are definitely biological differences between the sexes, they "don't believe those differences determine most of our behavior or limit the roles we can assume." For instance, Barnett and Rivers confirm that men have more testosterone on average, but also say that women can be just as competitive and aggressive—social constraints simply encourage women to express those impulses differently. *Same Difference*'s review of 1,500 studies in biology, primatology, anthropology, sociology, genetics, and managerial behavior led Barnett and Rivers to the conclusion that differences between males and females are far less than the differences *among* males or *among* females. As a result, they lament the history of women's depiction as a sacrificing caregiver and men as stoic breadwinners with little emotional capacity—fairytalelike stereotypes that are limiting for everyone.

Barnett and Rivers also indicate that fears in generations past that women would have difficulty both working and rearing children were unfounded. Their findings show that most children with working mothers show no major differences from children of stay-at-home mothers, and that working mothers seem to be more emotionally healthy and grounded. They also demonstrate that male partners of working women tend to accept their careers and often take on equal or more equal parentage.

In fact, in Barnett and Rivers' research, the group of people who seem to be experiencing the most overwhelming stress at work and in monogamous partnerships are men and women who believe in separate roles, but who are going through the motions of equal task delegation anyway. Most men and women are happier when there is greater equality in parenting, housework, and wage earning, but couples who continue to view women as naturally domestic and men as suited to the working world do not enjoy or feel competent at more evenly distributed roles. In other words, the perpetuation of theories of "sex differences" makes it difficult

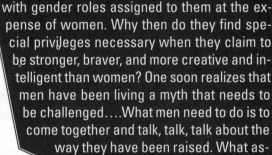

°MALE ALLIES:
Not all crusaders for helping women achieve equality are female. Jonah Gokova, the 2001 recipient of the Africa Prize for Leadership for his efforts to stop the spread of HIV/AIDS, is a male ally to the women of Zimbabwe. He writes, "Generally, men enjoy privileges associated with gender roles assigned to them at the expense of women. Why then do they find special privileges necessary when they claim to be stronger, braver, and more creative and intelligent than women? One soon realizes that men have been living a myth that needs to be challenged….What men need to do is to come together and talk, talk, talk about the way they have been raised. What assumptions about women and men have we picked up that have made us oppressive and unhelpful in creating meaningful relationships between men and women? Where do we need to change?"

JONAH GOKOVA

for those who believe them to excel or feel happy outside of archetypal gender roles. Since relationships with equal task delegation had been doing quite well according to most surveys before the new influx of sex difference studies, Barnett and Rivers challenge the merit of reinforcing archetypes once more and limiting both men and women's options.

As of the 1990s, almost a quarter of all workers with families were single mothers. How are today's workplaces adjusting to more working women and mothers? And how do gender archetypes affect their transition? In 1991, the National Research Council found that with more American women in the workforce, more households where both parents work, and more single-headed households who work, policies were not keeping up to provide support for families. Their suggestion manual, *Work and Family: Policies for a Changing Workforce*, points out that women's earnings have increased overall spending and the demand for labor. Statistically speaking, more American women who work also postpone marriage, have fewer children, and receive more education and training, which both increases their market worth and helps the economy. Given the new demographic breakdown, *Work and Family* suggests that Americans need more family benefits as well as more sick leave and family leave.

In *Reshaping the Work-Family Debate* (2010), lawyer and distinguished law professor Joan C. Williams concurs that rigid workplace policies that refuse to account for families' need for leave, flexible hours, and support for mothers make it more difficult for women to succeed. Williams also discusses how women in the workplace face a double standard; they may be promoted for embodying "masculine" leadership traits such as decisiveness and confidence, but are also often chastised for not being congenial enough once in a position of power. Depending on whether a male or female exhibits the quality, "assertive" or "direct" can easily be considered "abrasive" or "domineering." Williams notes that "men [express] positive feelings toward the good girls (who meet their expectations of femininity) and negative feelings toward the bad girls (who do not and are thus seen as selfish, aggressive, and cold)." She also asserts that women who act passive in order to get along with others find themselves at odds with any competitive women who are

JOAN C. WILLIAMS

determined to have a voice. Yet women who promote their own capability (which often raises performance ratings) are given a harder time by other women and are viewed as "distasteful" by men. Apparently, women are expected to be modest and cooperate, despite men being encouraged to compete and convey their worth. It seems that in America's workforce new strides for equality are being made, but some gender roles remain firmly in place, resulting in a hostile environment for women.

Even with somewhat more equal heterosexual relationships and more opportunities for women in the workplace, there is still clear disparity between what jobs men and women have access to and in their earnings. Just how equally are women represented in today's workforce?

### Gender Disparity by Industry
According to U.S. Department of Labor "Women in the Labor Force" report, February 2012

Majority Women

Majority Men

- Retail
- Health Services
- Social Assistance
- Education

- Book Publishing
- Real Estate
- Leisure & Hospitality
- Accommodations
- Food Service

- Agriculture
- Mining
- Construction
- Manufacturing
- Transportation
- Utilities

Though women make up the majority of workers in education, health services, and the financial activities industry, their access to certain specializations and all top-level jobs within those broad categories is much more limited. Furthermore, women are attaining more positions, but their salaries do not compare to men's, nor do they reflect their experience or education level. In spite of there being more women in financial positions, female financial managers make only 66.1 percent of male salaries for the same jobs. And while 36 percent of women ages 25 to 64 held college degrees, (as opposed to 11 percent in 1970), their earnings do not reflect their commensurate experience. Based on the wage gap of 77 cents to the dollar in 2009–2010, the average American woman makes approximately $431,000 less over a forty-year career than a man would in the same profession.

**DID YOU KNOW?**
Only 13 percent of America's engineers and architects, or 32 percent of physicians and surgeons are women.

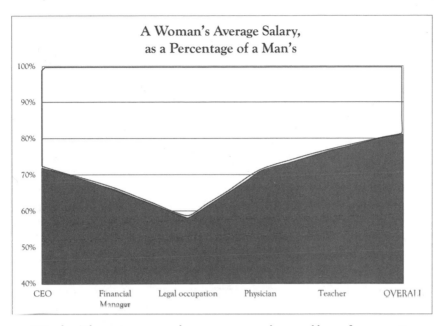

**A Woman's Average Salary,
as a Percentage of a Man's**

| 100% | | | | | | |
| 90% | | | | | | |
| 80% | | | | | | |
| 70% | | | | | | |
| 60% | | | | | | |
| 50% | | | | | | |
| 40% | CEO | Financial Manager | Legal occupation | Physician | Teacher | OVERALL |

We don't have to guess why women earn less and have fewer options in a society perpetuating gender archetypes that devalue femininity. Nor should we wonder why children often strive to emulate the messages around them that there are larger differences between men and women than among them. But besides a handful of sex difference studies, where are these messages coming from? What causes parents and educators, including those who don't actively believe in stereotypes, to behave in ways that teach young people to conform to gender norms?

Heteronormativity and archetypes have ample promotion in the media. From advertising and magazines to film and television, messages about what is "normal" are everywhere—and ripe for consumption. Children Now, an organization that examines the impact of media on children and youth, performed a study whose results demonstrate that depictions of men in the media reinforce their real-life social dominance. The study names some of the most frequent archetypes of men that appear in films and television shows: the action hero, the big shot, the strong silent man, the jock, and the joker.

## THE WAGE GAP CAN CHANGE

Feminist economist Lourdes Benería contends that many economists today who defend the free market accept women's current earning capacity as a fact instead of considering its circumstances and the potential for change. Benería denounces these economists for thinking that women should simply specialize in the areas that their acquired skills are preparing them for (e.g. running a household). She believes instead that the conditions which situate women as subordinates need to be altered.

Apparently, since the end of the "action hero" craze of the 1980s, more men are now portrayed in film and television as thoughtful, and also as caring about their appearance. Still, "manly" characters are generally allowed to exhibit few emotions, which are implied to be a sign of weakness or femininity. The majority of male characters in film and television are also depicted as heterosexual, and primarily associated with their work roles and problems therein. Male protagonists often use physical aggression or violence to solve those concerns. They also overwhelmingly receive social recognition, sexual interest from women, and other forms of prestige for being financially successful, maintaining control over situations and others, and for being attractive. Femininity in males is also discouraged by disproportionate media portrayals of brave and athletic "heroic" men, who may either exhibit ingenuity or sheer toughness to attract women and succeed in all areas of life. By contrast, masculine females and feminine males are scarcely shown in the media, except as marginal or humorous characters.

Both men and women are inaccurately portrayed in the media, but women are also just plain underrepresented. Alison Bechdel's syndicated comic strip "Dykes to Watch Out For" featured a simple test for popular films in 1985 to assess whether or not women were invisible (or treated as a mere object) in modern moviemaking. The criteria for the "Bechdel Test" simply states that in order to "pass," a film must have at least two female characters who talk to each other at some point in the film about something other than a man. Today (as in 1985), the majority of major Hollywood films fail this test. Even the rare films that do feature a strong female protagonist often situate her to mainly interact with men. As the Bechdel Test helps to demonstrate, when women do appear in movies (or television), they are often portrayed as one-dimensional sex objects—attractive and simple, with romance as their highest priority. Other times women are depicted as catty or manipulative go-getters, nagging wives, or maternal characters whose sole purpose is to provide care for other family members. More recently, there has also been a trend of hypersexualized female action heroes who are surrounded by (and validated by) men.

Since women in major Hollywood films are seldom developed into complex characters with motivations and thoughts of their own, it can be

## ALISON BECHDEL
Alison Bechdel's comic strip "Dykes to Watch Out For" was one of the first prominent (and ongoing) portrayals of lesbian life in American pop culture. Her Eisner award-winning graphic novel memoir, *Fun Home*, is one of the most widely-read literary accounts of struggling with gender identity and sexual orientation while coming of age in any language today.

argued that current representations of females in the media send girls and women the message that their primary function and sense of worth resides in attracting men. This trend also begins at a young age.

Commercials and print media present a complimentary problem. Constant images of airbrushed, extremely underweight women suggest that females should strive for an unhealthy and unrealizable ideal. Author and political consultant Naomi Wolf's *The Beauty Myth: How Images of Beauty Are Used Against Women* describes how these images promote the diet, cosmetic, and plastic surgery industries, and make American women perceive themselves as physically inadequate. To be fair, men are also overtly sexualized in the media, and given unrealistic images of bodies to aspire to. But even in commercials and print advertisements, their success is measured in a variety of ways. Like in films and television shows, men's "success" in advertisements and commercials is linked to their apparent jobs, fiscal status, cleverness, heroics, stoicism, prestige, social popularity, and physical strength, while women's "success" or status is most frequently conveyed through their physical attractiveness alone.

At first glance, it might seem odd that women are given so little airtime and depicted so shallowly. After all, females comprise more than half the population; one would assume that audiences would be invested in seeing themselves. Plus, wouldn't men be compelled to watch entertainment and news focused on female friends, co-workers, sisters, daughters, wives, and mothers—the women all around them? Is the devaluing of femininity in our society so profound that women are simply deemed uninteresting?

## GENDER PORTRAYAL IN CHILDREN'S MEDIA
In children's television programming there are roughly twice as many male characters, and female characters are dressed in "sexy" attire four times more often than males. In a study of G-rated films (1990–2005), only 28 percent of speaking characters were female, and four out of five had male narrators.

WOMEN OWN ONLY 6% OF US COMMERCIAL BROADCAST TV AND RADIO STATIONS.

Let's consider who owns media corporations, who writes and directs films and television shows, and who decides what makes it to the news floor. Here are some statistics:

# Employment Parity in the Media

Percent of professionals in the media who are women

### Career

| | |
|---|---|
| • Daily Newspaper Staff | 37% |
| • TV Programming Staff* | 27% |
| • Journalism Department Heads, Editors, Media Owners | 1% |
| • Journalists | 33% |
| • Directors | 7% |
| • Writers | 8% |
| • Executive Producers | 17% |
| • Producers | 23% |
| • Film Editors | 18% |
| • Cinematographers | 2% |

*creators, executive producers, producers, directors, writers, editors, and directors of photography working [in television] on situation comedies, dramas, and reality programs airing on broadcast networks*

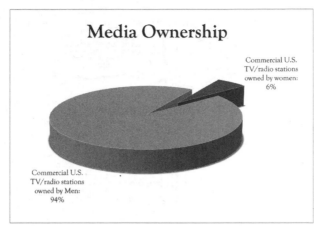

## Media Ownership

Commercial U.S. TV/radio stations owned by women: 6%

Commercial U.S. TV/radio stations owned by Men: 94%

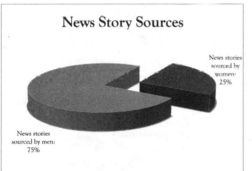

## News Story Sources

News stories sourced by women: 25%

News stories sourced by men: 75%

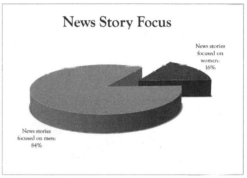

## News Story Focus

News stories focused on women: 16%

News stories focused on men: 84%

With so few women exerting any control over media-making in the United States and giving so little input into how they are rendered, is it any wonder that portrayals and images of women are misleading—or that their stories are few and far between?

Clearly, many parents' conditioning, some education policies, and the media still reflect gender archetypes. Unsubstantiated suggestions that the sexes have innate differences in both personality and aptitude continue to reinforce male dominance, heteronormativity, and a cultural emphasis on masculinity. Furthermore, gender roles in the workplace and in heterosexual partnerships are becoming more flexible, but have not yet achieved equality. In many ways, gender norms have also shaped our society's relationship to diverse sexual orientations. During the last century, while gender roles made (and in some cases lost) significant strides toward less rigidity, sexuality has been evolving alongside gender, both as a concept and as a human rights issue of its own.

# CHAPTER 5

# SEXUAL ORIENTATION

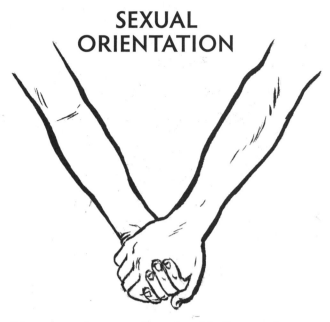

We can safely assume that sexuality existed before any human society delineated between gender identity, gender roles, the sexes, or sexual orientation. After all, humans were reproducing as a result of sexual intercourse long before we developed verbal language. But just as there have been many assumptions made about prehistoric people's distribution of labor, the idea that sexuality which results in reproduction is "normal" (and that other forms of sexual activity are deviations from that "norm") is rooted in a binary "either/or" construction of both gender and sexuality. Having explored the historical context for our society's gender archetypes, it can also be said that sexuality's "norms" are shaped by gender roles. Once we dispense with the notion that gender falls neatly into two categories, sexuality requires closer examination as well.

Everyone knows this story: Boy meets girl, roses, first kisses, walks on the beach, (and if all goes exceptionally well) a ring, a house, two kids, and a dog. There's nothing wrong with that image of a fledgling relationship, but it doesn't apply to everyone. That story could just as easily begin with "Boy meets boy," "Girl meets girl," "Genderqueer person meets girl," "Boy meets boy and girl," and so on. Apart from the obvious inadequacy of "boy meets girl," some couples prefer not to get married, many partnered people don't have kids, and not everyone wants to be in a long-term committed partnership of any kind. Many adults cannot afford a house; others prefer not to cohabitate with their romantic partner(s). Furthermore, some people don't experience sexual attraction and/or romantic attraction. All of these situations and options are perfectly normal; they have occurred both in our society and in different cultures around the world as far back as written history can document. But that first story of an archetypal heterosexual couple's (clearly stereotyped and oversimplified) courtship is the lifestyle that gets the most press, airtime, lip service, documentation, scholastic study, and both medical and legal recognition.

## TODAY'S CONSTRUCTION OF HETEROSEXUALITY

How do gender roles as they stand today affect the way that heterosexual men and women view their sexuality, and its meaning? Gender and queer studies scholar Eve Kosofsky Sedgwick believes that in a society where men and women differ in their access to power, there will always be important gender differences in the structure of sexuality. According to Sedgwick, to be female is to be defined in relation to the role of a lady—a role that takes its shape and meaning from a sexuality where one is not the subject but object. Feminist legal scholar Catherine MacKinnon argues that each facet of the female gender stereotype is sexual; that women's vulnerability represents easy access, and passivity indicates receptivity. She asserts that femaleness has come to mean femininity in all social realms, and by proxy sexual availability and attractiveness to men on their terms. MacKinnon's perspective illuminates how difficult it can be for modern men and women to see one another as individuals and not reflect the messages around them that women (even sexually empowered women) should be pursued by men who essentially employ different strategies to gain sexual access to them.

Another way of putting this might be that over the course of Western history, men and women's sexual involvement has been defined by an unequal power relationship where men had the upper hand. Therefore, when participating in sexual relationships, women have not always had agency. What's more, women have been treated as objects of conquest in every facet of popular and high culture, rendering their sexuality secondary to the desires of their pursuers. For men, the situation is arguably less oppressive, but they still face significant social pressure to pursue women, and some mixed messages about monogamy, how and when to show their emotions, and sharing fiscal responsibility with romantic partners.

## MONOGAMY

"Monogamy" means having only one sexual or romantic partner at a time; it can also be used to refer to having only one spouse at a time (as opposed to polygamy, where a man has more than one wife, or polyandry, where a woman has more than one husband).

Sexuality is about desire, human relationships, and in some cases, reproduction; in our society, most people are assigned as males or females, who are assumed to be attracted to one another. Heterosexuals are people who identify within this paradigm of being romantically or sexually attracted solely to the "opposite" assigned sex or gender—men who desire women, and women who desire men.

Since gender roles are based on a given society's ideas about gender and sex, it stands to reason that in a society where archetypal heterosexual men are overrepresented, and women are most valued for their sexual appeal to those men, other forms of sexuality would fall by the wayside. Nevertheless, other equally legitimate sexual orientations exist, and people who identify as lesbian, gay, bisexual, queer, and asexual are gradually beginning to gain more visibility, rights, and personal freedoms. Ironically, some of the communities and activist efforts of LGBTQIA people

> ## LOADED TERMINOLOGY: HETEROSEXUAL AND STRAIGHT
>
> The very term "heterosexual" assumes that there are only two sexes or genders, and that there is an "opposite" or "same" sex. Sometimes people who primarily identify as heterosexual prefer the term "straight," since it does not automatically imply that they are the "opposite" of homosexuals. The term "straight" has its own implications, however, of being "correct" (ie., that other orientations are "bent—a term that queer communities sometimes co-opt as their own).

were prompted by psychologists inventing terminology to describe sexual orientations and gender identities that they considered abnormal. As a result, it is useful to review the ways in which homosexuality has been studied academically, and how those studies have affected public policies and gay and lesbian people's lives.

Long before gay and lesbian studies or activism existed (or feminism and gender studies, for that matter), there were fierce debates about gender and sexuality. While many academic disciplines offer commentary on gender, such as history, psychology, law, women's studies, sociology, anthropology, biology, queer theory, and transgender studies, many viewpoints on the subject of sexuality fall into two categories: essentialist and constructionist theories. The ideas of essentialist and constructionist thinkers sometimes overlap, but each has distinct positions regarding how an individual's sexuality emerges or is formed.

Essentialists believe that identity is a natural and unchangeable fact, unique to each individual and determined at birth. They think that gender and sexual orientation has nothing to do with where someone is born, factors in their life, or society's influence. Essentialists do not believe that someone can "become" gay, straight, queer, masculine, or feminine; people are simply "born this way" with their gender and sexual preferences ingrained in them.

This group of thinkers considers sexual orientation to be purely biological, even genetic. They argue that homosexuality has always existed and continues to occur in cultures all around the world; therefore, it must be biological in nature. But while essentialists agree that sexual orientation is part of one's intrinsic identity, this does not necessarily mean that they all endorse a broad variety of sexual expression. In fact, some essentialists consider homosexual and asexual individuals a genetic error or abnormality.

Constructionists, on the other hand, do not reduce all sexual proclivities to a single, unchanging identity or predisposition that one has at birth. They contend that any given sexual act can mean a variety of things to individuals in different cultures, time periods, or relationships.

Readers should note that not all people, theorists, and social scientists who believe in social constructions of gender endorse constructionists views of sexuality.

As a result, constructionists do not think that one's sexual orientation can be understood as falling into one category with the same label irrespective of where or when one lives. According to these theorists, engaging in homosexual activity in 17th century Greece means something completely different from identifying as gay in 21st century America.

Constructionists also do not agree that identity is a constant or fixed state, instead arguing that it changes over the course of one's life in reaction to experiences and circumstance. Therefore, they generally support the idea that someone's gender can shift over the course of their life. Constructionists may also believe that someone can "become" (or cease to be) gay, straight, bisexual, asexual, or queer.

It may seem as though essentialists hold an inherently conservative point of view, but the stance that homosexuality is genetic or begins at birth has been invoked in civil rights struggles to gain rights for gay people. That said, should scientists discover a gene linked to orientation, it's possible that some people would once again view homosexuality as a disorder. Conversely, constructionist ideology, while typically politically progressive, can also be used to reinforce the idea that homosexuality is a learned behavior. Some homophobic groups have used constructionist arguments to encourage people to try to "quit" or change their sexual orientation. These groups consider homosexuality a decision or an unfortunate preference for particular sex acts rather than an identity. They therefore think that they can correct what they perceive to be negative behavior. Many other constructionists simply view orientation as an extension of gender, both of which can shift, but neither of which is the conscious choice of an individual.

Vicki Eaklor has noted that some gay and lesbian liberationists dislike the "born this way" argument because they think it implies an apologist "I can't help it" vibe that actually discourages difference.

Both essentialists and constructionists agree that humans have been attracted to their own assigned sex and/or gender and have participated in same-sex sexual acts throughout the course of history. They disagree, however, about whether or not these actions should be generally considered "homosexual" in the modern sense of the word. Constructionists, taking their cue in part from French philosopher and historian Michel Foucault (1926–1984), often assert that until the term "homosexual" existed, a preference for same-sex intimacy could not be considered part of a person's identity.

FRENCH PHILOSOPHER AND HISTORIAN MICHEL FOUCAULT (1926-1984)

---

## HOMOPHOBIC DISCRIMINATION

Homophobia describes negative behaviors, attitudes, or feelings toward gay, lesbian, or bisexual people based on their sexual orientation. The term "homophobic" is used in this book instead of "groups opposed to homosexuality" for the same reason that one would say "racist" as opposed to "groups opposed to people of color." It is the position of this book that sexual orientation is as intrinsic to a person's identity as race, age, or (dis)ability, and that opposing a specific orientation is by definition discriminatory. The word "homophobic" helps to convey that being "against" a sexual orientation cannot be considered a legitimate opinion.

---

The term "homosexual" began to emerge in medical literature around 1870 as a way of describing a type of person. Academics initially used this word to generalize about sexual behavior between people of the same assigned sex. Their manner of discussing homosexuality's characteristics bears resemblance to the way that psychologists sometimes label "a bipolar person" or "a borderline personality"—as if these terms can completely sum up an individual. In this way, "homosexuality" originated as a medical term indicating that a person attracted to the same assigned sex's entire world view factored into their sexual orientation.

**MICHEL FOUCAULT**
Although volume 1 of Foucault's *The History of Sexuality* predates gay and lesbian studies, it is often considered one of their most crucial texts.

As the general population became aware of this label, the first information that the medical community provided implied that homosexuality
was a disorder or medical condition.

According to Foucault, before the late 19th century, sexual behavior occurring between people of
the same assigned sex was considered a lure away
from the proper way of living. That said, neither
homosexual desire nor the practice of engaging in
same-sex acts was believed to be a personality trait.
When an individual had a relationship with someone of the same assigned sex, it wasn't understood
or discussed as being a way of looking at one's self
or the world. Instead, it was seen as an illicit activity that anyone might have a craving for, and give
into. Homosexuality was not defined in literature
as being separate from many other forms of behavior considered corrupt
or depraved at that time. As a result, Foucault claims that, prior to the
coining of the term "homosexual," these acts had a different meaning. Individuals may have had a sexual preference or inclination toward their
own sex or gender, but they would likely have considered it an anomaly
that fell outside of their regular social and home life. Prior to the existence of a word articulating homosexuality as a characteristic of an individual, it makes sense that societies practicing strict gender roles would

## FOUCAULT AND SEXOLOGY

Foucault argued that sexologists were not discovering an identity that already
existed, but that, by coining the term, they were actually inventing the very concept of homosexuality (even though sexual acts between people of the same assigned sex or gender had occurred prior). Furthermore, he did not believe that
the stigmatization of sexuality was completely negative and oppressive. Foucault admitted that regulation of behavior (such as laws forbidding certain sexual actions, medical diagnoses of certain sexual behaviors as "diseased," and
educational models that perpetuate these ideas) acts as a mechanism for normalizing certain behavior. Though he did not phrase it this way, his work can be
interpreted as asserting that the regulation of norms through repeated behavior can lead to a broad acceptance of any idea, including the notion that heterosexuality is "normal" and homosexuality is "odd." He clearly understood the
danger and likelihood that those who cannot or will not conform to heterosexual "norms" would be ostracized. Foucault recognized how oppressive social
regulation could be, but he also considered labels and sexology studies a pro-
ductive way to broaden human understanding of behavior and to generate
knowledge. Ultimately, he thought that any discourse about sex and behavior
leads to information, categories, and identities that give meaning to our actions.

view any sexual attraction to someone of the same assigned sex as superfluous.

Historians and sociologists do not agree on the date or reason that the meaning of the term "homosexuality" shifted, nor do they agree on how homosexuality evolved into an identity. While Foucault focused on sexuality's place in medical literature, John D'Emilio instead considers the rise of capitalism. He believes that there was a significant shift in all relationships when individuals started earning money to support themselves rather than functioning as part of a family in terms of all wealth distribution. Suddenly, people had the freedom to view families and sexual relations from an emotional point of view. Sexual intercourse and cohabitation became options and ways of creating meaning and personal happiness, instead of fundamental strategies for procreation and survival. In this light, one might say that homosexuality started to have cultural relevance (and relevance as an identity) once it was a viable life choice. Instead of thinking about sexual orientation as an urge indulged infrequently behind closed doors, one could embrace a preference for the same assigned sex and reject the traditional family model. In D'Emilio's opinion, it was at that moment that the term "homosexuality" started to apply to a way of being in the world.

A LONDON "MOLLY HOUSE" CIRCA EARLY 1700s.

Alternatively, British historian and gay rights activist Alan Bray contends that the origins of homosexuality as an identity can be dated as early as the late 17th century, when a subculture of molly houses emerged around the Thames River in London. These "houses" were both bars and actual residences; in both cases, they functioned as a network of locations for men to gather and flirt, engage in sexual activity with one another, drink, or just interact socially. Because these locations were considered a community with its own slang, fashion trends, gestures, and decorum, Bray argues that they demonstrate homosexuality existing as an identity. Therefore, he says that the clientele of molly houses embodied homosexuality's modern meaning, even if they lacked a cohesive term for it.

As with the examples just given, early academic efforts on the topic of gender and sexuality primarily address male homosexuality, leaving lesbians by the wayside. Female homosexuality was not given equal attention in medical journals during the time that male homosexuality was first emerging as a concept. In addition, the British judicial system (adopted by most of the West during their Colonial period) only criminalized male homosexuality, completely ignoring lesbian activity.

The female gender archetype in American and most Western European societies allows for mildly affectionate friendships between women with little social stigma attached. As homosexuality first emerged in the public's consciousness, there were far fewer assumptions made about two women with an intimate friendship than two men. Thus, among the theories for the lack of attention initially given to female homosexuality, one argument is that it was simply harder to identify. While lesbians were not heavily persecuted, they also didn't develop a community or identity that was socially acknowledged until far later than gay men.

Hoping to explain this phenomenon, in her book analyzing the evolution of contemporary lesbian identity, *Surpassing the Love of Men* (1985), Lillian Faderman wades through classical and modern literature to demonstrate how frequently relationships between women are depicted as sexual or romantic. She claims that prior to the 20th century, romantic relationships between women, including sexual ones, were common and in no way taboo. Occasionally, women who acted in a sexual manner in public were criticized for behaving in an unfeminine way, but not specifically for their attraction to other women.

Faderman states that lesbian love was seldom, if ever, persecuted before the 20th century, and suggests that any modern aversion to lesbians is likely a displaced fear about feminist politics. In other words, she believes that people today who have negative feelings about lesbianism are concerned about upsetting the traditional gender roles in our society. They care more about women assuming leadership roles in the workplace or politics than about women having sex with other women. Faderman also contests Foucault's assertion that medical texts gave rise to a modern lesbian identity (though she doesn't dispute their contribution to a gay male one). Instead, she argues that early sexologists classified love between women as "freakishness," and caused them to fear same-sex desire. She concludes that medical accounts of the term "homosexuality" actually delayed the formation of the lesbian identity and community.

No matter when the term "lesbian" emerged and its community coalesced, it can be commonly agreed that women's erotic desire for and involvement with one another has existed throughout all of human history. Given the variability of women's roles and how "woman" was defined in different societies, all of these women cannot be said to share one gender; still, accounts of lesbian sex acts encompass all social classes and exist in every culture. What varies in popular and scientific opinion, as with male homosexuality, is the supposed date and reason for this preference first constituting an identity in Western society.

Along with all of these suggested timelines for the evolution of homosexuality into an identity, an option, a community, or a category, there comes an inherent assumption that heterosexuality need not be described or commented upon. It is considered by many to be the natural way of conducting one's self in the world, while homosexuality is frequently marginalized as an alternative or a deviation from the norm. The ways in which typical parenting, education, science, and the media reinforce gender norms and heteronormativity have already been commented upon, but there are many other avenues through which homosexuality and other sexualities are either stigmatized or ignored altogether—including organized religion, psychology, and the marginalization of extant tribal groups' sexual practices.

Most major organized world religions either directly condemn homosexual behavior as a crime against the wishes of a higher power, or simply ignore its existence. It is actually strangely easy to leave homosexuality and homosexual relationships out of the religious historical texts of many cultures. This is because religious definitions of family generally focus solely on procreative genealogy or heritage. Since homosexual sexual activity and relationships did not historically produce children, they were not considered relevant to document, except, perhaps as examples of "misguided behavior." Therefore, when reading religious texts, it can appear as though prior to modern times, sexual relationships occurred almost exclusively within heterosexual family units. (There are, of course, notable exceptions to this, such as hijras in Hinduism).

There is also a particular tendency in Western society to whitewash over the existence of extant tribal groups' various cultural norms, which often include radically different gender roles and approaches to sexuality. Although cross-cultural studies of same-sex conduct are plentiful, their social significance and historical situations are equally varied, further reinforcing the inadequacy of the oversimplified Western binary of heterosexuality and homosexuality. It is sometimes tempting to compare these diverse same-sex sexual acts and orientations to homosexuality or bisexuality, but doing so would fail to account for the unique meaning and contexts in which they occur.

For example, Rudolf Gaudio's research details some West African same-sex sexual relationships between male-assigned Hausa, where either both partners identify as male or both identify as female. These Hausa are referred to as "kifi," which (roughly translated) means lesbianism. Hausa classify this particular kind of sexual exchange among males as "lesbian" because partners switch between penetrating and submissive roles. In these relationships, Gaudio says, "Neither partner seeks to exercise a kind of unilateral power over the other by virtue of gender, age, or wealth." Another, very different account of same-sex sexual conduct was documented by R. H. Mathews in the 19th century among tribes in Western Australia. Mathews reported that young boys in these tribes were sexual stand-ins for their sisters until the females reached the appropriate age to be married. After circumcision, a young man was given the younger brother of the woman he would eventually marry, with whom he was expected to masturbate and copulate.

In Gilbert Herdt's study of the Sambia, a New Guinea highlander tribe, he describes how boys perform oral sex on older unmarried youths. In Sambia culture, ingesting semen is considered necessary to help young boys grow up to be "physically strong, socially mature, and reproductively competent men." Once those boys reach adulthood, their sexual relationships are exclusively with women; the oral sex they perform and receive in youth is strictly a rite of passage. Victor Turner's 1950s fieldwork on the Central Bantu groups in Central Africa tells how boys there recover from circumcision in a sex-segregated lodge where they are told to rub the penises of the lodge-keeper (and anyone else present) so that their own penis will later grow. Judith Gay's ethnographic work offers same-sex sexual accounts of Lesotho girls, who have close emotional friendships with other girls until they marry, and traditionally touch their own and each other's genitals to lengthen their labias. Lesotho girls frequently fall in love with one another and may maintain these relationships past marriage. As just these few abbreviated examples illustrate, outside of Western societies, the variety of gender and sexual norms and practices are so diverse that they render a reduction of orientation to "homosexual" and "heterosexual" almost unintelligible.

Psychology is another avenue through which heterosexuality has been normalized in our society. A number of prominent psychologists, including Sigmund Freud, have asserted that homosexuality is a developmental stage through which most children or adolescents pass. These psychologists explain homosexual adults' continued preference for the same assigned sex or gender by saying that some people get inadvertently "stuck" in this adolescent phase. This description renders homosexual adults as immature or at fault for being attracted to their own gender. Most schools of thought in psychology no longer endorse this view, but the effects of its former popularity continue to resonate in mainstream culture.

It is unavoidable that the term "homosexual," at least initially, depended upon the prior term "heterosexual" in order to construct its meaning. In early academic work focusing on homosexuality, it was consistently discussed in contrast to heterosexuality. Because these early studies of homosexuality failed to analyze or deconstruct the heterosexual "norm," they inadvertently reaffirmed it as typical or "correct." Likewise, other categories of sexual orientation in our society partially depend upon the terms "heterosexuality" and "homosexuality" to construct their meaning, even if their views and feelings towards gender and sexuality have strikingly different characteristics from straight, gay, or lesbian people.

Many people are neither heterosexual nor homosexual. Bisexuality is another category of sexual orientation in Western societies where individuals of either gender are attracted to both male and female-identified people. Bisexuality should not be thought of as a combination of heterosexuality and homosexuality, however, as many contend that bisexuals are generally unconcerned with gender categories when considering their sexual attraction to an individual. Sean Cahill, the director of the National Gay and Lesbian Task Force Policy Institute, asserts, "Most bisexuals describe themselves as being emotionally, sexually, and/or romantically attracted to both women and men and feel capable of loving and forming relationships with either. To most bisexuals, the gender of the person they find attractive is substantially less important than who the person is."

Some members of the gay and lesbian community consider bisexual people privileged because they can choose heterosexual partners and avoid some of the scrutiny that homosexual relationships face. Many bisexual people would disagree with this assessment of their situation though, as their mere existence is frequently called into question by straight, gay, and lesbian communities who sometimes inaccurately claim that bisexuals are merely in a transitional phase or that bisexuals refuse to pick a gender of preference. As a result, many bisexuals do not feel that they belong in heterosexual or homosexual communities, as they are outliers in both.

A handful of feminist and queer theorists think that bisexual orientation offers a way to bypass gender and sexuality categories altogether.

Elizabeth Däumer, for example, believes that lesbian and feminist women are stuck in a binary framework of gender and sexuality because they constantly battle both homophobia and sexism. She suggests that bisexuals have a unique opportunity to take a more neutral vantage point from which to deconstruct "either/or" ideas of gender and sexuality.

Asexuality is another sexual identification that is often overlooked in mainstream society and also in academic studies of sexuality. Asexual people do not experience sexual attraction to anyone. They are not unable to have sex, and do not necessarily lack a sex drive (although some asexuals do not have one). Contrary to many misconceptions, asexuals are neither repressed, repulsed by sex, or in any way sexually dysfunctional. (Of course, some asexual people may experience sexual dysfunction or disgust towards sex, but those conditions or feelings are entirely separate from their asexuality). Quite simply, asexuals do not experience sexual attraction to other people. This does not mean that they don't feel romantically interested in men, women, men and women, or other genders, but any romantic feelings they may have are not accompanied by sexual desire. The asexual community is distinct from (but related to) demisexual people, who only experience sexual interest in someone after they have formed a strong emotional and romantic bond. Demisexuals do not describe this "secondary" attraction as having anything to do with the other person's personal appearance. Other individuals may identify as "gray-A," a term for people who experience very minimal or extremely infrequent sexual attraction. While some (but not all) asexual, demisexual, or gray-A people choose to abstain from sex, most people who choose not to have sex are not asexual.

Once something has become convention, it is very hard to look at it objectively. As gender studies and queer theorist David Halperin puts it, "If one could simply think oneself out of one's acculturation, it wouldn't be acculturation in the first place." At this point, heterosexuality has become so "normalized" in Western society that it can be difficult to think about it as being a concept or construct. We don't expect a heterosexual couple or their nuclear family unit to need context; there's nothing unique to us about their pairing. Our society seldom thinks of heterosexuality as a category that might be arbitrary. As the meanings of terms for other sexual orientations evolve within our society, it is increasingly possible to refuse to treat heterosexuality as the only "natural" or obvious world view.

IF ONE COULD SIMPLY THINK ONESELF OUT OF ONE'S ACCULTURATION, IT WOULDN'T BE ACCULTURATION IN THE FIRST PLACE.

In the meantime, modern definitions of homosexuality remain problematic and contradictory. In
*Epistemology of the Closet* (1990),
Eve Kosofsky Sedgwick discusses
two major contradictions in how homosexuality is currently regarded.
She claims first that there is no common consensus (among both gay-
positive groups and homophobic
persons) on whether homosexuals
should be considered a minority
group, or if, instead, sexual orientation is less categorical altogether and
more of a spectrum. In the latter
view, it is assumed that many hetero-

EVE KOSOFSKY SEDGWICK
(1950 – 2009)

sexual-identified people also experience some desire for their own gender. Sedgwick also stresses that there is a lack of agreement on whether
same-sex attraction is rooted in a homosexual person's identity falling
between genders, or if homosexuality more accurately reflects the lack
of cohesion within each gender.

Despite the inadequacy of a binary system, scientists continue to look
for differences in the brains of male- and female-identified subjects,
study chromosomal impact on secondary sex characteristics, and in the
last two decades, evaluate the possibility of a biological basis for homosexuality. Constructionists and essentialists remain at odds. Are all
people "born this way"? Conditioned this way? Predisposed? Is it our
brain, our genes, or outside influences that make us heterosexual, bisexual, gay, lesbian, transgender, asexual, or none of the above? These
question remain open to serious debate.

Early studies seeking a biological basis for homosexuality often experimented on rats or other animals to see if hormones or different forms of
breeding would produce "homosexual behavior." Such tests presupposed
the gender and sexuality of animals in ways that impose strangely narrow
definitions of what homosexuality means. For example, some studies labeled male rats who are on the receiving end of penetration as "homosexual," but ignored the rat who does the penetrating (perhaps assuming
him to be indifferent about whom or what he copulates with). Anthropologist Roger N. Lancaster comments in *The Trouble With Nature*
(2003) on the inherent assumptions of studies that use rats as analogues
for human sexual behavior. He finds it disturbing and misleading that "gay
and straight, male and female, are portrayed as deeply, radically different from each other—but humans and rats are not."

EARLY STUDIES SEEKING A BIOLOGICAL
BASIS FOR HOMOSEXUALITY OFTEN
EXPERIMENTED ON RATS OR OTHER ANIMALS
TO SEE IF HORMONES OR DIFFERENT FORMS
OF BREEDING WOULD PRODUCE
"HOMOSEXUAL BEHAVIOR".

Some of the first major scientific studies of homosexuality that modern researchers continue to reference were Alfred C. Kinsey's work. As early as 1948, his surveys of sexual behavior produced useful ways to categorize sexual behavior that are still in use today, including, perhaps most notably, a "rating scale" for the degree of homosexual or heterosexual inclinations in people (with zero as 100 percent heterosexual, and six as 100 percent homosexual). This scale placed sexuality on a continuum model, a considerable shift away from viewing homosexuality as a deviation from a heterosexual standard.

As Anne Fausto-Sterling points out in *Sexing the Body*, however, Kinsey mainly considered sexuality in terms of arousal, ignoring the particularity of relationships and their context. His linear scale has also reinforced the tendency of researchers to primarily examine people who identify as 100 percent homosexual or heterosexual in hopes of finding clearer or more exciting data. This uneven sampling method overrepresents two portions of the population and promotes the perception that most people are either "one or the other." Additionally, the mere assumption that there is an "opposite" gender or assigned sex reinforces a gender binary that makes "men" and "women" real and absolutely opposite categories. But while Kinsey's approach may seem regressive by current standards, by posing a spectrum of sexuality on which homosexuality and heterosexuality were opposite poles (with many shades of grey in between, and no "normal"), Kinsey revolutionized both of these archetypes.

ALFRED C. KINSEY
(1894 -1956)

Much of the current academic inquiry into sexual orientation's potential biological basis centers on neurobiological and genetic research. In 1991, Dr. Simon LeVay released a study stating that the hypothalamus in the brains of gay men and in those of straight men are measurably different in size. He was studying corpses, however, and because the brain structures he was examining were in adults whose brain structures could be related to social conditioning instead of a genetic predisposition for their orientation, the findings are controversial. Later that year, J. Michael Bailey and Richard C. Pillard's scientific team published a research study focusing on twins. Their team said that 52 percent of monozygotic twins identified as gay, as opposed to 22 percent of dizygotic twins and 11 percent of adoptive brothers. Given that a completely inherited trait should result in close to 100 percent of monozygotic twins exhibiting the same characteristic, Bailey and Pillard concluded that homosexuality must result from factors occurring both before and after birth.

Monozygotic twins share all of their DNA and come from a single egg. Dizygotic twins are fraternal twins who come from the same pregnancy but two eggs fertilized by two different sperm.

Then, in 1993, Dean H. Hamer's research team found that inherited polymorphic markers on an X chromosome had a strong parallel relationship to homosexual orientation. "Polymorphic" means a dissimilar trait from the majority or "rule," and some readers of the study took it to mean that homosexuality is simply a less common genetic expression, no different from left-handedness. Hamer's results do suggest the potential for orientation being inherited, but while claiming to have located genetic factors playing a role in 5 to 30 percent of gay men, Hamer was cautious about saying that the genes were deterministic. In an article he wrote in 1999

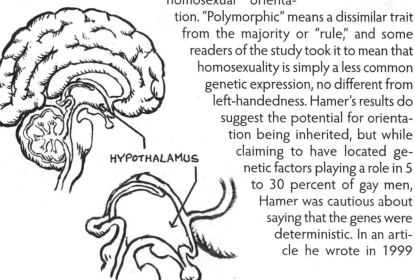

HYPOTHALAMUS

for *Science* magazine, he said that orientation was likely affected "by many different factors, including multiple genes, biological, environmental, and sociocultural influences." All of these results remain highly questionable, as LeVay, Bailey and Pillard, and Hamer's studies were all ruled inconclusive by the Council of Responsible Genetics, and Hamer was later investigated for scientific misconduct for suppressing data. The Council remarked, in particular, that since fraternal twins and other brothers have an equal genetic similarity, the higher number of gay fraternal twins in Bailey and Pillard's study probably demonstrated environmental factors impacting sexual orientation, not genetics at all.

When Dennis McFadden and Edward G. Pasanen published an exploration of the inner ears of lesbian women in 1998, a fresh wave of interest in a biological basis for sexual orientation arose. McFadden and Pasanen said that homosexual women's reaction to sounds were more similar to men than to heterosexual women. Despite the test not having a parallel result between homosexual men and heterosexual women, the study was cited repeatedly as "proof" that homosexuality was biological. McFadden also claimed that the cause of desire in men and women may have a different origin, but this statement is generally refuted by social scientists. In addition, it is obviously problematic for a study to base its findings on a biological similarity between heterosexual men and homosexual women, while simultaneously arguing that men and women's sexual orientations are unrelated.

The controversy over McFadden and Pasanen's work was closely followed by Bruce Bagemihl's book, *Biological Exuberance: Animal Homosexuality and Natural Diversity* (1999), an account of homosexual and transgender activity in more than 450 animal species. Some thinkers state that the mere presence of same-sex sexual activity in other species demonstrates that same-sex attraction is a normal occurrence in all of nature (not indicative of particular environments). The question of whether same-sex partnering in animals has relevance to the genetics or social construction of human sexuality, however, remains a fierce dispute.

In 2002, Toshihiro Kitamoto and his lab found that they could prompt same-sex sexual activity in male fruit flies to start and stop by disrupting transmissions in the flies' synapses. Rises and drops in temperature were

also key to the male fruit flies' shift in attention from females to males. This study was followed in 2005 by another research team led by Ebru Demir and Barry J. Dickson, who pinpointed a specific gene that appeared to determine fruit flies' sexual behavior. By swapping the typical male and female versions of this gene, the scientists were able to induce male and female fruit flies to pursue their own sex. It bears mentioning that humans, not sharing the fruit flies' invertebrate structure, are unlikely to have the same gene producing this trigger in fruit flies. Still, it appears that these fruit flies reacted differently to the pheromones (excreted chemicals) of other fruit flies on the basis of their sex, and did so because of this gene.

These results are also interestingly aligned with Dr. Ivanka Savic's research in 2005; she found two odors that humans emit which are potentially related to sexual arousal, and alleges that gay men and heterosexual men respond differently to those odors. Her research particularly indicated, using brain imaging, that gay men's hypothalamus reacted to those smells more similarly to heterosexual women's than to heterosexual men's hypothalamus. Then again, Dr. Savic  did not release accompanying results for lesbian women, and admitted that her results may simply demonstrate evidence of gay and straight men using their brains differently (which could be the result of their different social conditioning instead of biology). Dr. Savic believes that parts of the brain may be organized or structured based on sexual orientation instead of "biological sex," but also concedes that it is not yet possible to tell if these patterns in the brain are the cause of one's orientation or the effect of it. Her work would also seem to suggest that humans may be more attracted to people on the basis of particular brain structures and behavioral types, and that their sex or gender is actually less relevant. It is possible that desire is hugely related to hormones and smell, two things that vary within each gender, and can be altered by taking hormones orally; whether this would confirm or disprove "hard-wired" orientation is unclear.

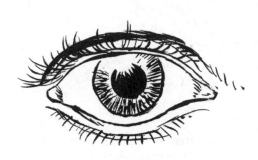

An interesting case for orientation being determined before birth was made in 2003 by Qazi Rahman, who considered eye-blink startle responses in gay and heterosexual men and women. Rahman saw a significant difference between heterosexual and homosexual women's blinking patterns, and contends that since startle responses are purely involuntary, this result demonstrates that orientation must not be a learned behavior. Like Savic, Rahman ignores the fact that, involuntary or not, any biological trait of grown homosexuals and heterosexuals may have been affected by environmental conditions and does not automatically indicate a predisposition for orientation. All the same, no differences were found between gay and heterosexual men in the study, and most scientists believe Rahman's results are utterly inconclusive.

In recent years, Dr. Anthony Bogaert's survey of men and their siblings has been regarded as significant in considering a potential biological basis for sexual orientation. Bogaert found that the chances of homosexuality in a given individual increased by 33 percent with each older brother. The study concluded that the only consistently significant factor in men identifying as homosexual is how many male siblings were born before them. As psychologist and neuroscientist Dr. S. Marc Breedlove told *The Associated Press* in a 2006 interview: "Anybody's first guess would have been that the older brothers were having an effect socially, but this data doesn't support that."

Bogaert's subsequent work with adopted sons further reinforces his conclusion that homosexuality is not related to the environmental effect of having older brothers in a household, but may be related to a mother's body changing during the gestation of males. There is no parallel for the orientation of women as related to their older siblings, however, as demonstrated by the work of Ray Blanchard and Richard A.

Lippa. This effect of fraternal birth order has also been reported in studies focused on male-to-female transsexuals in the U.K., Polynesia, and elsewhere. Those who disagree with the results of this work have argued that most of the studies performed on birth order used indirect reports to determine the orientation of participants' siblings and that all of the studies used misleading sample groups. Furthermore, a study replicating Bogaert's was performed in 2008 by Andrew M. Francis, who found very little evidence to suggest fraternal birth order's influence on same-sex attraction.

BRIZENDINE INTERPRETS SOME STUDIES AS SUGGESTING THAT PRENATAL EXPOSURE TO HIGHER LEVELS OF TESTOSTERONE MAY LEAD MALES TO HAVE MORE SAME-SEX ATTRACTION.

In *The Female Brain,* Louann Brizendine writes, "Sexual orientation does not appear to be a matter of conscious self-labeling but a matter of brain wiring." She bases this assertion on studies that, in her interpretation, demonstrate that prenatal exposure to higher levels of testosterone lead males to have more same-sex attraction. She believes a parallel overexposure can cause female brains to develop along more "male-typical" lines—affecting their behavior traits, rough play, and orientation. This analysis is problematic in several ways. First of all, as already discussed, researchers are seldom able to quantify the testosterone in unborn babies, making prenatal hormone tests unreliable. Additionally, according to Brizendine, males are born gay because they have more testosterone; gay men are, by her definition, essentially "more" male. Yet she also claims that females exposed to more testosterone will develop male traits, and a same-sex attraction to *females.* But if testosterone produces the effect of maleness, and "extreme" males (with extra testosterone) become gay, by Brizendine's own logic, would not these "masculinized" females become more attracted to *males*?

Although there are dozens of studies attempting to prove, one way or the other, if genetics determine sexual orientation, and if brain structure can be linked to sexuality in a gendered fashion, no one has reached conclusive or agreed upon evidence. Moreover, most biological studies of orientation presuppose the legitimacy of fairly narrow male and female sex categories. As Anne Fausto-Sterling notes, "We think of anatomy as constant, but it isn't; neither, then, are those aspects of human sexuality that derive from our body's structure, function, and inward and outward image." With the very categories of gender and sex in question, the possibility of scientifically studying orientation becomes uncertain. It is perhaps best to think about these studies not in terms of whether or not sexuality has a biological basis, but as a demonstration of the limits in current methods of answering that question, and the biases that make it difficult for scientists to evaluate their results.

Homosexuals do not only endure scrutiny about their sexuality from scientists, psychologists, or from those who consider their sexual orientation to be outside of the mainstream; they are also prohibited by law from expressing their identity in many parts of the world. Sodomy is a legal term used to describe "unnatural" sex, whose definition varies, but generally refers to oral sex, anal sex, or bestiality. Sodomy laws have most commonly been employed to restrict anal and oral sex between homosexual men, and remain in place today in 70 of the world's 198 countries. These laws originated from antiquated religious prohibitions against certain kinds of sex, such as the Buggery Act of 1533 in England, which was passed during Henry VIII's rule as a formalization of the ecclesiastical courts' rules, outlawing "unnatural sexual act[s] against the will of God and man." In practice, the courts applied this law to anal penetration and bestiality. Present day punishments for sodomy or homosexual acts in some countries include imprisonment, flogging (Yemen, Saudi Arabia), expulsion from one's homeland (Mauritania), and even death (Somaliland, Sudan, Saudi Arabia, United Arab Emirates, and Iran).

In the United States, sodomy laws historically fell under state jurisdiction (unless they related to the military, which is under federal law). Thirty-six states ended their sodomy laws before 2002, either through repeal or as the result of court cases; then, in 2003, the ruling in the *Lawrence v. Texas* Supreme Court case rendered sodomy laws unconstitutional. Before that case, the courts had upheld states' rights to individually consider homosexual sex illegal based on *Bowers v. Hardwick* (1986), a case whose ruling stated that there was no constitutionally protected right to engage in homosexual sex. Seventeen years later,

*Lawrence v. Texas* overruled that decision, asserting that laws which classify "consensual, adult homosexual intercourse as illegal sodomy [violates] the privacy and liberty of adults to engage in intimate conduct under the 14th Amendment."

While homosexual orientation and sex acts are no longer against the law in the United States, they are often met with serious civil ramifications. Homosexuals are excluded from many civil rights that protect the heterosexual population; for instance, in some states they are not protected against discrimination when seeking employment. Legal definitions of a family have also consistently left out homosexual pairings, rendering same-sex partners "illegitimate" and unable to receive many of the benefits married heterosexual couples receive. Some of these benefits include Social Security survivor benefits, federal tax benefits, as well as federal employee health and retirement plans. What's more, until very recently, openly gay, lesbian, or bisexual individuals could not serve in the United States military. This will be explored in more detail later on, but this disparity illustrates in plain terms the extent to which heterosexuality is considered the generic or mainstream manner of sexual conduct.

Another way to focus in on our limited ability to clearly define sexual orientation, or even homosexuals as a group, is to look at public health policies. In particular, the manner in which health policies have targeted and failed to reach people at risk for AIDS demonstrates our society's inability to adequately define sexual activity. In the early years of the spread of HIV, it was commonly misunderstood to be a disease transmitted primarily within the gay community. In fact, *The New York Times* initially reported in 1981 that it was a disease exclusive to gay men. By late 1982, doctors knew that HIV spread through blood and sexual contact, making it nonspecific to any one population, but significant damage had already been done: The early years of HIV/AIDS resulted in more severe discrimination and prejudice toward gay, lesbian, bisexual, and transgender people, especially gay men.

Gay rights activists were outraged when government agencies continued to group homosexual men alongside drug users and sex workers, calling them "risk groups" collectively.

AIDS educators eventually began to specifically admonish risky "practices," like unprotected sex and sharing needles, instead of making such inaccurate

Many people (both inside and outside of gay communities) do not view sex work as having an automatically negative connotation. Gay people simply did not want to be lumped together with other populations such that their characteristics and life choices were assumed to be synonymous.

generalizations. Unfortunately, this transition took time and cost many lives as the government refused to recognize that lack of condom use among heterosexual couples was also a leading contributor to the rapid spread of HIV.

---

**DID YOU KNOW?**

In some countries, including Germany, Australia, Finland, Canada, Russia, and the U.K. (as well as 34 U.S. states), you must legally disclose your HIV-positive status to all sexual partners. Intentionally or recklessly endangering someone by exposing them to HIV without their consent is illegal in many places—it can even be charged as murder. The Center for Disease Control (CDC) estimates that 1.2 million people in the United States are currently living with an HIV infection. One in five Americans with HIV do not know that they are infected.

---

Confusion about delineating same-sex sexual behavior from those who identify as homosexual still affects AIDS awareness today. For example, when attempting to educate people about safer sex practices, educators report finding it difficult to reach men who have sex with other men but do not consider themselves gay (MSM or "Men who have Sex with Men"). While the Center for Disease Control believes that MSM comprise roughly 2 percent of the U.S. population, they were "61 percent of all new HIV infections in 2009. MSM accounted for 48 percent of people living with HIV infection in 2008." As such, AIDS programs currently group individuals based on their sexual activities as opposed to the identities that they claim. This may be a more effective way of reaching certain individuals at the moment, but it's also an antiquated way of approaching homosexuality, comparable to medical literature categorizations of the 1800s. But then, many dispute if and when someone's orientation can be labeled at all, as well as whether engaging in specific sex acts defines someone as gay, straight, queer, bisexual, or none of the above.

So what is homosexuality, in its modern conception? It is generally agreed that this term currently describes sexual attraction to people of one's own gender. There are clearly people who identify as the gender matching their assigned sex and who are attracted to people of that same gender. But the term "homosexual" is inflammatory and loose in several regards. Some people will not acknowledge the sexual orientation of anyone who has not yet engaged in sexual activity. Others claim that bisexuality doesn't exist, or that it is a liminal period before ascertaining one's primary preference. Much of the population isn't familiar with transgender people's experiences, and wouldn't intuit the orientation, for example, of a female-to-male transsexual who is in love with another man (such couples typically identify as gay men). How should a woman who is only attracted to bisexual men identify her sexual orientation? If a woman who identifies politically as a feminist lesbian is in a monogamous marriage with a man that she loves, might she also identify as heterosexual or bisexual?

It is clear that the term "homosexuality" does not cover the full array of sexual preferences, orientations, or identities any more than heterosexuality does. Likewise, the two terms together also fail to add up to a full or meaningful understanding of how we regard gender and desire. By looking more closely at heteronormativity we may come to understand why the terms we use to describe sexuality and gender are confusing and incomplete. The practices, media outlets, and institutions that privilege heterosexuality and traditional gender roles as "natural" within society need a closer examination. As we examine gender roles and sexual conduct variance across cultures it becomes quite clear that neither are as objective or natural as we are led to believe.

## CHAPTER 6
# GAY AND LESBIAN ACTIVISM

Having acknowledged the limits of the heterosexual and homosexual binary, debated where the term "homosexuality" came from, and explored some academic ideas about gender and sexuality's origin within an individual, there is still a tremendous source of knowledge about sexual orientation that has not yet been discussed: gay and lesbian people themselves. Gay men, lesbian women, and bisexuals have been significant in shaping American society. LGBT people have been some of our most famous artists, musicians, writers, actors, and athletes, and have served (openly or closeted) in almost every public office. They have not, however, been treated equally by the apparent heterosexual majority, nor given much visibility in American history lessons.

## A Brief List of Celebrated LGBT Americans

**Writers:** William S. Burroughs, Truman Capote, Michael Cunningham, Bret Easton Ellis, Allen Ginsberg, Amy Lowell, David Sedaris, Gore Vidal, Tennessee Williams

**Politicians:** Sam Adams, David Cicilline, Barney Frank, Rives Kistler, Victoria Kolakowski, Harvey Milk, Annise Parker, Stu Rasmussen, Gerry Studds

**Actors:** James Dean, Ellen Degeneres, Angelina Jolie, Nathan Lane, David Hyde Pierce, Lily Tomlin

**Artist/Musicians:** Josephine Baker, Samuel Barber, George Gershwin, Janis Joplin, Little Richard, Robert Mapplethorpe, Meshell Ndegeocello, Gus Van Sant, Andy Warhol

**Athletes:** Glenn Burke, Billie Jean King, Ryan Miller, Will Sheridan, Brian Sims, Sheryl Swoopes

As aforementioned, being attracted to someone of the same assigned sex was first referred to as homosexuality in the 1870s. Prior to that, romantic friendships between women and between young girls appear to have been regarded as normal and bore no social stigma since at least the Renaissance. Lacking the very concept of a "lesbian," two women in the late 19th century could live as a sort of unrecognized couple and have a relationship that would likely be considered homosexual by today's standards. Though women might have felt guilty about having oral sex, vaginally stimulating or penetrating

> ### IN THE CLOSET
> "Closeted" is a slang term for gay, lesbian, bisexual, or transgender people who do not disclose their orientation or gender identity to friends, family, or publicly for a myriad of reasons, ranging from job safety concerns to fear of harassment.

## CONSIDER THIS...

Given the inadequacy of gender categories and broadly accepted definitions of sexual orientation, there is no way to know for sure whether heterosexuals actually comprise the majority of any population.

one another, they would probably have compared these sex acts to solo masturbation. Any discomfort or moral confusion would be related to having "sex without marital duties," which was seen as indulgent or misbehaving at that time. It's unlikely that women would have considered their affections or sexual interest in one another as abnormal in any way.

Shortly after the term "homosexuality" was coined, sexual relationships between people of the same assigned sex were suddenly denounced by psychologists as an "inversion," or a reversal of one's gender, regardless of whether individuals exhibited strong feminine or masculine traits. Some sexologists grouped everyone who was attracted to people of their own sex or gender and likened them to transgender or transsexual people, even though most of the people being studied identified in accordance with their assigned sex.

> A congenital disorder is "[an] abnormality of structure and, consequently, function of the human body arising during development."

As science began to replace religion in much of liberal society as the most highly regarded (and a more "objective") way to view the world, many white middle class European values were culturally imposed as an amalgam of what was "normal" and "healthy." Anything that fell outside those boundaries was attributed to poor genes. As such, women in romantic friendships who would once have been called "sinners" for inappropriately enthusiastic sexual behavior were now assumed to be "inverted" for their sexual preference for the "wrong" gender. Likewise, a man who was attracted to other men was assumed to be genetically more feminine than a "normal" man.

Around 1893, many sexologists also began to claim that same-sex attraction was a congenital disorder arising due to a hereditary malfunction that occurs in parents who lack "strong enough" sex characteristics. In other words, they attributed homosexual orientation to a lack of masculinity or femininity inherited from one's parents. This view of gay and lesbian people was aligned with the taxonomy of the time, which assigned classifications to any behavior not contributing to psychologists' vision of humans "moving forward." During this period, evolution was a fashionable concept and a moral code was temporarily attached to it. Along with the new popularity of Darwinism came an assertion that patriarchy (and heterosexuality) was best for society, as it would maintain gender roles that led to reproduction. As we've seen, even though evolution is generally viewed today as progressive and morally neutral science, in the late 1800s and early 1900s, theories of natural selection also reinforced archetypal gender roles and linked feminism and homosexuality to abnormality.

> Taxonomy is the science of naming and classifying species.

For generations, romantic friendships between females had carried a connotation of a virtue and idealism specific to two women's affection for one another. Sigmund Freud, on the other hand, defined heterosexual genital intercourse as "normal" sexuality, and believed that any other sexual conduct was a perverted result of developmental inhibition. He considered homosexual orientation a return to instincts that healthy infants normally grow out of. After he visited the United States in 1909, Freudian theory gained traction in popular culture.

AFTER SIGMUND FREUD'S VISIT TO THE UNITED STATES IN 1909, FREUDIAN THEORY GAINED TRACTION IN POPULAR CULTURE.

Soon, magazines and other media started to paint romantic alliances between women as dangerous, morally wrong, or even nymphomaniacal—as if their same-sex attraction came from an escalated sexual hunger that forced one's desire to extend beyond normal boundaries.

Another popular school of thought in science at that time was eugenics, "the science of using controlled breeding to increase the occurrence of desirable heritable characteristics in a population." Many who believed in eugenics also feared that women who sought other women as life partners would dilute the intellect of the greater population, largely because some of the most well-educated women were taking women lovers or roommates in order to pursue further studies and employment. Eugenicists dually cited the goal of a career and a partnership with another woman as two interwoven aspects of a morally depraved woman. Indeed, it is possible that much of the stigma against homosexuality originated in academics, psychologists, and sexologists who feared that women were beginning to seek occupations, independence, and not necessarily planning to marry men or have children.

Not surprisingly, these ideas about female homosexuality roughly correlate to the first period of time when women's suffrage was at the forefront of American politics. By the late 19th century, working class women could get employment in factories, service and clerical work, and a growing number began moving to the cities for jobs. Between 1870 and 1900, the female labor force tripled in America, at more than twice the rate of the increase in the actual female population. Women who shared living arrangements in the working class at that time were often simply forming

alliances to gain space. But as Lillian Faderman points out in her history of lesbian life in 20th century America, sexologists were happier to acknowledge romantic arrangements between working class women than between upper class women; they likely misrepresented the frequency in both groups.

As upper class women started to take jobs in women's colleges and social reform work, some cultural feminists declared that male values were the cause of "industrialization, war, and mindless urbanization." They sought female allies and equal employment opportunities. Before the term "lesbian" existed, many romantic friendships between women had taken place in these women's colleges without any particular back-

lash. In fact, some women continued on to academic appointments without marrying and would cohabitate with their same-sex partner in what was then referred to as a "Boston marriage." Yet by 1920, undergraduate lexicons were ripe with Freudian terms and "intimacy between two girls was watched with keen distrustful eyes…one looked for the bisexual type, the masculine girl searching for a feminine counterpart, and one ridiculed their devotions."

As such, few upper class women at that time wanted to be known as a "lesbian" unless they were staunchly disgusted by men; even those who had romantic or sexual relationships with other women would not claim homosexual orientation lest they be considered mentally ill or "inverted." Despite the new stigma and the end of women's "romantic friendships" (as they had been so casually called before), over time, awareness of the term "lesbian" gradually led to the creation of lesbian communities.

Women who were devoted to one another now had an articulated basis for unity and new concepts to describe the feelings that they had for each other. Before WWI, female attraction between people of the same assigned sex was accepted but largely private, preventing lesbians from finding one another socially. The new linguistic distinction between ambitious women (who sometimes took a female lover in lieu of a man) and "lesbians" (who are exclusively attracted to other women) recognized a distinct lesbian identity. This minimal visibility was all it took for lesbians to begin establishing communities and a culture of their own.

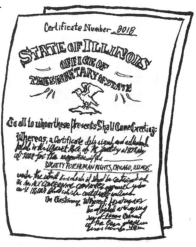

Following relatively close on the heels of the initial cultural stigmatization towards same gendered attraction and the subsequent formation of lesbian communities, some people started to organize politically to achieve better treatment for gay and lesbian people in mainstream society. The 1924 charter of the Chicago Society for Human Rights marks the earliest American organization lobbying for tolerance of homosexuality. Thus began a period of advocacy referred to as the "homophile movement."

The activists involved in the homophile movement were not yet seeking specific rights or acceptance from mainstream society. Many of these activists accepted the claim that homosexuals are mentally ill (or the alternate claim that homosexuality comes from a hereditary genetic flaw), but they also invoked the Declaration of Independence and stated that homosexuals have a legal right to pursue happiness. They hoped that if the rest of the population saw homosexuality as a psychological aberration that couldn't be helped, then at least gay men and lesbian women would be treated less severely. This was probably the first instance of the "born this way" argument.

The homophile movement's beginning was also concurrent with a brief reprieve from some of the harsher condemning of gays and lesbians in a

**HARRY HAY (1912 - 2002)**
LABOR ADVOCATE, TEACHER, AND EARLY
LEADER IN THE LGBT MOVEMENT

few select parts of the country as the Jazz Age and Prohibition took over. For a brief period, during those prosperous times of the 1920s, a more hopeful and progressive tone took hold in the urban underground. In Harlem, an African-American renaissance of music and culture occurred in covert nightclubs and speakeasies where liquor was illegally distributed. Cabarets and costume parties sparked a new community where disparate ethnicities and sexual orientations came together, and white and black homosexuals alike built alliances to push for societal change. Quickly following the stock market crash of 1929 and Prohibition's repeal, however, the Harlem gay subculture waned, and those who had been open about their sexuality in the "roaring twenties" were deemed indiscreet or indecent.

The next major homophile group didn't emerge until 1950, when Harry Hay and a group of men in Los Angeles formed the Mattachine Society. The Mattachine Society considered homosexuals "a population unaware of its status as 'a social minority imprisoned within a dominant culture.'" Their goal was to inform homosexuals that there was an establishment profiting from oppressing them. They organized group sessions to talk about homosexuality, where homosexual identity fit into the rest of society, what caused attraction to the same assigned sex, and to share personal experiences. This served mainly as a practice in building camaraderie; in a culture where their identity was either invisible or largely shunned, this was no doubt of huge significance to its gay members.

The Mattachine Society was mainly made up of men who were concerned with male issues; they didn't include lesbians or any lesbian agenda in their discussions. The group was essentially kept secret to protect its members, and because the founders were very leftist in their politics, they originally developed their organization from within the Communist Party. When communism became an incredibly hot topic in the 1950s, the Mattachine Society seceded from communist leadership and evolved into a more civil rights-focused group, seeking equal representation under the law. Their legacy was the establishment of pickets and court suits as effective means of producing change, a practice that would define gay and lesbian activism for future generations seeking civil liberties.

Another important homophile group also formed in the 1950s: the Daughters of Bilitis. This organization was openly political and sought to change the negative ideas about lesbianism that were then rampant

in mainstream society. There were certainly some lesbian members of the Daughters of Bilitis, but they did not openly declare themselves a homosexual group; they also overtly accepted psychologists' diagnosis of homosexuality as a disorder. The Daughters of Bilitis' propaganda described their members as women who were concerned for homosexuals and believed they ought to be sympathized with rather than persecuted. They petitioned the government, published newsletters and pamphlets, and attempted to get politicians to endorse their cause.

The Daughters of Bilitis advised lesbians to assimilate into the rest of society by dressing in a "feminine" fashion, and did not associate with anyone who lived outside of gender norms, such as butch lesbians or drag queens. The motive for this decision to exclude some lesbians and members of the gay community in favor of a more "normative" gender expression seems to have been politically motivated in and of itself. The Daughters speculated that if they represented themselves as nonthreatening to mainstream society and projected an image of lesbians as essentially "just

## BUTCH AND FEMME

The terms "butch" and "femme" can be used to describe some lesbians and some gay men as masculine and feminine, respectively. Butch and femme can refer to masculine and feminine types of behavior, expression, and fashion, or to individuals who assume a masculine or feminine role in a gay or lesbian couple. That said, many lesbians and gays do not identify as either butch or femme; they may be more androgynous, have a more fluid gender expression, or simply not ascribe to archetypal roles. Likewise, though butch/femme pairings are a common representation of gay and lesbian partnerships in the media, many gay and lesbian couples are not comprised of one butch and one femme partner.

## DRAG

Drag attire refers to any clothing that is generally associated with one gender being worn by a person of the "opposite" gender for performance, sexual, or entertainment purposes. People of all genders and orientations may wear drag, which has a wide range of artistic and cultural traditions. Men disguised as women have been part of folk traditions in rituals and performances for centuries. In England, Elizabethan theatre (including Shakespeare's plays) originally featured all-male actor ensembles, and female parts were played by men wearing drag. The term "drag queen" is often used to refer to men (gay, bisexual, or heterosexual) who dress in drag for performance or personal enjoyment, but who are not necessarily transvestites or transgender. Drag queens may wear wigs, prosthetic body parts, and elaborate and flashy costumes. "Drag king" can refer to the female equivalent of a drag queen, but has many meanings; it most frequently describes a woman assuming an intentionally masculine image when performing that does not match her sexuality or gender identity offstage.

like the rest of society" (with the exception of their gender of sexual preference), they would be awarded jobs and better treatment. The Daughters of Bilitis may have been relatively conservative by today's standards, but for the 1950s they also had quite a radical manner of working toward social change. They took aim at the same institutions that the gay liberation would soon target, including the police, organized religion, medical professionals, the press, and the federal government.

For context, it is important to know that as more homophile organizations formed in the 1940s and early 1950s, the government was entering a period of intense persecution and paranoia about the supposed threat of communists. In the midst of Cold War-era persecution and J. Edgar Hoover's expansion of the FBI's surveillance into citizens' privacy, Republican rabble-rousers claimed that communists had wormed their way into the government. They accused both communists and homosexuals of being psychologically unbalanced and a national security threat due to their "un-American" morals. Republican declarations that homosexuals were "weak" and could be easily blackmailed by communists to tell state secrets resulted in a period known as the "Lavender Scare." Homosexuals were often kept from entering the country during this period. For years following Roosevelt and Eisenhower's presidencies, civil servants were interrogated by government officials about their sexual relationships and social alliances; dozens of gay men, lesbian women, and their friends were fired from federal appointments. A congressional committee studied this supposed threat for months in 1950, but never found a single true example of a lesbian or gay person giving up state secrets.

Having never been significantly challenged by the nonconfrontational tactics of the homophile movement, gross mistreatment of gays and lesbians continued on into the otherwise increasingly liberal 1960s. In addition to habitual verbal harassment, job and housing discrimination, and unprovoked assaults upon gays and lesbians—all of which had occurred for decades—raids on bars that allowed gay people to socialize freely became increasingly common in the 1960s. On June 27th, 1969, police raided a New York bar called the Stonewall Inn that catered to poor and particularly marginalized members of gay communities, including homeless youth, transgender people, drag queens, and hustlers. Perhaps for the first time, gay and drag queen bar patrons fought back against the police, sparking a chain reaction of riots and protests in Greenwich Village in the days that followed. This event culminated in residents of the Village forming new, more radical gay and lesbian activist groups and designating places for gay men and lesbians to be open about their sexual preferences.

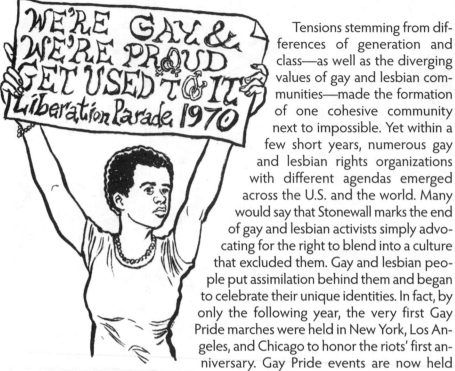

Tensions stemming from differences of generation and class—as well as the diverging values of gay and lesbian communities—made the formation of one cohesive community next to impossible. Yet within a few short years, numerous gay and lesbian rights organizations with different agendas emerged across the U.S. and the world. Many would say that Stonewall marks the end of gay and lesbian activists simply advocating for the right to blend into a culture that excluded them. Gay and lesbian people put assimilation behind them and began to celebrate their unique identities. In fact, by only the following year, the very first Gay Pride marches were held in New York, Los Angeles, and Chicago to honor the riots' first anniversary. Gay Pride events are now held throughout the month of June internationally, and June 27th in particular is highlighted to commemorate the beginning of a stronger push for gay and lesbian rights.

While the homophile movement sought gradual acceptance through educating people about homosexuality, the next wave of organizers represented a more militant force; their movement was known as gay liberation. Gay liberationists rebelled against the "status quo," and the values and structure that presented heterosexuality as the general or "normal" orientation. They debated gendered behavior, the nuclear family model and monogamy, and looked down on assimilation. They also promoted a distinct gay identity, and took pride in appearing different from the heterosexual "majority."

Gay liberation began in the late 1960s and early 70s during a new culture of protest in the United States. Black militants, student radicals, and hippies were raising their fists against the Vietnam War in street battles, protest

QUEER THEORIES SCHOLAR
ANNAMARIE JAGOSE (B. 1965)

marches, the takeover of universities, and even bombings. Until gay liberation, the formerly docile and policy reform-based nature of gay and lesbian movements had contrasted sharply from the direct-action and sometimes violent methods of the rest

of America's counterculture. Queer theory scholar Annamarie Jagose notes in *Queer Theory: An Introduction* that gay liberation now more closely aligned with the vision of the 1960s, and insisted that the system "would never be radically transformed by those who were invested in it."

Unlike the homophile groups before them, gay liberationists didn't seek increased social stature, but instead aimed to overthrow the institutions that marginalized homosexuality and considered it an ailment. Dissatisfied with the homophiles' fear of challenging the psychiatric diagnosis of homosexuality as a form of mental illness, they asserted a new politically-charged identity for gay people. They sought not only to gain recognition for homosexuality as a legitimate identity, but also to eradicate fixed notions of femininity and masculinity in hopes of liberating other groups who they perceived as similarly oppressed. Gay liberationists believed that by refusing to conform to the "normative" sex and gender representations they saw in the mainstream media, they would eventually put an end to the binary categories of heterosexuality and homosexuality.

## AUTHOR'S NOTE ON COMING OUT AS A YOUNG PERSON

This book is not meant to be a call to arms for coming out. Coming out can be an expression of pride, but disclosing your LGBTQIA status can be dangerous as well. It's also not a one-time thing. For those who are not cisgender, or who do not identify as heterosexual, the challenge to claim one's identity and face potential discrimination, misunderstanding, or ill treatment can occur daily. Everyone needs a support system of family and friends, financial stability, and a safe place to live. As a general rule, "coming out" should only be encouraged for financially-dependent young people when a LGBTQIA individual has adequate reason to believe that at least one family member or guardian will be supportive. Alternatively, you might want to try talking about your identity or orientation with a trusted friend, contacting a local support group for LGBTQIA people and their families, or attending a Gay-Straight Alliance meeting at a nearby school. **If things get tough, and you need support, please call The Trevor Project's crisis hotline for lesbian, gay, bisexual, transgender, and questioning youth at (866) 488-7386.**

It was popularly imagined during the 1960s and early 70s that if people were less sexually repressed, gender would be of less significance, and a new freer sexuality for all would then emerge. The ideal that gay liberationists (and some other hippies, radicals, and feminists) sought was a world where people would continue to fall in love and have relationships, but would no longer need to commit to a particular label signifying their preferences, orientation, or even their gender. Gay liberationists also advocated that sexual intercourse should be recognized as a morally neutral form of pleasure and a way of relating to people instead of being seen as having a purely reproductive function.

Gay liberationists started to promote the "coming out" narrative as a potent manner of sparking social transformation. They referred to this declaration of their orientation as a kind of "consciousness raising," and advocated that gay people should announce their identity to their family, friends, co-workers, and publicly until it was no longer seen as a shameful secret, but, as Jagose called it, "a legitimately recognized way of being in the world." In this way, gay liberation was closely tied to second wave feminism, as their own consciousness raising groups provided gay men with a forum for discussion and personal growth. Second wave feminists assumed that gay men and straight women would have the experience of oppression in common, and that by working together they would become more empowered and come to understand the homophobia and sexism in America's dominant culture.

The feminists who aligned themselves with the gay liberation movement figured that gay men shared a subjugation comparable to the one that women faced surrounding their own sex lives. Even during and after the 1960s "sexual revolution," women who were open about their sexual needs or desires received criticism for not being "ladylike," and women who took on stereotypical masculine roles, clothing, or careers were treated as outcasts in many social situations. With this in mind, many feminists thought that gay men were being similarly ostracized for falling outside of the male gender archetype in terms of their sexual preference and demeanor. At the same time, gay liberationists figured that by "coming out" they were challenging a system that kept both gay men and straight women down and presented certain gender roles as natural.

By the late 1970s, gay liberationists' radical tactics fell out of favor when a more formal agenda was adopted to seek specific gay and lesbian civil rights. Nevertheless, their movement had a number of lasting effects. The term "gay" emerged as a more appropriate way to describe the identity of some people with an attraction to the same assigned sex or gender, leaving the term "homosexual," with all of its pathological implications, largely by the wayside. Gay liberationists achieved a public identity for gay men that was based on more than their sexual orientation

## TERMINOLOGY SWITCH: HOMOSEXUAL TO GAY

In the 1960s, the word "homosexual" fell out of popular favor because of its association with 19th century theories about sexuality. Many people felt that saying "homosexual" would continue to reinforce the idea of same-gendered attraction as deviant, or even as a psychological disorder. Disagreeing with those implications, they instead adopted the word "gay," which had gradually grown in popular usage for several decades. Since "gay" was formerly used to describe women of questionable morals in the 19th century, redefining it was meant to somewhat sarcastically counter the idea that homosexuality was a negative alternative to "normal" heterosexuality. Employing the term "gay" helped to articulate a group of people's orientation without the clinical history of sexology attached. Gay (or queer) is also sometimes used as slang to refer more broadly to LGBT communities as a whole, but this is somewhat controversial because doing so can make other identities less visible, and it is less clear when someone is solely referring to gay men.

and which was politically effective. They also articulated a substantial and influential critique of gender as an oppressive construction that elevates the status of heterosexuals above everyone else.

Before gay liberation ceded to agendas for particular civil liberties, however, lesbian feminism emerged as a separate movement that shared a strong opposition to marginalization and to restrictive gender norms. Fundamentally, while "lesbian feminism" describes a range of different political and theoretical positions, most lesbian feminists agreed that lesbianism could offer feminists a model for transformation. They held that a woman's act of choosing another woman as a lover was a political statement in a society run by heterosexual privilege. For this to extend to truly liberating women, lesbian feminists believed that open female sexuality and sisterhood among women would need to expand dramatically.

Although there were some feminists in the gay liberation movement and a handful of open lesbians in the women's movement, lesbians found that their voices were given far less weight and they eventually converged to seek their own agenda. There were a number of reasons for this exclusionary behavior towards lesbians by both gay men and straight feminist women. First of all, it might seem like common sense to assume that all homosexual people would have merged during gay liberation and agreed that patriarchy oppresses lesbians along with gay men and feminists who deviated from gender norms of the era—but this simply didn't happen. Gay men and lesbian women may have attraction to same-sex partners in common, but their gender identities have resulted in numerous cultural differences between them. Gay men and lesbian women really should not be construed as "two genders within one sexual [orientation] category." Having been organized along the lines of their gender for centuries, gays and lesbians have important

At the very least, one cannot deny the analogy of sexually active males (gay or heterosexual) being applauded by their peers for their conquests, while similarly sex-positive females are often degraded for their "promiscuity" or "slutty" behavior. Clearly, masculine sexuality has a much greater degree of freedom and legitimacy in our society, the trickle-down effect of which has a profound effect on relationships (gay and straight), as well as on male and female-specific culture.

and distinct histories and experiences specific to their gender identities, which surpass their orientation.

For example, lesbians lack the economic and cultural privilege of men and commonly assert that their love relationships have different qualities from the partnerships between gay men. Masculine sexuality has been given legitimacy and some freedom of expression for many generations, which has resulted in different gay male cultures and attitudes toward sex than that of lesbians. Gay men are popularly associated with a variety of high culture, such as ballet, fashion, musical theater, and interior design, and stereotyped as having obsessive interest in actresses and other pop stars. Their relationships, though often long-term and committed, are often caricatured as a string of indiscriminate sexual encounters based on physical appearance alone. Lesbians, by contrast, are usually stereotyped as seeking love and companionship in a feminist, women-focused, or women-only environment.

The category of lesbian also transcends clear-cut gender definitions of man and woman. In the past, butch and femme archetypes were more expected and rigid than today, but lesbians are still commonly represented as falling into these categories, neither of which describes the archetype of a woman in our society. Furthermore, according to Monique Wittig, being a lesbian has economic, political, and ideological implications beyond being simply a sexual orientation, because in all three of these areas of life, a lesbian is distinct from any other woman. Lesbians are neither socially defined in relation to their partnerships with men or to childbearing, nor do they concern themselves with provoking desire in men. Yet, as women, access to employment and fiscal independence has been historically more difficult for lesbians than for gay or straight men, made more difficult by discrimination against their orientation. Additionally, as mentioned, homosexuality is almost exclusively legally defined along the lines of sodomy and gay sex acts. As a result, lesbians have been both less exhaustively persecuted and less visible or acknowledged.

"For what makes a woman is a specific social relation to a man, a relation that we have previously called servitude, a relation which implies personal and physical obligations as well as economic obligation ("forced residence," domestic corvée, conjugal duties, unlimited production of children, etc.), a relation which lesbians escape by refusing to become or to stay heterosexual."
—MONIQUE WITTIQ

## COMPULSORY HETEROSEXUALITY AND LESBIANS

In her essay "Compulsory Heterosexuality and Lesbian Existence," the prominent lesbian feminist and poet Adrienne Rich explained how lesbians' voices have been stifled and excluded by those who consider their plight merely a female version of male homosexuality. She contended that equating lesbians with gay men on account of their shared stigma and same-gendered attraction erases lesbians' distinctly female experience, especially since women's stories and viewpoints are already marginalized in mainstream society. Rich further defined heterosexuality as an institution "systematically working to the disadvantage of woman" and coined the term "compulsory heterosexuality" to mean that as long as heterosexuality was considered more acceptable, primary, or normal, the term "lesbian" will be a derogatory word "and will be used…against women."

ADRIENNE RICH (1929-2012)
PROMINENT LESBIAN FEMINIST
AND POET

Even though some gay liberationists teamed up with feminists, and even worked against the oppression of women, their organizing efforts almost always left out lesbian organizations and individuals. Ultimately, lesbian feminism largely considered gay men—as men who enjoyed much of the privilege afforded to heterosexual men—to be "part of [the] oppressive social structure [that they were] committed to overthrowing."

It is also a common misconception that, as women frustrated with sexism and discrimination towards women's sexuality, lesbians

## GAY MEN AND (STRAIGHT) FEMINISTS

Despite not including lesbians in their activist efforts, it's worth noting that most gay men of the time aligned with feminists and stated that they found chauvinism distasteful. Some gay liberationists argued that they did not participate fully in the dominant (heterosexual) male culture, and therefore were more willing than straight men to acknowledge women as equals.

must have played an active role in first and second wave feminism. Contrary to this notion, early feminists often distanced themselves from lesbians because they feared that associating with them would damage their project of equal rights for women, which they saw as a more fundamental goal than securing equal rights for a minority of women who openly identified as lesbians. A parallel may be drawn to the exclusion of African-American women from early suffrage efforts, wherein their minority status was treated as a liability to the "greater effort" to liberate—mainly straight, white middle class—women.

## NOW AND THE LAVENDER MENACE

NOW, the largest feminist organization in the U.S., eventually included the lesbian agenda in their activities, but until the early 1970s they consistently kept a conservative stance on how the women's movement should seek better footing. Much like the homophile movement, NOW avoided radical solutions; their immediate aim was passing laws to limit sex discrimination, and they discussed their goals in terms of equal rights instead of women's liberation. Some members were cited as referring to lesbians as "a lavender menace" (an allusion to the "Lavender Scare" of President Truman's term) because there was public antipathy for the lesbian stereotype of being both "anti-men" and masculine in attire and appearance. Ultimately, NOW members feared that lesbians' demeanor was too extreme to be accepted by mainstream society and would undermine feminist gains.

As a result of NOW and other organizations' limited acceptance of lesbians, at the Second Congress to Unite Women on May 1, 1970, a group of radical lesbian feminists decided to protest against the fact that no open lesbians were on the program. During the first session of the Congress, they flipped off the lights and stood up wearing purple T-shirts with the words "Lavender Menace" silkscreened on them. They read from a manifesto emphasizing the importance of inclusivity in the women's movement and outlined how both sexism and discrimination against lesbians could be eliminated. The paper they read, "Woman-Identified Woman," describes lesbianism not just as a sexual orientation but also as a way of living that emphasizes the love of one's self and all women. These radical lesbians were part of a small group of lesbians who **did** think that gay men, straight feminist women, and lesbians should form an alliance. Eventually, this idea would take root in the queer movement and some modern LGBT organizations, but it took decades to seed.

They may have held different ideologies and agendas, but both gay liberationists and lesbian feminists sought to transform the social morays and structures of an American society that oppressed them. Each group sought to demonstrate that an identity based on attraction to the same assigned sex or gender was as legitimate as heterosexuality, and each was eager to make notions of gender and sexuality more malleable. Finally, given their shared opinion that people would become more "bisexual" if the stigma was removed from female sexual expression and if gender archetypes were less predominant, it appears that gay liberationists and lesbian feminists shared a constructionist viewpoint.

Following the free love movement and radicalism of the late 1960s, mainstream American society began to explore a new fascination with sex for its own sake, without much of the taboo that had formerly been

## PANSEXUALS AND GENDER FLUIDITY

By saying that people had the potential to become more universally "bisexual" and remove gender archetypes, gay liberationists and lesbian feminists likely meant—in today's terms—that people could become both more pansexual and gender fluid. Pansexuals (also called omnisexuals) identify as having the potential for sexual attraction, romantic love, or an emotional connection to people of all gender identities. Pansexuals may refer to themselves as "gender-blind," meaning that gender and assigned-sex do not affect their level of attraction to a given individual. Gender fluidity denotes the gender identity of someone who feels like a mix of the two dominant genders, but may feel more male or more female on any given day. This identification has no relationship to an individual's genitals or their orientation.

attached to it. Women had long been told by both popular culture and religious institutions that sexual intercourse was only acceptable in the context of marriage and for the purpose of producing a family (or in some cases, to please their husband); suddenly, they were finding increasing social acceptance in pursuing their own enjoyment. Throughout the 1970s, X-rated movies became accessible to the general public, adult bookstores emerged, and gay men took out personal ads for sex partners. But as heterosexual couples thumbed through the best-selling *The Joy of Sex* in search of the multiple orgasm, some lesbians felt somewhat left out.

Having never considered their orientation to be purely about sex acts, lesbianism was to some extent inextricable from the strain of feminism that celebrated women culture and love of all women. Many lesbians who had been socialized as females in our society felt no more able to have purely lust-based relationships than heterosexual women of the previous era, and they entertained few casual encounters. Lillian Faderman contends that lesbians were having less sex in committed relationships than heterosexual couples, because both (female) parties had been socialized to be the recipient of (male) sexual advances; as a result, neither would be a trained initiator. As the 1970s progressed, feminists and lesbians diverged into two different schools of thought concerning their identity, both sexual and otherwise.

Cultural feminists considered women's culture different and better, and advocated for intimacy and nurturing the connection between women. As such, they were uncomfortable with sexual exploration that emulated any shred of male sexuality. Cultural feminists distrusted the long-term effects of pornography, along with violent or even mildly dominant sexual roles, including butch and femme identification, which embodies strongly dichotomous masculine and feminine traits. They worried about the potential for women to objectify women the way that men had in the past, and stressed the political significance of these feelings.

By the 1980s, another group of lesbians who considered themselves sexual radicals had taken an opposing stance. They felt that lesbians needed to end their sexual repression and that equality meant access to any kind of safer sex that appealed to them (just as, they contended, men had enjoyed for centuries). They were frustrated with having been left out of the pleasure-seeking of the 1970s and wanted to claim new sexualized identities for themselves like many gay men and heterosexuals had done. Some sexual radicals began to partake in pornography and role-playing that had originated in gay male and in straight culture, arguing that doing so would extend and intensify the sex life of long-term lesbian relationships. They rejected the idea that claiming masculine sex roles could reaffirm patriarchy. Instead, they wondered if the effects of female socialization might be doubled in lesbians and said that cultural feminists were reinforcing traditional notions of what femininity looked like.

So as cultural feminists continued to hold essentialist notions of women and believe that sex had strong moral connotations, sexual radicals were intrigued by working out feelings about power and polarities through taking on new roles in sex play. They resented how feminists of the previous decades had desexualized female clothing; despite their desire to end the objectification of women, radicals thought sex acts themselves were morally neutral. Sexual radicals didn't conceive of women as innately different or better, but sought the freedom to try out forms of dominance and submission. They were interested in exploring these new roles, media, and kinds of sex that were no longer solely a male privilege. Conversely, cultural feminists were concerned that women who participated in this sort of sexual exploration had absorbed patriarchal values that validate one person having more power than another in a relationship or sexual encounter.

Over time, cultural feminists, sexual radicals, gay liberationists, lesbian feminists, and other marginalized groups advocating for equal rights on the basis of gender and sexual orientation evolved toward a variety of new philosophical positions. Yet as feminist, gay, lesbian, bisexual, and transgender activists alike began to focus on gaining specific rights under the law, they began to find a lot more common footing. As early as the late 1970s, but gaining significant steam in the 90s, LGBT organizers began addressing the wrongs inflicted by a legislature that alternately ignored and actively discriminated against them.

---

## LGBT, GLBT, LGBTQ, AND LGBTQIA

LGBT, GLBT, and LGBTQ are acronyms that collectively name lesbian, gay, bisexual, and transgender people. Originating in the mid 1980s and becoming more popularly used in the 90s, the term LGBT was meant to take the place of the phrases "the gay rights movement" or "the gay community," which were often used to refer to lesbian, bisexual, or transgender individuals that did not feel included in the term. The decision to put "L" first in the acronym has historically been a political one; often the person employing it was asserting that lesbians are underrepresented compared to gay men. Other times it is a more arbitrary choice of an individual or group. LGBTQ is meant to signify the range of gender identities and sexualities, and is also used to refer to anyone who does not identify as heterosexual or cisgender, such as genderqueer folks. The sometimes present "Q" denotes queer, and the more recent LGBTQIA adds in an "A" for asexual (or sometimes ally), an "I" for intersex, and/or also doubly use the "Q" to represent "questioning" individuals.

---

One might say that Stonewall was not the beginning of the gay and lesbian rights movement, but the moment where the public became aware of it. Similarly, in the course of developing a more seemingly inclusive and policy-based approach to seeking rights, and subsequently adopting the LGBT (or later LGBTQIA) acronym, activists' efforts gained increasing visibility. That visibility was not equally distributed, however, as bisexuals, transsexuals, and transgender activists were sometimes exploited by gay and lesbian rights activists who allowed them to contribute to "the cause" while deprioritizing their needs and goals. The addition of the "B" and "T" letters to the acronym LGBT has been criticized by some bisexual and

DURING WWII THE MILITARY CONDUCTED PSYCHIATRIC EVALUATIONS ON ALL SOLDIERS. HOMOSEXUALITY WAS CONSIDERED PROOF OF A MENTAL ILLNESS, PUNISHABLE BY IMPRISONMENT AND DISHONORABLE DISCHARGE.

trans people who consider it a purely symbolic gesture.

Instead of pushing for more universal transformation and a hope that society would reframe their ideas of gender and sexuality as a whole, the majority of LGBT rights activists worked for local initiatives to change laws and policies to make life safer for gay and lesbian people (and to a lesser degree, bisexual and transgender people). Whether the gender categories of man and woman were social constructs or not, the realistic need to live dignified lives, free from extreme poverty, persecution, and violence came to the forefront of the larger organizations fighting for LGBT rights. Among their key goals, they focused on attaining different forms of status that many felt would lead to fiscal and social equity, including same-sex marriage, rights in the workplace, and the ability to serve in the military.

One of the most hotly disputed civil liberties sought by LGBT activists is the right to serve in the military. Since the Revolutionary War, sodomy had been grounds for discharging a soldier from the military, but the exact rules governing homosexuality have evolved over the last century. During WWII, the military conducted psychiatric evaluations on all soldiers, and homosexuality was considered proof of a mental illness, and punished if discovered after induction by imprisonment and dishonorable discharge. Regulation 615-360, briefly in effect between 1944 and 1947, even made it policy to commit gay service members to military hospitals before discharging them. In 1947, the form of discharge was separated into two categories, undesirable and dishonorable, depending on whether or not a service member had same-sex sexual contact while in the service.

Between the 1940s and continuing during the Vietnam War, gay men were allowed to serve in the event of a shortage of service members. But in 1982, the Department of Defense formally issued a policy stating that homosexuality was incompatible with military service. This policy was received with a great deal of skepticism and increasing anger from LGBT communities and others throughout the 1980s and 90s. President Clinton attempted to overturn the ban on gay service when he was first elected, but Congress pushed the ban into federal law before he could, and a "compromise" measure, "Don't Ask, Don't Tell" was put into effect instead in 1993.

"Don't Ask, Don't Tell" prohibited military personnel from discriminating against or harassing closeted homosexual or bisexual service members or applicants, but barred openly gay, lesbian, or bisexual persons from military service. It asserted that openly serving homosexuals would "create an unacceptable risk to the high standards of morale, good order, and discipline and unit cohesion that are the essence of military capability." Gay, lesbian, and bisexual service members were not allowed to disclose their orientation, or speak about their relationships. In recent years, surveys of service members revealed that few believed that allowing open gays, lesbians, and bisexuals would negatively affect military order and effectiveness. President Obama signed the repeal of "Don't Ask Don't Tell" in 2010, allowing gay, lesbian, and bisexual people to serve openly in the U.S. military for the first time. The United States continues to prohibit openly transgender people from serving in the military.

Marriage equality—the right of two people of the same legal sex or social gender identity to marry—continues to be a major civil liberty issue today. Proponents of gay marriage seek the same rights afforded to married heterosexual couples, including the transfer of wealth between partners, hospital visiting rights when their partner is ill, court-litigated distribution of assets if they divorce, and the assignment of rights if one partner should become incapacitated (comatose, mentally ill, etc.). They contend these are basic and universal human rights that should be extended to any long-term couple that wishes to commit to one another, without gender or sex as a limiting factor.

"Denial of access to marriage to same-sex couples may especially harm people who also experience discrimination based on age, race, ethnicity, disability, gender and gender identity, religion, and socioeconomic status," said the American Psychological Association in 2004.

Opposition to marriage equality commonly stems from the use of the word "marriage" or concerns about tradition and parenting. The Defense of Marriage Act of 1996 (DOMA), a definitive policy in the contest over marriage equality, defines marriage as purely between "opposite sex" couples and explicitly allows states not to recognize unions made legally in other states whose laws protect them. Yet studies show that allowing marriages recognized by society may dramatically increase the health of gay people. Given reports of the American Psychological Association (APA) on the effects of multiplying risk factors for LGBT individuals, it is probable that denying gay and lesbian couples access to marriage and its benefits institutionally sanctions and reinforces other forms of discrimination that LGBT people face.

Same-sex marriages are currently legal in ten countries, and vary by state in the U.S. on the basis of legislative marriage laws and court cases that have dealt with equality legislation. Same-sex couples can become legally wed in nine states and the District of Columbia, but their unions are only recognized on the state level. Some states also allow civil unions or registered partnerships, but LGBT advocates claim that these carry a "separate but equal" stigma and that civil unions currently have limited rights compared to married couples. Civil unions also make couples more vulnerable when crossing state lines, seeking Social Security, or filing taxes, since some states refuse to properly honor their legality. In 2011, President Obama declared DOMA unconstitutional and directed courts to stop defending the law, but the House of Representatives has since said they would continue to defend the act, so it is still in dispute.

---

### Federal Protections Denied Same-Sex Couples Without Gay Marriage

- Joint parental rights over children
- Joint adoption
- Next-of-kin status (in the event of death or a medical decision)
- Domestic violence protection orders
- Spousal veterans benefits
- Social Security benefits
- Medicare
- Wrongful death benefits for surviving partner/children
- Bereavement/sick leave to care for partner or children
- Child support
- Joint insurance plans
- Welfare/public assistance
- Joint housing for elderly couples
- Credit protection

Gay and lesbian rights groups have also made significant efforts to pass legislation to fight discrimination against LGBT people in the workplace. Wisconsin banned employment discrimination based on sexual orientation in 1982, making it the first state to do so. Minnesota was the first state to ban employment discrimination on the basis of both sexual orientation and gender identity when it passed its Human Rights Act in 1993. Sixteen states currently have some form of policy protecting both orientation and gender identity discrimination in the workplace, and five more states protect orientation alone. Five states have regulations to protect orientation and gender identity for public employees, specifically, and five others protect just orientation for public employees.

## THERE TO PROTECT US?

In 2005, Amnesty International released a report based on more than 170 interviews with LGBT survivors and allies, as well as surveys of dozens of police departments, and extensive further research. "Stonewalled: Police Abuse and Misconduct Against LGBT People in the U.S." details the routine practices of verbal abuse, harassment, physical assault, selective enforcement of the law, profiling, and nonenforcement (in the case of hate crimes and domestic violence) that police officers across America inflict upon LGBT people. The report also showed that transgender people, especially trans women and young people, receive the most frequent and extreme brutality from police officers.

The United States still has not passed the Employment Non-Discrimination Act (ENDA), a proposed bill that has been introduced in each Congress since 1974. ENDA would federally ban discrimination against employees on the basis of sexual orientation or gender identity. Although President Obama supports the passage of ENDA, prior Presidents have threatened to veto it, and many advocacy organizations were divided over transgender inclusion in the bill, which some felt would make it more difficult to pass. The proposed bill does not cover employees of small businesses, religious organizations, or the military, nor does it require that same-sex partners would receive benefits afforded to married or domestically partnered couples. As it stands today, people can still be fired solely because they're gay, lesbian, or bisexual in 29 states, and for transgender identification in 34 states.

MATTHEW SHEPARD
(1976 - 1998)

There are a number of other critical issues and rights that LGBT activists in the U.S. have ardently sought to resolve over the last few decades, such as housing discrimination, homelessness among LGBT people, unequal access to adequate health care, unsafe schools for LGBTQ youths, bullying and assault, and increasing AIDS awareness. Activists seeking better treatment for LGBT people face an array of obstacles, not the least of which includes misconduct or mistreatment by police officers, health care professionals, teachers, religious leaders, and even social workers who are ostensibly there to protect them. Some American LGBT activists are also attempting to fight state-sanctioned violence in other parts of the world, such as assault, torture, or the death penalty inflicted upon LGBT people by their governments as punishment for their orientation or gender identity.

In the U.S., abroad, and even in countries where there were never explicit laws against homosexuality, LGBT people remain frequent targets of violence, ranging from bullying and assault to homicide. LGBT hate crimes statistically result in particularly extreme brutality against victims who frequently do not know their attacker(s). In other words, the attack is often motivated by a person's real or perceived sexual orientation or gender identity alone, not any personal relationship or transgression between the attacker(s) and victim. In an effort to reduce violence against LGBT people, President Obama signed the Matthew Shepard and James Byrd, Jr. Hate Crimes Prevention Act in 2009, expanding upon federal hate-crime legislation to include crimes motivated by a victim's actual or perceived gender, sexual orientation, gender identity, or disability. Even so, hate crimes directed at LGBT people are difficult to address because of ongoing societal discrimination and inequity. These crimes remain underreported by both prejudicial authorities and by victims who may wish to avoid drawing attention to their status or who do not expect proper treatment by police and the court system.

Today, while progress is being made to end hate crimes, discrimination, homophobia, and transphobia, there are still many obstacles to obtaining equality for LGBT people. Long-standing legislation, institutions, and cultural values that stigmatize LGBT individuals obstruct potential policy-making that could help to ensure more material equity. Despite what we know about the diversity of gender roles worldwide, gender archetypes and heteronormativity in American society relegate LGBTQIA people to "other" status. But as new information and diverse views of gender and sexuality become more prevalent, more people are rethinking their "either/or" formulations of male and female, heterosexual and homosexual. Some advocate instead for a more inclusive umbrella term for those who renounce archetypal heteronormative roles: "queer."

FEMINISM WILL DEFEAT ITS OWN GOAL IF IT CONTINUES TO FOCUS ON THE CATEGORY OF "WOMEN" AND ASSUME THAT WOMEN HAVE A NATURAL UNITY OF EXPERIENCE.

POST-STRUCTURALIST PHILOSOPHER JUDITH BUTLER (B. 1956)

CHAPTER 7

# QUEER THEORY

While attempting to remove the stigma against diverse sexual orientations, lesbian feminists and gay liberationists raised new questions about gender identity and sexuality. Debates about whether an individual's identity exists distinct from their chosen actions were exacerbated by the rhetoric surrounding the AIDS epidemic. And in the background of the new LGBT focus on obtaining civil liberties, some theorists began to rethink the idea of identity categories altogether.

Philosopher Judith Butler, for example, predicted that feminism would defeat its own goal of gender equality if it continued to focus on the category of "women" and assume that women have a natural unity of experience. In *Gender Trouble: Feminism and the Subversion of Identity* (1990), she explains that then-current theories of sexuality were ignoring sexual orientation's dependence on fairly consistent gender categories. Butler witnessed how people not adhering to the cultural norms for their assigned sex (or whose orientation does not align with their sex or gender) lacked coherent descriptive terms, and were consequently reduced to an aberration or abnormality in society's eyes.

Instead of conceding that gay and lesbian activists should seek to make same-sex desire as "natural" as heterosexuality, Butler argued that gender is a cultural fiction that makes some identities invisible and consistently delegitimizes gay and lesbian people. Since current representations of gender offer privileges to heterosexuals, Judith Butler suggested that "deconstructing normative models of gender" would help gay and lesbian people to gain legitimacy within society at large.

If gender is just a series of repetitious actions, like Butler says, then by claiming a queer identity, one asserts that the "innate" correspondence between cisgender people and their assigned sex is a facade.

Rather than viewing gender as a bond between people sharing similar experiences and attributes, Butler believes "gender is the repeated stylization of the body, a set of repeated acts within a highly rigid regulatory frame that congeal over time to produce the appearance of substance, of a natural sort of being." She further asserts that heterosexuality is not merely one of the options within the sex/gender system. Instead, Butler believes that the sex/gender system invents the very concept of heterosexuality (and its assumed naturalness) through repetition of gender identity norms.

David Halperin added onto this argument that "homosexual" was not a name for something natural, universal, or static any more than "woman" is. He thought all identity categories were far too narrow and rigid, implying a fake unity that inevitably excludes some people and regulates everyone's ideas of behavioral and sexual options. Halperin contends that identity categories are arbitrarily constructed to concentrate on particular bodies (almost as a method of organization), but come to be considered natural groupings over time. For example, one might refer back to how psychologists at the turn of the 20th century suddenly began encouraging parents to dress their infants and toddlers in new gender-specific clothing and colors, and to teach children gender-appropriate behavior lest they not acquire it. Today, it seems "unnatural" to many parents to avoid the gender-specific clothing, colors, toys, and activities that they expect their children will prefer. Halperin felt that this sort of mechanism (and potential domino effect) applied to all identity politics and labels, including sexual orientation categories. Many other theorists in the late 1980s and early 90s (such as Teresa de Lauretis, Eve Kosofsky Sedgwick, Diana Fuss, Gloria E. Anzaldúa, and Valerie Traub, to name a few) were also engaged in discourse about the insufficiency of identity categories, which eventually led to queer theory.

---

**GENDERED ADVERTISING**

If readers have any remaining doubt that toys are so strictly gendered that it would be difficult for children to think a "boy" or "girl" toy can be used by the opposite assigned sex (and therefore is an option for any kid), take a look at the Gendered Advertising Remixer designed by Jonathan McIntosh to empower youth to understand and take control of the gendered messages being sent to them. Check out: http://www.genderremixer.com/.

---

But what does "queer" mean? There are many definitions of queer, some of which contradict one another. Ultimately, as David Halperin says, being "queer" is an identity "without an essence." "Queer" is unavoidably a bit ambiguous and vague as it refutes the conventional ideas of sexual identity that are familiar to most people in our society. "Gay" and "lesbian" refer to sexual orientations whose definition depends on existing gender categories. By contrast, "queer" suggests a new form of self-identification for both gender and sexuality at once. It points directly to a contradiction between the external world's observations of one's characteristics and self-definition, refuting the idea that people can fit into a narrow category.

Perhaps "queer" may be best described as a position rather than an identity. By taking the position of "queer," an individual places themself specifically outside of that which privileges heteronormativity. To be queer, by that definition, is to reject the notion that heterosexuality is "normal," "natural," or above and beyond any other gender identity and sexual orientation pairing. "Queer" is also sometimes used as a political synonym for all things non-heterosexual. As such, there are many gay, lesbian, and bisexual people who also identify as part of the queer movement. Accordingly, some transgender people who are also gay, lesbian, bisexual, or genderqueer may concurrently identify as queer. Queer can also be employed as a verb; to "queer" one's gender or a space or topic means to make it more inclusive or merged, and less singular or homogeneous.

Because queer theory destabilizes the idea that sexual orientation is properly paired with particular genders, queer also implies that cisgender people—whose bodies, identities, and assigned gender all match—are no more normal or more natural than people with any other gender identity. In fact, the queer movement is meant to include anyone who claims to be against the very concept of a "normal" gender or sexual identity; it is a stance against the idea that anyone who deviates from heterosexuality (or homosexuality) or identifies outside of gender norms is abnormal or "other." "Queer" avoids the dichotomy of straight

Some trans communities use a similar description for transgender identity. They mainly emphasize gender as unstable, however, and therefore contend that sexual orientation (and its lack of coherence) follows from gender definitions, since an "orientation" can scarcely be understood without a primary definition of who one is oriented to.

and gay, masculine and feminine, and does not inherently expect that identity needs to be constant or consistent. Additionally, some people of color employ the term "queer" to help describe the disparate but related identities of their current citizenship, where their family emigrated from, their ethnicity, and/or the language(s) that they speak.

Like other constructionist theories, queer theory implies that gender's meaning can change. Judith Butler and some other early queer theorists wondered if an individual's gender is a development of their repeated actions, not an innate quality. They generally agreed that gender only acquires a meaning with any sense of permanence when someone's actions conform to a societal standard over a period of time. The way queer theorists saw it, in the event that regulations on behavior are perpetuated long enough, they come to be perceived as a natural category with innate meaning. According to this theory, heterosexuality became "naturalized" as a result of people repeating archetypal gender identities until they become our idea of an "original." For example, because Western women were frequently told that being passive or meek was attractive, and enough of them followed suit, it was eventually assumed that women were by nature more submissive and demure than men. Likewise, dressing in drag attire may depict archetypal women or glorify the archetypal female form, but those performing as women in this way are rarely considered "natural" or "real" women by heterosexuals. Queer theorists might argue that this is because drag does not fall under the regulations for what "woman" means in this society, and because drag does not occur with enough frequency to force a redefinition of "woman."

As queer theory emerged, many theorists, including feminist scholar Elizabeth Grosz, grew frustrated with the expectation that gender must "be understood as a kind of overlay on a pre-established foundation of sex—a cultural variation of a more or less fixed and universal substratum." In other words, it was then (and is still) commonly believed that while men and women may vary between cultures, the "male" and "female"

GENDER MUST BE UNDERSTOOD AS A KIND OF OVERLAY ON A PRE-ESTABLISHED FOUNDATION OF SEX - A CULTURAL VARIATION OF A MORE OR LESS FIXED AND UNIVERSAL SUBSTRATUM.

FEMINIST SCHOLAR ELIZABETH GROSZ

sexes are a fairly universal given. Nevertheless, Grosz asserts that queer theory opened the door for the idea that bodies may not divide neatly into two types. The idea of "queer" made it possible for many people in our society to consider for the first time that one's sex might not have innate properties. After all, the manner in which these "sexes" were established has seldom been addressed or acknowledged in any academic field. Although intersex people have sparked debates about the adequacy of gender categories, only a very small handful of scientists have developed theories suggesting that we count beyond two sexes.

As discussed earlier, there are varied notions of what one's sex is truly defined by. Anatomical, chromosomal, and hormonal variations are only three of the myriad ways by which we suppose one's body to have a pre-set biological type. Furthermore, we have seen the difficulty and unreliability in using these axes as a means of generating consistent and distinct categories. When the "natural foundations" of both gender and sex began to come into question, the stage was set for the queer movement.

Long before queer theory, in the 1910s and 20s, the word "queer" was used to describe men who were attracted to one another, specifically referring to those who were very masculine and did not have a flamboyant demeanor. Over the next several decades, "queer" was transformed into a derogatory term for anyone with a non-heterosexual orientation. Even so, by the early 1990s, with identity politics raging, a number of new definitions of orientation and gender arose, and perhaps chief among them, the term "queer" reemerged with its current meanings attached.

It is generally agreed that the queer movement was a reaction to constructionist concerns about universal terms. The cultural shift away from using the term "homosexual" and the reappropriation of "gay" demonstrates an example of how our society had negatively labeled some people who were attracted to their own gender, and how those who were so labeled came to see themselves more positively. "Queer," on the other hand, wasn't a new label for an already existing identity. Instead, it was an assertion that identity is always contextual and comes with qualifications.

The position of "queer" was developed by theorists who questioned both the universality of "women" as a category and "race" categories as collective descriptions of many diverse cultures' experiences. Queer theory did not arrive as the next wave of gay and lesbian activism or feminism; instead, these movements coexisted and reacted to one another's ideas. Some gays and lesbians were committed to fairly stable identities in order to fight for political gains; others, some of whom adopted the label "queer," found the descriptors of "gay" and "lesbian" somewhat limiting and bound up in antiquated concepts of gender. Early queer theorists thought that there were limits to the effectiveness of any category aiming to generalize about a group for a political purpose. Even though most individuals think of themselves as separate and real with perspectives that are personal and unique, some queer theorists considered identity to be formed almost entirely as a result of one's culture and environment.

People's self-concept, wherein we consider ourselves whole and self-determining, results purely from the mediums through which we describe ourselves and create an identity.

ROLAND BARTHES
(1915-1980)

Roland Barthes, for example, a French literary theorist and philosopher, articulated that people's self-concept—wherein we consider ourselves whole and self-determining—results purely from the mediums through which we describe ourselves and create an identity. Barthes questioned the supposedly obvious "truth" of identity that has for so long been a cornerstone of Western civilization. He posited that humans are unable to think freely because society prescribes much of our identity; therefore, a person is unable to separate their "self" from environmental conditioning.

Drawing on Barthes' analysis, Annamarie Jagose surmises that queer theory considers a constant identity to be a "sustaining and persistent cultural fantasy." Instead of focusing on how people in a group are alike, trying to see similarity between other groups' ideologies, or suggesting that anyone assimilate to find unity, early queer thinkers focused on difference and unique formulations of one's self. Queer theorists typically agree that identity politics are flawed, not just because one sexual or gender identity is limiting and fails to account for cultural differences, age, race, and other factors, but also because they don't consider a "self" something static or even necessarily real.

There are some individuals who oppose the term "queer" simply because its previous meaning was once derogatory. Proponents contest, however, that this reclaiming of the term is a powerful way to devalue homophobia. They believe that "queer" represents a new model for gender and sexuality. Moreover, if the word "queer" continues to hold some stigma, most queer activists feel that the discomfort it provokes can be useful, as it forces people to think about issues surrounding gender and sex. They figure that the very use of the word "queer" can be a launching pad for transforming public perception of archetypes.

Other people who dislike the term are worried about the possible negative impact on public perception of gay, lesbian, bisexual, and transgender people, some of whom align themselves with the queer movement. Because "queer" is often used as an umbrella term for everyone expressing a non-heteronormative sexual practice or identity, it can be misunderstood as including illegal practices, such as pedophilia. Those who promote the term's usage argue instead that including some marginalized groups whose interests aren't represented elsewhere (such as those who practice safe sadomasochistic sex) is essential. As a result, they consider it a necessary challenge that "queer" may be misunderstood by the mainstream as being in support of unsafe practices.

Many queer people also contend that gender fluid, intersex, and transgender people are typically left behind in gay and lesbian activism. They worry that the implied unity under the terms "gay" and "lesbian" fail to include those who consider "man" or "woman" an incomplete description of their way of interacting with the world. They also assert that some people who are attracted to the "opposite" gender or assigned sex do not find the term "heterosexual" an adequate way to describe their orientation, particularly if their gender expression does not wholly conform to any archetype.

But while some people consider queer theory a kind of natural progression away from the archetypes of the past, there are some advocates of gay and lesbian culture who take issue with the androgynous imagery and propaganda surrounding queer activism. Some queer advocates have critiqued the flamboyant archetypes celebrated in gay pride, in favor of promoting a variety of gender identities that don't necessarily fall into strict male or female roles. As a result, some individuals in LGBT communities worry that "queer" devalues masculinity and femininity. They don't want any new politics to silence the members of their communities who do identify strongly with their gender or assigned sex. For example, they would not want to see a very masculine transgender man feel "not queer enough" because he doesn't present himself in a gender-ambiguous fashion. Likewise, many fear the potential loss of hard-won visibility and legitimacy for feminine lesbians' identities.

Essentially, though some queer advocates would prefer to move away from the "either/or" construction that underlies homosexuality and heterosexuality and perpetuates an "us vs. them" mindset, many gay and lesbian people still feel invisible or degraded in our society and want to continue to celebrate their uniqueness, their sexuality and their identities—which can include archetypes. Gay and lesbian criticisms of queerness are often related to concerns that they will once again become marginalized, this time for their gender identity instead of their orientation. They don't wish to lose the history that they have as a collective political force, and sometimes profess discomfort about the androgyny that is celebrated in the queer community.

On the other hand, queer theory was influenced by lesbian feminism's attention to gender, their framing of sexuality as institutional, and their critique of heteronormativity. The biggest difference is this: Queer theory takes a fully unique stance in rejecting the notion of sexuality's "automatic" relationship to gender. Gay and lesbian cultures often affirm that people are born "naturally" gay, heterosexual, or bisexual, and that this should be celebrated; as such, they do not necessarily allow for fluctuation in one's orientation over the course of one's life, an important tenet in queer formulations of sexuality.

In fact, many queer people and queer theorists do not tie attraction to gender identity at all, and describe their sexual attractions to others as being strictly on the basis of that individual's personality or presentation of self (much like pansexuals). The basis for their attraction may include someone's body or appearance, but isn't necessarily driven by their gender or limited by what sex organs that person may or may not possess. Put simply, some queer people consider themselves attracted to different individual people, not necessarily people of one gender, one assigned sex, or of a specific sexual orientation. Others may be asexual, and might not be interested in sex with anyone, but identify as queer as a political statement or to differentiate their status from that of the heterosexual population. And still others may be gay, lesbian, bisexual, transgender, intersex, questioning, or claim any number of other labels regarding their sexuality and gender; these individuals usually adopt the label "queer" for its philosophical stance on gender and sexuality and its general ambiguity regarding static identities.

Whatever their affiliations and other labels, queer proponents routinely deny the idea that groups of people across time and cultural lines can form under one heading and it mean the same thing. That is, they don't believe that the word "lesbian" would, for example, mean the same thing to a cisgender Japanese woman living in San Francisco in this decade as an African-American transgender woman living in the Harlem Renaissance in the 1920s. Thus, they don't find the term useful as a blanket statement to describe all self-identified women who are attracted to one another. They commonly reiterate how the word "lesbian" was sometimes used in the past to describe women who weren't necessarily interested in one another sexually, but who were politically advocating for women's autonomy.

---

**YOUNG PEOPLE, LABELS, AND INCLUSIVITY**

Today, some young people do not want to identify as gay, straight, or bisexual because they don't want to be cut off from their friends or affiliate themselves narrowly. Others simply do not wish to base an "identity" on who they are attracted to. In both of these situations, some claim the term "queer." Because queer takes a position against norms even more than it articulates any orientation of its own, it can also serve as a placeholder for many people who dislike labels.

---

To be clear, this is just an example and not specifically an issue that queer politics has with lesbianism—most queer people deny "natural" categories of women and men with equal or more vehemence. Many queer-identifying people and their allies fear that these archetypes perpetuate heterosexuality's elitism and valorize stereotypes surrounding what masculinity and femininity look like. By pushing for more ambiguity, however, they evoke concerns from gay, lesbian, and heterosexual people alike that those who choose willingly to express themselves along more archetypal lines of femininity or masculinity will become ostracized, or thought of as antiquated and "square." Queer theories promoting gender fluidity can sometimes be interpreted as depicting feminine women (including lesbian or feminist women who are femme) as passive, reactionary, or even brainwashed. They are also accused of portraying heterosexual and masculine men as almost automatically misogynous and uninformed.

Some other objections to queer theory come from activists for LGBT equality who think that queer theory is more concerned with institutions and academic theories than politics that change people's lives at the ground level. These opponents express concern that arguments for queerness are privileged and inaccessible or incomprehensible to the general public, and may damage the collective political force and recognition that gay and lesbian people have claimed. They worry that queer theory distances its advocates from the grassroots activism whose successes have made life more tenable for many gay and lesbian people, as well as achieving better opportunities for women. Queer proponents, by contrast, may consider it inaccurate to treat "gay and lesbian people" or "women" as coherent categories in this way. They argue that not all women have been helped by or included in feminism, and that many people who may be attracted to the same assigned sex or gender are marginalized by gay and lesbian activism and its goals, including transgender and bisexual people.

Obviously, there is some concern that queer constructions undermine the identities of those who fit comfortably into the "norms" established around gay, lesbian, man, and woman in our society. But while some queer proponents call gay and lesbian categories "dated," or say that gay and lesbian people are gradually assimilating into the rest of American society (except for who they sleep with), this is not the queer consensus by any means. And although some gays and lesbians do seek a sense of belonging or inclusion, others celebrate their difference from mainstream culture; in a way, this is not so dissimilar from queer attempts to distance themselves from the very idea of gender or sexuality "norms." What's more, many LGBT individuals also align themselves with the queer movement or identify as queer themselves. Queer movements typically seek to be inclusive of people who are marginalized by other activist groups related to sexual orientation, including LGBT people whose goals are not addressed by gay and lesbian rights groups. The categories are by no means mutually exclusive, and in many instances fight for visibility, equal treatment, and social justice hand-in-hand.

Ultimately, despite sharing a sense of marginalization from the mainstream, each identity, orientation, and position within the LGBTQIA acronym may have some different ideas about what an ideal society would look like. Queer people and theorists advocate stepping away from norms, deconstructing sexuality's basis on gender, and rejecting heteronormativity. Gays and lesbians and their advocates hold more than one position, but tend to focus on their desire for visibility, acceptance, and the freedom to have a distinct culture from the heterosexual population. While diversity within one's gender identity is clearly represented within their communities (butches, bears, and drag queens, to name a few), there is generally some continued investment in distinctly masculine or feminine expression. At the same time, bisexuals may align with gay or lesbian communities, queer people, both, or neither. And again, some gay and lesbian people identify as queer as a description of their political or gender identity, while separating that identification from their (gay or lesbian) sexuality. Yet others identify as gay, lesbian, bisexual, transgender, or even mainly heterosexual in terms of their orientation, and also identify as queer because of fluid or transgressive sexual preferences.

There are also many people who do not feel that their identity matches either gender archetype. Some may consider themselves gender nonconforming; others identify as genderqueer. Once claiming a genderqueer identity, an individual may (or may not) choose to adopt a new public persona, including changing their name, seeking hormones to adjust their bodies, and/or changing how they articulate and present their gender. For example, they may eschew the pronouns "he," "she," "him" and "her" in favor of the more androgynous "they" or invented gender-neutral pronouns like "ze" and "zer," "s/he," "hir," "one," "zher(s)," "zhim," "mer," "hu," "hus," "hum," and "'e" or "'s." (The last two are neutral replacements for "his" and "hers").

They may also seek intentional androgyny in their fashion and grooming or alternate their style on a frequent basis, depending on the gender they wish to express at a given time. People who identify as genderqueer often align themselves with the aspect of queer theory advocating the mutability of identity, and oppose generalizations about groups that leave others at the margins. Genderqueer people whose gender identities are multiple or dissimilar from either gender archetype sometimes additionally identify as transgender.

Gay and lesbian identities can offer unity and potential political effectiveness. The rituals of "coming out" and celebrating gay and lesbian pride are profoundly important to many

## GENDER-NEUTRAL LANGUAGE

One issue that divides LGBTQIA advocates, feminists, and social justice proponents in general is the use of gender-neutral language. Many supporters contend that using pronouns that don't specify gender or include multiple genders reduces assumptions about people's assigned sex. They also advocate phrasing things in a manner that does not leave anyone out. Others simply believe gender-neutral language promotes a less sexist society and a more complete history (or "herstory") that includes women's voices more visibly. Opponents, on the other hand, think that placing a heavy emphasis on gender-neutral language is a "political correctness" campaign that polices people's speech to the point of making communication more difficult. They feel that requiring the usage of gender-neutral pronouns alienates people who would otherwise be more supportive of LGBTQIA and women's issues. This stance, however, does not address the identities of people whose gender is neither male nor female (or may be both), for whom gender-neutral pronouns are simply accurate.

people as a way of asserting the validity of their identity. Still, some queer people and queer theorists question the generalizations inherent in gay and lesbian categories, as well as in "men" and "women"; they instead advocate for more varied gender expression. They usually support a sexuality rooted in individual attraction instead of permanent affiliation with a group that symbolizes an orientation towards one or more archetypal genders. Queer people reconceptualize "coming out" as something that happens continuously in different contexts. They argue that instead of focusing on claiming a potentially transitory identity that forces us to choose and possibly leave behind communities, we need to rethink gender and sexuality entirely. Many queer people advocate for valuing all genders and sexual expressions equally. This also serves as a method of including transgender and bisexual people, who may otherwise disregard either their gender(s) or the range of their orientation in order to belong to a non-heteronormative community. For instance, bisexuals frequently choose to associate primarily with gay or lesbian communities, but feel obligated to ignore that they are also attracted to people of the "opposite" assigned sex

---

## POLYGENDER QUESTIONS

In *Sexing the Body*, Anne Fausto-Sterling posed the question, "If an animal (or person) were extremely masculine (by whatever measure), did that mean he or she would, by definition, be unfeminine? Or [are] masculinity and femininity separate entities, able to vary independently of each other?"

Perhaps there is an important rhetorical question to ask concerning queer theory, masculinity, and femininity: Is there necessarily a relationship between these two qualities? Cannot someone feel both masculine and feminine, and does one in any way actually negate the other? Often times these two qualities are thought of on a scale where a person is expected to fall somewhere between the two, either right at the archetypal poles (cisgender male or female) or more or less in the middle (androgynous and some genderqueer people). Maybe there's another way to think of this, which includes the possibility of plurality. Some people express gender identities that include both masculinity and femininity—not necessarily a "bit" of each, but potentially embracing both wholly (polygender and some genderqueer people).

---

or gender.

And where do transgender and transsexual people fit into queer theories of gender and sexuality? Transgender communities have a close relationship with queer ideas about gender despite the fact that some trans people strongly identify as men or women. That said, there are certainly transgender individuals who do not personally identify as queer, and a number of discrepancies between queer and trans theories. Furthermore, transgender and transsexual people have their own unique history of activism and economic disparity related to the criminal justice system and the medical community's assessment of their gender identities. By considering the ways in which transgender and transsexual people have struggled for fair treatment in mainstream society, from medical and mental health institutions, and even within LGBTQIA communities, we will see how the extreme inequity they continue to face represents a challenge for all social justice movements that aim to promote inclusivity.

VICTORIAN TAXONOMIST
RICHARD VON KRAFFT-EBING
(1840-1902)

# CHAPTER 8

# TRANSGENDER CONTEXTS AND CONCERNS

Many factors have contributed to American society's views and treatment of transgender people. Among them, Western medical and psychological views have strongly influenced public perception of transgender experience. These views have both contributed to the pathologization of trans experience that many trans people and modern psychologists refute, and in some cases, assisted trans people in making changes to their body. Before there were scientific terms for transsexual and transgender identities, a Victorian taxonomist named Richard von Krafft-Ebing was studying forms of social defiance, and became fascinated by individuals who would likely be called transgender or transsexual today. In the late 1800s, Krafft-Ebing had begun to establish categories for behavior and activities which he believed constituted psychosexual disorders, including homosexuality, which he saw as a form of gender variation that could either be acquired or innate from birth.

His most extreme category for deviation, which he called "metamorphosis sexualis paranoica," was his classification for those who identify as members of the "opposite" gender from their assigned sex. Among these individuals, Krafft-Ebing grouped anyone who wanted to change their genitals or secondary sex characteristics. With very limited knowledge of gender identities which deviated from the dominant male and female archetypes in Western Europe, Krafft-Ebing thought that their desire to change their bodies was a form of psychotic impulse, similar to extreme masochism. Likewise, when German physician and sexologist Magnus Hirschfeld coined the term "transvestite" in 1910 to describe people who periodically wear clothes of the "opposite" gender, he viewed it as a grave mental illness, only slightly less severe than those who identified as a different gender than their assigned sex.

The term "psychosexual disorder" refers to a sexual problem which is believed to be psychological rather than strictly physiological or biological.

MAGNUS HIRSCHFELD (1868-1935)
GERMAN PHYSICIAN AND SEXOLOGIST

157

ENDOCRINOLOGIST HARRY BENJAMIN FIRST POPULARIZED THE TERM "TRANSSEXUAL" IN HIS MEDICAL LITERATURE ON GENDER DYSPHORIA.

Western academics' rather condemning reactions to similar types of gender expression continued until the 1950s, when German endocrinologist Harry Benjamin first popularized the term "transsexual" in his medical literature on gender dysphoria. He viewed transsexualism as "the intense and often obsessive desire to change the entire sexual status including the anatomical structure. While the male transvestite *enacts* the role of a woman, the [male] transsexualist wants to *be* one and *function* as one, wishing to assume as many of her characteristics as possible, physical, mental, and sexual."

Another important contributor to early studies of transgender people was British physician and psychologist Havelock Ellis. It may be said that Ellis and Magnus Hirschfeld established the difference between trans identification and homosexuality. Like Krafft-Ebing, Ellis viewed transvestitism as a form of "inversion" where individuals imitated or identified with that which they admired—in this case, the "opposite" sex. He guessed that chemical imbalances caused transsexuality; thus, he described transgender identification as being a transitional form of sexuality.

Benjamin, on the other hand, believed that transsexualism is caused by psychological, hormonal, and physiological influences, and can also be spurred by traumatic events. He considered transvestitic behavior a social (and nonsexual) problem wherein transvestites want society to adapt to their desire to lead lives as a different gender without needing to change their body, an impulse that he considered narcissistic and self-involved. Transsexuals, by contrast, were described by Benjamin as having a split between the soma (body) and one's psyche. Because many of the trans people who came to him reported feeling

"Dysphoria" is another term that Hirschfeld coined to describe a person's discomfort with their assigned sex.

HAVELOCK ELLIS (1859-1939), PSYCHOLOGIST, WRITER AND SOCIAL REFORMER.

that their bodies were incorrect, Benjamin saw their identification as a medical condition needing treatment. Benjamin considered the trans experience a type of dissociation from one's body, which is beyond any person's power to completely control or change.

---

## BEHAVIOR THERAPY AND TRANS IDENTITY

Although Benjamin advocated for tolerance for trans people, "curing" trans identification was still considered a goal by practitioners of the time, and the generally accepted first course of action for "treating" gender identity disorder was behavior therapy. Since then, counseling undertaken with the aim of "converting" a trans person to identify as their assigned sex has almost entirely fallen out of favor within the medical community. Likewise, practitioners largely frown on counseling that encourages trans people to adopt behaviors to better fit the cultural "norm" for their assigned sex. Such behavior therapy is widely considered to be typically ineffective and potentially traumatizing.

---

This description paints trans identification as a type of illness, which many transgender people refute, but at the time this view was considered very progressive because Benjamin advocated for tolerance for trans people. He suggested that psychiatrists' role with transsexuals was to attempt to bring a person's mentality back into harmony with their given body, and if this proved impossible, then sexual reassignment surgery (SRS, also known as gender reassignment surgery) ought to be considered as a treatment.

Sexual reassignment surgery was first attempted by German doctors in the late 1920s and early 1930s, but the first widely known SRS operation was performed upon Christine Jorgensen in 1952, who had formerly served in the U.S. Army. Unlike the surgeries performed in the 1920s and 30s, Christine underwent hormone therapy, a practice that would become standard for most transgender people seeking surgeries (and many who haven't desired accompanying surgeries). The practice of taking estrogen or testosterone (often combined with other hormones) helps some trans-identified people to alter their secondary sex characteristics, such as tone of voice, facial and body hair,

CHRISTINE JORGENSEN (1926-1989)

and the ability to tone and build musculature. This may assist an individual in appearing more "feminine" or "masculine."

There are a variety of surgeries that trans people may seek to alter their bodies. Transgender people may desire chest reconstruction surgeries (or "top" surgeries that offer chest contouring) or breast augmentation. They may undergo a hysterectomy and oophorectomy (removal of the uterus and ovaries, respectively), and/or genital reconstruction surgeries such as scrotoplasty (the creation of testes) and phalloplasty (the construction of a penis) or metoidioplasty (altering the clitorus' position to better approximate a penis). Alternatively, they may seek an orchiectomy (removal of the testes), labiaplasty (creation of a labia and clitoral hood) and/or vaginoplasty (construction of the vulvo-vaginal complex). Some trans people also obtain plastic surgeries of other kinds to change their facial structure and other contours of their body.

In the 1960s, the Harry Benjamin International Gender Dysphoria Association created a set of guidelines to ensure that psychiatric professionals treating transgender people aimed for their comfort and well-being. The standards of care were also meant to ensure that only strong candidates for successful surgeries received them. Before this criteria, however, most countries failed to offer medical options for altering one's gender, and many nations criminalized trans identification or expression. In the meantime, scores of completely illegal and untested methods of treatment were exercised by so-called medical professionals, to the detriment of trans people's health and safety; in many cases, these procedures resulted in death or severe disfigurement. Benjamin's set of protocols outlined how individuals who wanted hormonal or surgical transition to another sex should be guided by medical professionals. While this new standard of care was not compulsory, it had a large impact on the medical establishment's view of trans identity and resulted in many advancements in surgeries for transgender people.

## CRIMINALIZATION OF TRANSGENDER IDENTITY

There are now many countries in which people can legally change their gender (including on one's birth certificate), but there are also countries which still punish homosexuality with imprisonment, torture, or death—some of which consider trans identity to fall into the category of homosexuality. In fact, in the United States at the turn of the 20th century, gender nonconforming people were often excluded from citizenship under statutes that policed homosexuality by excluding sexually "degenerate" people from immigrating.

Although Dr. Benjamin established standards of care for transgender people and helped the medical establishment to form guidelines for their treatment, he is also responsible for the term "Gender Identity Disorder" (GID) making its way into the American Psychiatric Association's *Diagnostic and Statistical Manual* (*DSM*). One who is diagnosed with such a disorder can be considered ill, unstable, and potentially in need of treatments that they may not want; DSM diagnoses can also have negative consequences for one's ability to obtain medical insurance. Yet while many insurers do not yet cover hormones or surgeries for trans people, once there is a term for a mental disorder in the *DSM*, the potential for medicare and other insurances to help pay for treatment becomes possible. As such, Benjamin is viewed as a polarizing figure by many. He both made it safer for transgender people to obtain surgeries to alter their bodies, and simultaneously made these surgeries more difficult to obtain for anyone who failed to fit the American Psychiatric Association's definition of GID. And as he said himself, "The psychiatrist must have the last word."

It can be very challenging to gain authorization for sex reassignment surgery, which, it bears mentioning, in its very name presupposes that any trans person desiring body alteration is attempting to go from one sex to another. The "standards of care" for transgender people are not legally enforced—surgery and distribution of hormones are left up to physicians' personal discretion—but they are the suggested guidelines which most medical professionals adhere to. Often, trans people seeking SRS must be diagnosed with dysphoria or GID by a psychotherapist or counselor. That therapist can then refer them to an endocrinologist who distributes hormones (testosterone, estrogen, and others). In some cases, physicians who have a history with a patient will prescribe hormones themselves. In others, counselors or physicians may write letters stating that a patient is of sound mind and capable of giving informed consent for body alteration or surgery. The standards of care suggest that daily expression of a gender different from the one assigned at birth is necessary before one should undergo body modifications, and insist that one's trans identity must have been present consistently for at least two years.

## REAL LIFE EXPERIENCE

Often the requirement for being cleared for sexual reassignment surgeries is one year of Real Life Experience (RLE); that is, having presented one's self as "the gender one is transitioning to" for at least one year. This, again, assumes that trans experience follows a binary that many trans people refute. Some transgender people seeking surgeries to alter their body do not identify as "male" or "female"; others do not believe that body alteration will result in their having only one gender, or in fully changing their gender.

In considering GID, it's quite hard to ignore its timely first appearance in the *DSM-III* in 1980—the same edition that removed "homosexuality" as a disorder. Without pre-homosexuality as a clinical diagnosis that mental health professionals were supposed to keep an eye out for in children, many of the very same gender nonconforming kids were heretofore labeled as "pre-transsexual." In her book, *Gender Shock*, Phyllis Burke remarks dryly how the decision to eliminate homosexuality was made in 1973, giving those who "wished to continue treating nonconforming children...seven years in which to develop a new category of illness."

The *DSM-IV* offers symptoms for diagnosing GID, including "strong and persistent cross-gender identification (not merely a desire for any perceived cultural advantages of being the other sex)." Among children, boys with GID supposedly "have little interest in cars and trucks" and girls with GID "prefer boys' clothing and short hair." There's almost no differentiation between gender nonconformity and GID, and the standard implies that "normal" is the opposite of what a kid with GID does. To be diagnosed with gender identity disorder, one must know in their gut that they're in the "wrong" body—and some people do feel that way—but who is to say if that is because of the regulatory constructs around them?

The *DSM-V*, as it is currently proposed, will change the term "Gender Identity Disorder" to "Gender Dysphoria" in response to criticisms that GID is stigmatizing. It will also offer separate diagnoses for transgender children and those who begin to trans identify in adolescence or adulthood. Additionally, the primary definition may be changed to "a marked incongruence between one's experienced/expressed gender and assigned gender, of at least six months duration," which more closely reflects the language many trans people use to describe their experience. Its supporting indicators for children, on the other hand, continue to include "strong rejection" of gender-typical toys, games, activities, and clothing. (For adults, more of the definition relies on one's desire for—or to be rid of—primary or secondary sex characteristics.) In both

## INTERSEX CHARACTERISTICS AND GENDER IDENTITY DISORDER

Interestingly, if a person has physical intersex characteristics, their experience cannot qualify as GID, even if they were raised as one gender and identify as another. One can infer that this is because the discomfort intersex people may feel about their body appears to have a clearer biological basis. By making this demarcation, however, the DSM further pathologizes the transgender person's experience as a "mental disorder," which many psychologists and trans people rebuke.

the current and proposed versions of the *DSM*, an individual with gender dysphoria (or GID) must exhibit "evidence of clinically significant distress or impairment in social, occupational, or other important areas of functioning." Since the *DSM* is a manual for diagnosing mental health concerns, it is somewhat understandable that transgender experience is defined therein relative to how it can complicate one's mental well-being. But because insurance providers usually only cover treatments for people with clinically diagnosed GID, a healthy trans person who wishes to alter their body may be forced to seek a diagnosis that negates their mental stability.

Many health professionals today endorse the decisions of some trans people to seek body alteration surgeries or hormones. They may also endorse a change of gender role without medical treatment, if a trans person prefers that course of action. These health professionals may agree that the decision to modify one's body should reside with the patient. They may also be aware of the astronomical suicide rate, and high instances of depression, anxiety, and drug abuse among transgender people, which are generally understood to be symptoms of the great duress trans people can face in our society (not tied to an innate mental instability related to trans identification). The results of many surveys and case studies imply that the mental health concerns of transgender and transsexual people are equally the result of society's reactions to their gender expression, and the disparity of opportunity, health care, and income that they face, not solely due to their gender identity. Even so, many health professionals agree that empowering trans people to seek surgeries or hormones to alter their gender expression can help to alleviate some of the societal difficulties trans people face.

---

### SRS AND SOCIAL JUSTICE

The APA Task Force on Gender Identity and Gender Variance's 2008 report says that for transgender people seeking surgeries, "Sex reassignment resulted in improved mental health, socioeconomic status, relationships, and sexual satisfaction." From Benjamin onwards, this is the general medical and psychiatric assessment; the endorsement of SRS is implicit in both the APA's suggestions and the "standards of care." Furthermore, according to the report, "The needs of transgender people are inextricably linked to broader issues of human rights and social justice." Providing transgender people with proper health care must include facilitating the self-determination of their gender; as such, denying them access to surgeries and/or hormones is considered by many to be a human rights violation.

A handful of theorists believe that treating sex assignment discomfort with surgery cannot liberate or help achieve gender equality, such as Dwight D. Billings and Thomas Urban. They argue that categorizing trans experience as an illness and "fixing" it through surgery and treatment which expect the individual to express their gender along very specific lines is an automatic step backward. In fact, Billing and Urban state that doctors have "invented" the concept of a transsexual by requiring a lifelong story of discomfort with one's body in order to be rewarded with surgery—a narrative that is sometimes mimicked or faked by those who desire body modification surgeries for other reasons.

Billings and Urban imply that treating transgender people with sexual reassignment surgery results in compulsory heteronormativity all over again. After all, they figure that a transitioned person is expected to essentially disappear back into society within a now more traditional gender role. That said, Billings and Urban are also assuming that trans patients aren't conscious of these mechanisms; they disregard the potential for trans people's informed political agency. Many trans people and their allies today assert that body alteration surgeries and hormones can be empowering, but also take issue with how the medical establishment only allows gender-normative body alterations and denies surgery to those that resist a naturalized view of gender. They say it is time to promote self-determination and end constraints around the amount of time one is required to express a specific gender before gaining access to surgeries.

In his critique of the medical community's "gatekeeper" stance towards body modification for trans people, legal activist and theorist Dean Spade refers to Neil Gotanda's theory of "hypodescent." Gotanda identifies the racist mechanism in considering anyone with a trace of African ancestry to be black. Given the

> "I'm supposed to be wholly joyous when I get called 'sir' or 'boy.' How could I ever have such an uncomplicated relationship to that moment? Each time I'm sirred I know both that my look is doing what I want it to do, and that the reason people can assign male gender to me easily is because they don't believe women have short hair, and because, as Garber has asserted, the existence of maleness as the generic means that fewer visual clues of maleness are required to achieve male gender attribution. This 'therapeutic' process demands of me that I toss out all my feminist misgivings about the ways that gender rigidity informs people's perception of me."
> — Dean Spade, "Mutilating Gender"

common application of this "rule," Gotanda thinks that considering one's self "white" also validates an idea of white racial "purity" that makes all other races subordinate. Spade contends that gender has a similar problem, where if one claims to belong to a single (static) gender category, it reaffirms a gender binary. With this chain reaction in effect, he wonders about the limits of achieving social justice through surgeries for transgender people; after all, their goal is often to make others perceive a trans person as more naturally or purely fitting one gender or another.

Furthermore, because one must "inhabit and perform 'successfully' the new gender category" in order to be diagnosed with GID (or "gender dysphoria" in the proposed *DSM-V*), which is typically necessary to gain access to surgeries, the medical institutions that offer surgeries also reinforce the very norms and archetypes that transgender people are attempting to overthrow. The necessity of "passing" as one or another gender in order to obtain a surgery limits the potential for someone to claim an identity outside of "male" or "female" archetypes. As a result, other emergent categories get swept under the rug.

So how did theorists get from Harry Benjamin's early work on tolerance and SRS for transsexuals to considering whether normative gender roles should be the goal of body alteration surgeries? For starters, the newer term "transgender" is generally credited to Virginia Prince, a transgender activist who published *Transvestia* magazine and advocated for freedom of gender expression from the 1960s to 90s. "Transgender" was first used in the 1980s to describe people who fall somewhere between transvestites and transsexuals. At that time, the term was understood as referring to someone who "permanently changed social gender through the public presentation of self, without recourse to genital transformation." Such individuals were not dressing as another gender temporarily for personal preference or for sexual excitement (as some transvestites do), but rather because they felt that their gender had been incorrectly assigned.

"Transgender" became something of a buzzword in the early 1990s, after it was popularized by Leslie Feinberg's pamphlet *Transgender Liberation: A Movement Whose Time Has Come*. Feinberg called for all marginalized and oppressed persons who feel ostracized because they differ from society's norms for gendered behavior, appearance, or demeanor to join together. Ze thought that all such individuals ought to strive for political, economic, and social justice as a team. Feinberg revised the usage of the term "transgender" to be an umbrella term for a community that includes transsexuals, butch lesbians, those who dress in drag, intersex people, masculine women, effeminate men, tomboys, and anyone else who wanted to claim the term.

The popular understanding of the term "transgender" was also affected by Sandy Stone's 1991 "The 'Empire' Strikes Back: A Posttranssexual Manifesto," an essay denouncing feminists who were critical of transsexualism. Some feminists who were fighting for gender equality at that time and trying to do away with antiquated gender roles saw transsexualism as an embodiment of outdated masculine and feminine stereotypes. They said that by altering their bodies, trans people were alienating themselves from their personal history. These feminists thought that transsexuals seeking body alterations were misrepresenting themselves.

ZINES RANGE FROM HANDWRITTEN TO SILKSCREENED PUBLICATIONS, AND TYPICALLY HAVE SMALL PRINT RUNS.

In Stone's manifesto, she sternly rebuked these arguments and instead suggested that people abandon notions of "authenticity" altogether. She said that if transgender people no longer attempted to "pass" as non-transsexual men and women, it would give way to broader understanding and empower individuals to define for themselves how to embody their gender. Stone declared this call to arms in hope of generating a mass movement of affirmation and strength that would parallel the first wave of "coming out" for gay people. Alongside this effort, in 1991 trans activist Jamison Green also transformed a San Francisco support group for FTMs (female-to-male transsexuals or transmen) into the first worldwide organization for advancing transgender rights: FTM International. The organization almost immediately began printing newsletters that explained the variety of forms that masculinity can take.

JAMISON GREEN (B. 1948)
TRANS ACTIVIST, CO-FOUNDER
OF FTM INTERNATIONAL

## THE 1990S, TRANS ACTIVISM AND TRANS STUDIES

Stone, Green, and many other trans activists' efforts coalesced around the early 1990s to bring new ideas about trans identities into the mainstream. In the wake of the AIDS crisis fueling generalized LGBT activism, specific transgender activism emerged from the broader queer movement. Feminists and gay and lesbian rights activists had already blamed gender roles for restricting the career aspirations, personal expression, and sexual proclivities of many. But now it seemed that assumptions about biologically determined sexes (male/female) with corresponding fixed social categories (man/woman) were failing to describe the lived experiences of many people who fell outside that binary. These individuals were beginning to gather organizing strength and raise their voices in both queer and trans movements.

Perhaps partially as a result of the explosion of the internet, and definitely due to the efforts of growing support groups and activist communities within the trans population, the term "transgender" exploded in 1995, and came into much wider usage. Though not everyone agrees on its political or social implications, "transgender" is easily the term of choice for a variety of activities and observable occurrences which demonstrate that gender is more diverse and complicated than the dominant binary notion of sex and gender. To say one is "transsexual" used to be a strictly medical definition, but it is now used by some people as an expression of living as a gender other than the one they were assigned at birth, regardless of whether or not they have undergone surgery or take hormones. In other words, "transitioning" between genders can now be personally determined and defined.

Instead of trying to articulate a spectrum that would place trans identified people arbitrarily in the middle, or looking for a neurobiological issue that would explain why trans people do not conform to supposedly innate male and female archetypes, some academics began to question the framework underpinning the two categories' origins. Transgender studies became a new academic field that explicitly recognized gender as another system (like race, nationalism, or economic class) in which diverse humans who are modified by many factors are reduced to overly simplistic labels. Perhaps for the first time, the academic community actively attempted to accommodate the variety of lived gender experiences instead of trying to par them down to two clearly inadequate categories.

167

Some transgender or transsexual individuals identify either as an MTF (a male-to-female trans person, trans woman, or someone who was assigned "male" at birth and now identifies as female) or an FTM (a female-to-male trans person, trans man, or someone who was assigned "female" at birth and now identifies as male). In either case, being transgender or transsexual is not an attraction-based identity like gay, lesbian, and bisexual identities are. Nor does the term signify a privileging or preference for being "other" than heterosexual in the way that queer theory mobilizes individuals to dispense with norms around sexuality. One might say that, in general, transgender experience focuses on gender identity (the "I") as opposed to orientation (who one is attracted to or oriented "at").

## TRANS IDENTITY AND ORIENTATION

Regardless of whether they physically transition, transgender people have a sexual orientation independent of their gender; that is, a trans woman may have been identified (or assigned) as a gay or straight man before transitioning, and may or may not have a different orientation after transitioning. She might be a lesbian or consider herself heterosexual, but this orientation has nothing to do with her body or social status as a woman.

Drawing on European perspectives of explored, conquered, and colonized cultures and ethnographic work over hundreds of years, trans studies took the longstanding Western academic interest in sex and gender, kinship and behavior, and offered it a new narrative. Trans theorists reconsidered medical interventions that forced surgery on intersex infants, the regulation of homosexuality, and the ways that different cultures treat gender variance. The field's objective can be best understood as seeking to destabilize views that treat gender as a subjective representation of an objectively knowable sex. Trans activists and theorists point to a new way to consider "how bodies mean, how representation works, and what counts as legitimate knowledge."

For many, the assumption that one's assigned sex is demonstrated socially by a gender role and understood subjectively as a gender identity (ie., "a [biological (or assigned sex)] male is a [social] male who [subjectively] identifies himself as such") continues to be instinctual. This ingrained notion of gender and identity as mimetic of one another—a real thing with reflections—is based on a European worldview that puts biological matter (and objectively knowable information based on matter) at the center of all understanding. It assumes knowledge to be, if not fixed, than at least following a consistent pattern of change that can be accessed through individual perception.

When one considers sex chromosomes, anatomical sexual parts, and reproductive sexual acts, however, attempting to bind them all as inextricable qualities following one rule is impossible. For when one looks to transvestites, butch women, and drag queens, the idea of one's sex completely determining identity and gender becomes deeply troublesome. Most trans scholars consider the "wholeness" of one's body (and the idea that one's sex represents that type of body) to be socially constructed. This position not only rejects the idea of universal experience (or "women's"/"men's" experience), but also takes a powerful stance against the notion that bodies are static objects. Instead, it treats the body as a composite of individually evolving parts which together function as an interface with the outside world. And while subjective knowledge is certainly given validity elsewhere, the assertion in transgender studies that personal experience is equally legitimate to other forms of supposedly more objective ways to "know" is an important and highly controversial claim.

---

## TRANSGENDER PEOPLE IN THE MEDIA

Trans people were once largely excluded from representations in popular culture, except as "humorous" characters meant to be degraded. Currently, many of the major films and commercials that feature transgender people or characters still portray them as either disturbed or as trying to "trick" people into believing that they are cisgender; their "coming out" is generally reacted to poorly by other characters who express fear, disgust, confusion, or anger. Such examples excuse prejudicial behavior, reinforce stigmatization, and no doubt counteract trans efforts to gain social acceptance. Trans activism has sought more recognition among other gay and lesbian activists and feminists for decades. As transgender people gain visibility and support both within and outside of LGBTQIA efforts, they aspire to be more fairly represented in the media as well.

---

Regardless of its importance, most of our society is not exposed to transgender studies, and it often upsets those who see biological sex and social gender as neat and tidy. Trans people are sometimes perceived as though they are making a false representation of an underlying "true" gender or sex by distorting their appearance. They are made to justify or prove their experiences to a society that reinforces heteronormative and gender normative narratives.

Trans activists ask why it should be an issue, morally or ethically, how individuals experience and present their gender in different ways. They also contend that it is essential to address the violence and injustice inflicted on people with atypical gender expressions.

In 1975, a network of trans support group leaders aligned themselves with the U.S. activist group Transsexual Action Organization. This affiliation eventually led to a 1992 uprising in the U.K. regarding transgender rights that spawned the Gender Recognition Act (GRA), passed in 2004 by the U.K. parliament. The GRA offers transsexuals legal recognition as the sex that corresponds to their gender identity, and includes the right to a new birth certificate and the ability to marry as their new legal sex. No similar or corresponding law exists in the United States. While activists in the U.S. continue to seek legal support for trans rights, the U.K. has traditionally focused more stringently on effecting policy change.

So what rights and protections are trans activists so ardently seeking from the U.S. government? For starters, trans people are seeking better avenues for getting their birth certificates and driver's licenses changed to match their gender identities. Mainly, though, the legislation they seek represents protection from a society with seemingly inflexible institutional barriers to their safety, success, health, and visibility. This may sound a bit theatrical, but consider the following:

**It is legal in more than half of the U.S. to fire someone purely on the basis of their trans identification (37 states as of 2009).**

**GLSEN's 2007 survey says that over 85 percent of trans-identifying students report verbal harassment, and nearly half (49.5 percent) report physical harassment or (34.1 percent) physical assault.**

Basic needs like going to the bathroom can become terrifying for trans people who are commonly assaulted when perceived as being in the incorrect bathroom for their gender. Cops often look the other way when transgender people are physically or sexually assaulted, and consistently fail to implement the few nondiscrimination laws that are in place to protect trans people. Edu-

cators fail to inform (or are disallowed from informing) students about why bullying trans kids is wrong. Many companies and employers come up with random excuses for not hiring (or for firing) trans people, particularly if they are visibly transitioning from one gender presentation to another. In these cases, there isn't always a way to prove that

discrimination is at the helm, but the disparities are clear and compelling. Violence against trans people continues to be prevalent, both
in the U.S. and worldwide, including higher murder rates, frequency of
sexual and physical assault, and other severe mistreatment.

Legislators have long questioned the need for better protective
measures and laws governing trans discrimination, partially because
there simply weren't raw statistics or funded studies to demonstrate
what kind of significant damage was being caused. Today, we finally
have these figures.

A staggering 61 percent of American trans people report having been
physically assaulted as a result of their gender identity, and 64 percent report having been sexually assaulted. Given underreporting, actual figures of drastic mistreatment are no doubt significantly higher.

The National Center for Transgender Equality and the National Gay
and Lesbian Task Force formed a research partnership in 2008 to "address
the lack of hard data on the scope of anti-transgender discrimination."
Their National Transgender Discrimination Survey found that without
question, discrimination was rampant across all aspects of life and all demographics for transgender people. The study also discovered that for
transgender people of color, disparities were particularly widespread, as
respondents who fit both of those demographics were four times more
likely to be making less than $10K a year than the "average" citizen.

One might ask how this discrimination plays out on a day-to-day basis
for the trans population. To begin with, access to health care from medical professionals who are familiar with trans needs can be hard to come
by, and some medical professionals may refuse to treat trans people.

---

# Trans Discrimination in
# Health Care*

**Percent of trans population who report they:**

- Were refused health care    19%
- Taught their provider about trans health    50%
- Postponed medical care when sick or
  injured fearing mistreatment by health care    28%
  providers

*based on data from National Transgender Discrimination Survey*

---

**41 percent of adult trans persons have attempted suicide at some point in their life, as opposed to 1.6 percent of the overall population. By this estimate, trans people are 26 times more likely to attempt suicide than cisgender people. Studies indicate that this statistic reflects the effects of severe discrimination on trans people, not a medical issue.**

The percentage of trans people who are HIV-positive is four times the national average, and is currently at 24.9 percent for black transgender persons—a daunting statistic that is likely related to poverty and lack of access to health care and sex education. San Francisco Human Rights Commissioner Cecilia Chung has pointed out that frequent police profiling of transgender women as sex workers encourages a population already at high risk for HIV to refuse condoms from outreach workers. Not only does this poor quality of available care negatively affect the trans population and their friends and family, but it also represents a potential economic crisis as transgender individuals continue to be both prevented from obtaining the care they need and unable to afford what treatment is available.

In addition to health care, the education system plays a significant role in the unequal treatment of trans people. Here are some figures:

---

# Trans Discrimination in Education*

**Percent of trans population who report they were:**

- Harassed in grades K–12                          78%
- Physically assaulted in school                  35%
- Sexually assaulted in school                    12%
- Expelled just for identifying as transgender     6%

**51% of those harassed, assaulted, or expelled later attempted suicide**

*based on data from National Transgender Discrimination Survey*

---

It is important to keep in mind that the statistics on these experiences in grades K–12 are based on a sample of transgender people who were open about their trans status when in school. It's difficult to gauge how much worse these statistics might be if they also included people who were incorrectly perceived as trans or who were not openly transgender.

What's more, genital status alone is used to determine where one is grouped in most substance abuse treatment programs, rape crisis centers, homeless shelters, and in prison. Transgender people are almost always placed in the wrong facility for their gender, and are also frequently denied necessary medical treatment in prison—including hormone therapy. If a trans person is in the middle of a health care crisis cannot obtain gainful employment, is thrown out of their household by transphobic family members, or develops a drug or alcohol problem, the institutions supposedly there to protect and serve them can become unsafe places where violence and sexual abuse may occur due to their gender expression. For example, MTFs placed in men's prisons and jails are thirteen times more likely than cisgender inmates to be sexually assaulted or raped. Transgender people are also far less likely to be able to afford strong legal counsel than cisgender people.

The NTDS study clearly demonstrates that many institutions in our society are implicated in the oppression of transgender people. On the positive side of these frightening statistics, it was also found that among transgender people whose family accepts their identity, rates of incarceration, homelessness, drug and alcohol use, and suicide attempts drop dramatically. Unfortunately, only 43 percent of the trans people surveyed reported that their family accepts their gender identity.

In addition to concerns about public policies and laws to protect them from discrimination, trans people are also attempting to change how transsexual and transgender experience is viewed by the medical establishment. Activist groups such as Transgender Nation (a subsection within the San Francisco chapter of Queer Nation) began protesting against Gender Identity Disorder's inclusion in the *DSM* as early as 1992. Some activists cite neurobiological studies, which demonstrate that many trans people have brain structures akin to their gender identity even before hormone treatment; they argue that such research

---

### TRANSPHOBIA

Transphobia describes negative behaviors, attitudes, or feelings toward transgender or transsexual people based on their gender expression. The term "transphobic" is used here instead of "groups opposed to transsexuality" for the same reason that one would say "racist" as opposed to "groups opposed to people of color." It is the position of this book that gender identity is as intrinsic to a trans person's construction of self as race, age, or (dis)ability, and that opposing a gender identity is by definition discriminatory. The word "transphobic" helps to convey that being "against" a gender identity cannot be considered a legitimate opinion.

clearly distinguishes trans experience from a mental illness. These studies are controversial, however, and are viewed by many as skewed by the same binary presuppositions as sex difference studies. Regardless, the branding and stigmatizing nature of being diagnosed with GID, while sometimes a conduit to receiving a desired surgery, remains a harsh reality for many trans individuals who do not feel that their identity is a disease or disorder. This binding label is additionally troublesome to individuals who may not seek to transition neatly from one gender archetype to another.

## DIVERSITY WITHIN TRANS COMMUNITIES

It's worth noting that trans people do not necessarily have a great deal in common beyond having a gender identity that doesn't conform to society's norms; being transgender is not a leisure activity, a lifestyle, or even a preference. A trans person's feelings related to their body and gender are also not all neatly tied up into MTF or FTM categories. Many trans people do not wish to change their body and do not think of themselves as a "man/woman trapped in a woman/man's body." Some transgender people identify as male or female but do not consider their body parts to have a great deal to do with their gender. Others may wish to alter their body or take hormones despite not identifying with one specific gender, and may identify as genderqueer or "third gendered," among many possible terms. Still others may identify as gender fluid, and experience their gender as ever-changing, or as a mix of genders.

While more recent queer theory tends to stand in alliance with trans experience, some queer and feminist thinkers have questioned the validity of a transsexual fully becoming a "woman" or "man" through changing their sexed body. The concept of socially constructed gender, which most queer communities embrace, reinforces the idea that one's environment and culture shapes gender roles and gender experience—a position that can be at odds with some trans individuals, who may believe their gender is innate. Transgender people may assert that they have always identified as their gender, and that their assigned sex was simply incorrect. As aforementioned, some feminists felt challenged by trans identities and wondered whether trans women had the same claim to their frustrations with sexism (or if they were perpetuating archetypes). Transgender theorists, on the other hand, contend that the term "woman" invokes the issues and concerns of only a portion of feminists (most of whom are in the demographic majority), while sometimes ignoring the class, racial, and religious concerns of other women. For example, when generalizing about "women's concerns," many women of color and their experiences get sidelined. The trans disagreement with universal terms for "woman" and "man" generally resonates with queer communities' ideology; yet, in practice, queer activists are sometimes less inclusive of highly masculine or feminine individuals in their more androgynous communities. On the other hand, some trans communities also seem to preference trans male and genderqueer identities over trans women. Ultimately though, trans theories challenge feminists and other LGBT activists to reconsider any exclusionary practices that limit the number of participants in the fight to end discrimination and injustice based on gender.

To further explain why "authenticity" should not be an issue when considering transsexual and transgender people, Dean Spade argues that, in his experience, most trans people do not actually seek to become a "real man" or "real woman" by passing as non-trans. Instead, they simply do not believe that there is meaning in these categories and may feel that transforming their bodies will allow them to be more comfortable with their gender identity. Indeed, it's very possible that theorists who think that transsexuals ascribe to dichotomous gender ideas have based their research on the most popular stories of transsexuals among non-transsexuals (which were given preference because they reinforced normative gender expression). Spade also points out that the speakers in such narratives may have constructed the stories strategically, in hopes of winning tolerance or acceptance for transsexuals. Surgery can obviously offer access to a new appearance and new types of sexual activity, but it can also be sought for the purpose of breaking with social norms about male and female roles, or to further someone's personal definition and expression of their gender. Spade himself defines "transgendered" as simply anyone "who [transcends] traditional stereotypes of 'man' and 'woman.'"

Given their shared frustration about binaries and related oppression, transgender people, feminists, and queer communities have some parallel concerns, and their respective academic theories are influenced and informed by one another. As discussed, queer theory emerged in the late 1980s and early 90s during the AIDS epidemic, which made it necessary to rethink the relationship between orientation, self-identification, and sexual activity. This shifted the gay and lesbian rights movement in both Europe and the U.S., and to some extent deflected the focus away from gaining protections for specific minorities facing discrimination. Suddenly, the transgender population had a microphone to speak out against the expectation that they fit neatly into a binary, but had little support in seeking legislation to protect them.

**THOUGHT EXPERIMENT!**

Do you think a cisgender female or cisgender male is "less" female or male if they behave in a manner that our society does not consider "feminine" or "masculine"? What do statements like "be a real man" or "behave like a lady" actually mean?

# A CROSS-CULTURAL LOOK AT TRANSGENDER ROLES

Many cultures have more than two genders. In fact, gender fluid, intersex, and trans people have been acknowledged in other countries for centuries. Arabian xanith, Indian hijra, Thai kathoey, Brazilian travestis, and Polynesian mahu are a few examples of complicated gender identities that don't fit neatly into "male" or "female," and in some cases hold an elevated or celebrated position of power within their respective societies.

In many instances, these individuals are delegated ceremonial or spiritual roles. On the other hand, they may also be harassed, abused, or ostracized from their respective societies when not serving a religious function. Some perform as sex workers. Omani xanith, for example, are transgender MTFs who have sex for money with non-transgender men, and are perceived in Omani culture as neither male nor female. They are barred by law from dressing in female-specific garments, and typically wear men's robes in pastel shades; when testifying before court, xanith have twice the "vote" of a non-transgender Omani woman's testimony.

Thailand's kathoeys (loosely translated as "ladyboys," or people who are assigned as male at birth, but express various "feminine" characteristics), by contrast, may occupy positions as various as soap-opera stars and models, to kickboxing champions, musicians, or just about any other vocation one might seek. Additionally, as mentioned before, in some Native American cultures, gender-variant individuals are known as "two-spirit" people, and are typically held in particularly high esteem. Some tribes, such as the Zuni, have religious stories in which two-spirit deities have brought peace to warring nations or otherwise aided humanity; therefore, they generally treat two-spirit people with great respect.

XANITH

MAHU

TRAVESTIS

KATHOEY

HIJRA

Transgender studies scholar Jay Prosser argues in *Second Skins: The Body Narratives of Transsexuality* (1998) that early queer theory glorified drag while discouraging transsexual identification, which was sometimes viewed as essentialist. Some transgender people also feel that the queer movement privileges and promotes sexuality-specific ways of differing from heteronormativity. Conversely, the transgender population is more concerned with gender identity than desire or sexual orientation. As a result, they place much more emphasis on race, class, age, disability, and nationality within the communities they engage. Ultimately, just as butch lesbians have sometimes cited androgynous queers as unintentionally undermining their visibility, transgender people and the feminist and queer communities find themselves occasionally at odds with one another. Nevertheless, much of trans theory emerged from the broader queer movement, and they share an opposition to universalizing the experience of "men" and "women," as well as a stance against heteronormativity.

One thing is for certain: trans phenomena renders the dichotomy of a male and female binary deeply troubled. If your gender can be fluid or has the potential to change, then narrow definitions about sexuality become almost meaningless. And when one considers the importance placed on who people are attracted to, how much of the homophobia we see around us can be linked back to cultural discomfort with gender nonconformity?

Although there are many cultures where transsexuals have an integral (or at least acknowledged) role, the United States' medical and psychological traditions have long problematized gender identities that do not conform to Western male and female archetypes. Transgender studies argue instead that varied experiences of gender are morally neutral and carry enormous weight and validity to those who identify outside our cultural "norms." Besides, is not everyone's body image and sense of identity somewhat altered by the lens of gendered expectations that society imposes?

Still, for much of the cisgender and heterosexual population, trans people represent the most flagrant deviation from their "norms" and assumptions about male and female roles in our society. Moreover, as those who were present at Stonewall can attest, in spite of their critical participation, the trans population and their concerns have often been left behind in gay and lesbian activism and feminist efforts. Attaining equality for more easily assimilated gay, lesbian and bisexual individuals may have simply seemed more attainable by activists at the time, who prioritized issues such as gay marriage and the ability to serve in the military, neither of which is usually a key concern to trans individuals (though even today, after the repeal of "Don't Ask, Don't Tell," trans people are still not allowed to serve in the U.S. armed services). Instead, trans people are seeking better access to health care, jobs, and bathrooms; the option to legally change their sex on birth certificates and driver's licenses; trans-inclusive policies in jails, homeless and rape shelters; better implementation of existing nondiscrimination policies; and methods to address bullying in schools.

Nowadays, the LGBTQIA umbrella is expanding to be ever more inclusive, and despite varying backgrounds and identities, many people see the importance of strategic alliances between marginalized communities. Others feel that these alliances reinforce generalizations and minimize the visibility of diverse populations lumped together under the terms "LGBT" or "LGBTQIA." Given that trans issues have been so frequently ignored in LGBT efforts, some trans activists also assert the necessity of co-organizing in social justice movements with other marginalized communities experiencing oppression whose social justice concerns are not specific to their orientation, such as people of color, the elderly, young people, low income people, and HIV-positive people. Fundamentally, at the root of many arguments between disparate groups about gender and sexuality lies fear of being ostracized, silenced, marginalized, misunderstood, and mis- or underrepresented.

Gay, lesbian, bisexual, transgender, queer, questioning, intersex, and asexual individuals may not share personal interests, political affiliations, a belief system, or even all of the same views on gender and sexuality. They all do, however, experience state regulation of their bodies, structural inequities, lack of representation, and social stigma. As trans discrimination bears clear links to systemic forms of violence such as sexism, classism, ableism, ageism, and racism, it cannot go unrecognized without creating a tremendous burden on the nation's health care system and economy. Many transgender people believe that everyone has a role in fixing transphobia and other forms of discrimination that afflict this country, which will require rethinking the sex-gender system and implementing policy changes at all levels.

# LOOKING FORWARD

After reading this book, it is hopefully clear that gender norms and heteronormativity are deeply problematic in our society. It is misleading and disingenuous to divide people into categories of "men" and "women," whose most basic definitions are based on reproductive abilities alone. In doing so, our society negates variety in gender identification and expression. To date, no convincing argument exists for sex differences determining personality or aptitude; such ideas reinforce an oppressive history of devaluing both femininity and androgyny.

There may be a fundamental difference between most male- and female-assigned people that has significance beyond reproduction. But since humans are more varied within each sex than between the "two," how crucial could such a trait be? Over-emphasizing a 1 percent genetic difference whose implications remain unclear while neglecting differences *within* the sexes is personally irresponsible, and becomes politically criminal when institutions create and enforce policies on its basis. Furthermore, does it really matter whether or not people are born with a biologically-determined sexual orientation? In either case, one's identity is no less legitimate. People have diverse traits. All people deserve respect, basic freedoms, protection under the law, and equal representation.

**We should not need to prove our experiences, defend our realities, or negotiate basic human rights. But we do.**

Significant strides have been made in recent years on behalf of gay and lesbian rights. Yet transgender, intersex, and asexual people have seldom been served by these gains. Conservative media pundits and new legislative policies restricting women's access to reproductive health care are actually moving us backwards. And even in the best of cases, there remains a large division between the law and day-to-day reality for all LGBTQIA individuals and for women in our society. Equal opportunities for everything from jobs to representation in the media simply do not exist. And while advocating for policy change is important, it is not enough. Legal equality alone will not ensure material change. Laws aren't always enforceable. Not everyone can afford adequate legal counsel. Sometimes police and service providers abuse their power. Often, elected politicians, the media, and even educators treat women as a minority and LGBTQIA people as a special interest group. They are wrong. We are everywhere. If we are to address these wrongs, perhaps we need to ask: Which Americans experience oppression so severe that their basic human needs and ability to pursue a safe and prosperous life are fundamentally denied? Unfortunately, there are many valid answers to that question.

Women make up slightly more than half our population. There should be no question of women's relevance to our society's well-being. Yet despite mountains of evidence that they have equal aptitudes in every area, women's abilities are still held to different standards than men's. Sex difference scientists, the media, and much of our nation's educational curricula continue to imply that women are less important, have less to say, or can lead less effectively. Women's wages are lower, their choices are fewer, and they face roadblocks to reproductive health care and respectful treatment on a daily basis.

Some Americans continue to view any sexual orientation besides heterosexuality as "different," "abnormal"—sometimes even sick or morally wrong. The same goes for transgender people and others whose gender does not align with their assigned sex. Many people who do not fit our society's gender norms for men and women find themselves marginalized or simply left out. LGBTQIA people's social, emotional, fiscal, and physical well-beings are challenged and obstructed by institutions that privilege norms. They are misrepresented in the media, underrepresented in the law and public policy, and generally ignored altogether in public education.

Race, age, class, disability, and citizenship add a further dimension to the sex and gender system in our country. While this book cannot address those overlaps, it is clear that literally everyone other than an affluent, able, straight white male is disadvantaged in our society. Moreover, the intersections of oppression are often more than the sum of their parts. For example, disabled youth in this country experience so many barriers to accessing information and opportunities that it boggles the mind. Likewise, to be a woman of color in America means more than simply experiencing both racism and sexism; in addition to more overt prejudice, they may experience discrimination from both men of their own race and from white women who share their gender.

Many of the queer young people interviewed for this book expressed frustration with not knowing how to distinguish different forms of oppression at work. They asked how they are supposed to know if someone is reacting to their sex or gender, their race or ethnicity, their orientation, age, class, disability, or creed. They wondered how to correct the frequent and often incorrect assumptions about their identities. One teenage queer activist suggested that, "Perhaps the biggest obstacle we face is the lack of solidarity between movements." After all, it's easy to get caught up in labels that divide people, even among those who strive for social justice. It feels especially discouraging when diverse needs and identities cause conflict among activists and young people. We so obviously cannot afford to have in-fighting among advocates for equality and visibility. With so many people facing similar or related obstacles around discrimination, oppression, and state violence, it's obvious that nothing is more important than allies.

Equality will continue to be resisted by those who wish to preserve privilege and by those who are simply uneducated about these issues. But it helps when people are exposed to the concerns of diverse populations. It helps when we can put a name, a face, a personality to all of these ideas of gender and sexuality. Knowing people who we like that embody diverse genders and sexualities makes all the difference. Spreading awareness and forging such friendships and alliances begins with personal accountability and allyship.

---

### WHAT IS AN ALLY?

Allyship has many definitions. Here's one aimed at promoting effective collaboration: Allies recognize that differences between people are frequently used to discriminate against some while privileging others. They understand that this situation is unacceptable and are willing to stand behind those whose voices are silenced and whose rights are denied. Allies speak up when others express intolerance or ignorance. They reiterate the fundamental similarities of us all while acknowledging, accepting, and educating others about differences. Allies challenge policies, structures, and institutions that result in disadvantaging or hurting people; they work to create a more compassionate world, using their skills and talents to help society become more open and supportive of all people—no matter how they define themselves. Allies refuse to settle for the status quo.

---

Creating an inclusive culture or society requires persistent day-to-day action on the ground level, but the work is a lot lighter if everyone contributes. What does a culture that's actually inclusive look like? Perhaps it's something fairly nonhierarchical where all voices are valued and considered before decisions are made. That would better reflect the democracy that our country's founders intended. After all, the original model was meant to liberate people who had been persecuted for their religious and political stances, and to eliminate the inequities of an economic system based on inherited social class. It was meant to embolden those who had been undervalued elsewhere. So let us begin here and now to forget no more voices. In empowering everyone to participate and be heard, we can better embrace the full range of human potential.

LGBTQIA people and women need not just safe space, but space that allows people to thrive. We need not just visibility, but accountability, as well as equal and accurate representation. Policy changes and education reform are, of course, key. But most of all, we need to work together.

# HERE'S WHAT YOU CAN DO

**LEARN.** Educate yourself about these issues, and then educate others.

**GET INVOLVED.** Seek out local organizations that support initiatives to address issues facing LGBTQIA people, women, and other marginalized groups—or start your own. There are also many places you can volunteer to effect immediate and direct change in your community, like AIDS clinics and youth shelters. This is a great way to meet other people who share your interests and commitment to social justice.

**GIVE.** If you can, donate to those who are undertaking efforts on behalf of underrepresented people in America or elsewhere, both inside and outside of LGBTQIA communities, for women and for other genders. Even small contributions are truly instrumental in grassroots organizations. If you do not have money you can spare, promoting others' work, or assisting in fundraising efforts can be equally valuable.

**PARTICIPATE IN POLITICS.** Read newspapers, watch the news, and seek varied and alternative news sources for more rounded perspectives. Write to your local, state, and national political representatives about unfair or discriminatory public policies. Write to international lawmaking bodies and aid organizations abroad to show your support for progressive legislation. If you are 18 or over, make sure to vote. Attend open community meetings to demonstrate support for issues you're concerned about. Go to rallies and demonstrations that peacefully protest oppressive practices, and build consensus that lawmakers cannot ignore.

**TAKE CARE OF YOURSELF.** Participating in efforts to increase awareness and eliminate oppression can be emotionally draining. Remember that you are a better advocate and example when you are capable of listening with patience and compassion. Try not to overextend yourself. This is about teambuilding. You can't do it all alone.

**MOST IMPORTANTLY: Be accountable and sensitive to oppression around you in your everyday life.** Speak up when you notice someone's voice or opinion being silenced. Be friendly and supportive of those who are different from you. If you aren't sure about someone's identification, ask rather than assume. Start conversations that will encourage thoughtful, nonconfrontational discussion that can help others to examine their stances on these topics. Challenge norms. Ask questions. **LISTEN.**

# RESOURCES

The bibliography of this book includes many books, articles, websites, a few films and lectures, interviews, and more, all of which helped to inform this book (but not all of which the author endorses). The purpose of this resource guide is to intentionally curate a much shorter list of a few key sources. The books, zines, and websites selected provide crucial information not always found in the mainstream media. They also provide visibility to underrepresented voices, and in some cases, access to necessary support.

## SUPPORT NETWORKS, EDUCATIONAL RESOURCES, AND ADVOCACY:

**The Trevor Project** (National organization providing crisis intervention and suicide prevention services to lesbian, gay, bisexual, transgender, and questioning youth) http://www.thetrevorproject.org/
**If you need help, for 24/7 support call: 866.4.U.TREVOR**

**Reteaching Gender and Sexuality** (Intergenerational team of mediamakers and community educators who facilitate dialogue on gender and sexual diversity in communities, among students and with practitioners in youth-serving professions) http://www.reteachinggenderandsexuality.org/

**PFLAG: Parents, Families and Friends of Lesbians and Gays** (Support for families and friends of LGBT people) http://community.pflag.org/

**Safe Schools Coalition** (International public-private partnership in support of gay, lesbian, bisexual, and transgender youth; offers resources for educators, parents/guardians, and youth) http://www.safeschoolscoalition.org/

**National Runaway Switchboard** (LGBTQ-friendly assistance for runaways, homeless and at-risk youth, and their allies) http://www.1800runaway.org/

**Accord Alliance** (For intersex care and questions) http://www.accordalliance.org/about/our-mission.html

**The Silvia Rivera Law Project** (Provides free legal services and referrals on issues impacting transgender, gender nonconforming, and intersex people) http://srlp.org/

**National Gay and Lesbian Task Force** ("Committed to building LGBT power from grassroots efforts") http://thetaskforce.org/

**National Center for Trans Equality** ("Dedicated to advancing the equality of transgender people through advocacy, collaboration, and empowerment") http://transequality.org/

## BOOKS AND ZINES:

*Queer America: A People's GLBT History of the United States* by Vicki L. Eaklor (Cultural and political context for gay, lesbian, bisexual, and transgender experience in America from 1890 to 2009; series edited by Howard Zinn)

*No Turning Back: The History of Feminism and the Future of Women* by Estelle B. Freedman (Cross-cultural history of feminist movements and political concerns, women's representation, and economic positioning)

*Asexy Life: On Asexuality and Challenging Heteronormativity* by n.b. (What asexuality means; stories and accounts from asexual people)

*Sexing the Body* by Anne Fausto-Sterling (Gender politics and scientific deconstructions of sex, gender, and sexuality)

*Queer: The Ultimate LGBT Guide for Teens* by Kathy Belge and Marke Bieschke (The 411 for any gay, lesbian, bisexual, transgender, or questioning teen)

*Gender Outlaws: The Next Generation* edited by Kate Bornstein and S. Bear Bergman (Trans and genderqueer voices and essays)

*Learning Good Consent* by Cindy Crabb (Assault prevention and verbal consent)

*Brain Storm: The Flaws in the Science of Sex Differences* by Rebecca M. Jordan-Young (On weaknesses in brain organization theory and methods of conducting sex difference studies)

*Queer Youth Cultures* edited by Susan Driver (Essays on political and artistic cultural practices of queer youth, from zine-making to organizing resistance)

*Teaching for Diversity and Social Justice: A Sourcebook* edited by Maurianne Adams, Lee Anne Bell, and Pat Griffin (Resource for teachers who want to be accountable to diversity)

*Normal Life: Administrative Violence, Critical Trans Politics, and the Limits of Law* by Dean Spade (Rethinking law, the justice system, social services, and strategies for seeking justice and equality, particularly as relates to trans people)

*Exile and Pride: Disability, Queerness and Liberation* by Eli Clare (Queer and disability politics; introduction to understanding oppression)

*Same Difference: How Gender Myths Are Hurting Our Relationships, Our Children, and Our Jobs* by Rosalind Barnett and Caryl Rivers (Sex difference science and its flaws, misleading data and effects)

*Delusions of Gender: How Our Minds, Society, and Neurosexism Created Difference* by Cordelia Fine (Society's construction of gender through parenting, education, and neuroscience)

*GenderQueer: Voices From Beyond the Sexual Binary* edited by Joan Nestle, Clare Howell, and Riki Wilchins (Stories and essays from people who identify outside the gender binary)

*My Gender Workbook: How to Become a Real Man, a Real Woman, the Real You, or Something Else Entirely* by Kate Bornstein (Guide to discovering, rethinking, and understanding your gender identity)

*Queer Theory, An Introduction* by Annemarie Jagose (Academic introduction to queer theory)

*Odd Girls and Twilight Lovers: A History of Lesbian Life in Twentieth-Century America* by Lillian Faderman (History of lesbian life, culture and experience in America)

*Gender Trouble: Feminism and Subversion of Identity* by Judith Butler (Crucial queer theory text)

*The Second Sex* by Simone de Beauvoir (Crucial feminist theory text)

# TIMELINE

*Since few American history books include significant LGBTQIA and feminist perspectives, issues and events, here's a timeline of some of their overlapping evolution:*

## SOME SUCCESSES AND SETBACKS IN THE FIGHT FOR LGBTQIA AND FEMINIST RIGHTS AND VISIBILITY IN THE U.S.

1828     The phrase "crime against nature" is first used in the Criminal Code of the United States to refer to same-sex sexual acts

1890     National American Woman Suffrage Association (NAWSA) is founded (women's rights organization, primary group responsible for winning women's right to vote)

1892     First known use of the term "heterosexual" in the U.S., *Chicago Medical Recorder*

1930     Hollywood Production Code goes into effect; bans references to homosexuality in American films

         Magnus Hirschfeld (having founded the Institute for Sexual Science in Berlin in 1919) visits the U.S. to lecture to various medical facilities and organizations, pushes for the decriminalization of same-sex sexual acts

1935     Committee for the Study of Sex Variants is founded in New York City

1947     Institute for Sex Research (Kinsey Institute) is founded at Indiana University

         *Vice Versa,* the first known lesbian newsletter, is published by "Lisa Ben"

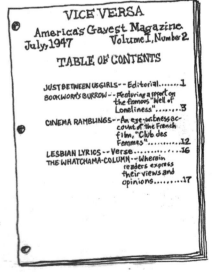

1950     "Lavender scare": It is revealed that 91 homosexuals had been fired from the State Department. because they were considered national security threats; congressional committee spends months studying this "threat," finds zero examples of gay or lesbian civil servants revealing state secrets

1951     *Stoumen v. Reilly:* California Supreme Court upholds rights of bars to serve homosexuals

         Mattachine Society, a homophile organization began by Harry Hay is 1948, is officially founded in Los Angeles

1952    The American Psychiatric Association (APA) describes homosexuality as a "sociopathic personality disturbance" in its first *Diagnostic and Statistical Manual (DSM)*

Immigration and Nationality Act (McCarran-Walter Act) bans homosexual immigrants

1953    Christine Jorgenson returns to the U.S. after MTF surgery in Denmark, first widely publicized "gender reassignment" operation

Executive Order 10450 makes homosexuality grounds for dismissal from federal employment

*ONE* magazine begins publication, first pro-gay magazine in wide circulation

1955    Daughters of Bilitis is founded in San Francisco, first homophile organization for women

Evelyn Hooker begins publishing studies of homosexuals without psychological disturbances, demonstrates that homosexuals are equally likely as heterosexuals to be "in their right minds"; pushes for homosexuality to cease being classified as a mental disorder

1961    José Sarria is the first openly gay person to run for public office in San Francisco

Illinois is the first state to repeal its sodomy law

Motion Picture Production Code is reversed, allowing depictions of homosexuality in American films

1964    Civil Rights Act creates protection against racial and sex discrimination

The very first pickets for gay rights are held at the U.S. Army induction center and Cooper Union, (both in New York City)

1965    Pickets for gay rights are held at Independence Hall on July 4th, as well as at the White House, United Nations, Civil Service Commission, Pentagon, and State Department

First gay sit-in is held at Dewey's restaurant in Philadelphia

Council on Religion and the Homosexual (San Francisco) holds a press conference to report police harassment

San Francisco's first drag ball is held, blatantly ignoring a police picket line

1966    National Organization for Women (NOW) is founded

1967    Student Homophile League at Columbia University is the first formally acknowledged student group of its kind (essentially an early Gay-Straight Alliance for students, or GSA)

1968    APA revises classification of homosexuality to a "non-psychotic mental disorder"

Civil Rights Act expands protections of 1964 to include protection from housing discrimination related to race, religion, and national origin (in 1974 expanded to include gender; 1988 expanded to include disabilities and families with children). Also protects civil rights workers.

1969    Gay Liberation Front founded in New York City

Stonewall riots, June 27–28, violent demonstrations against police raids of the Stonewall Inn, a bar in Greenwich Village (New York City) that had many gay and drag queen patrons

1970    Jack Baker and Michael McConnell are the first American gay couple to apply for a marriage license, denied; later established their legal relationship via adult adoption

First gay studies class taught at University of Nebraska

1971    NOW "acknowledges the oppression of lesbians as a legitimate concern of feminism" (formerly excluded them)

1972    First Gay Community Services Center opens in Los Angeles

Parents and Friends of Lesbians and Gays (PFLAG) is first established

Title IX of Education Amendments bans sex discrimination in publicly funded education

First gay studies program, California State University at Sacramento

National Bisexual Liberation Group is formed in New York City

1973    APA removes homosexuality from its list of mental disorders

National Gay Task Force is founded in New York City

Lambda Legal Defense and Education Fund is founded in New York City

1975    Sergeant Leonard Matlovich is discharged for being gay, appears on the cover of *Time*

1977    National Lesbian and Gay Health Foundation is founded

       *Soap* introduces a gay character to its long-running and popular TV show

       White House staff holds first-ever meeting with gay and lesbian leaders

1978    California voters defeat antigay Proposition 6 "Briggs Initiative," that would have banned homosexuals from working in public schools

       International Lesbian and Gay Association is founded

       San Francisco Supervisor Harvey Milk and Mayor George Moscone are murdered; both were prominent gay rights activists, and Milk was openly gay

       The U.S. State Department announces that it will begin considering job applications from lesbians and gays for employment in the foreign service

       Artist Gilbert Baker creates the Rainbow (Pride) Flag as a positive alternative to the Pink Triangle—a symbol used by Nazis to identify homosexuals

1979    First National Third World Lesbian and Gay Conference is held

       Dan White is convicted of voluntary manslaughter for the deaths of Harvey Milk and George Moscone; following the sentence, White Night Riots ensue as a protest from the gay community, over 160 people are hospitalized

1980    Harry Benjamin International Gender Dysphoria Association is founded

       Socialist Party nominates David McReynolds, an openly gay man, as its presidential candidate

       Black and White Men Together, a gay multiracial multicultural organization committed to overcoming racial barriers, is founded

1981    AIDS is first reported in *The New York Times* and *San Francisco Chronicle*

1982    Wisconsin becomes first state to pass a law banning discrimination based on sexual orientation

1983    People with AIDS Coalition is founded

       Gay men are federally prohibited from donating blood

1984    Discovery of virus causing AIDS, later named HIV

1986    *Bowers v. Hardwick:* Supreme Court upholds Georgia's (anti)sodomy law

       Antigay amendments introduced to bills in Senate

       New York City passes nondiscrimination law to include sexual orientation

       FTM International founded ("Female-To-Male" transsexual network)

       Gay Activists Alliance of Washington, D.C. adds "Lesbian" to its name, as does National Gay Task Force

| 1987 | *The New York Times* first uses "gay" in place of "homosexual" |
|---|---|
| | The AIDS Coalition to Unleash Power (ACT-UP) is formed in New York; three weeks later they protest on Wall Street to bring attention to the AIDS crisis |
| 1988 | National Coming Out Day begins (annual event, Oct. 11th) |
| 1989 | First gay and lesbian studies department, San Francisco City College |
| 1990 | Simpson-Mazzoli Act passes, removing the "sexual deviation" clause used to exclude homosexual immigrants |
| | Americans with Disabilities Act is passed by Congress |
| | Hate Crimes Statistics Act is passed, requiring the Attorney General to collect data on crimes committed because of the victim's race, religion, disability, sexual orientation, or ethnicity |
| | Ryan White CARE (Comprehensive AIDS Resources Emergency) Act is passed |
| | "Outing" controversy begins when publication *OutWeek* "outs" Malcolm Forbes |
| | *Journal of the History of Sexuality* (peer-reviewed academic journal) begins circulation |
| | Queer Nation is founded in New York City |
| | North American Bisexual Network is formed (later renamed BiNet USA) |
| | National Bisexual Conference is held for the first time |
| 1991 | First major study claiming sexuality may have a genetic basis is published |
| | Day of National Coordinated Action, protesting military policies against gay soldiers, is held on April 10 |
| | Gay and Lesbian Civil Rights Bill is reintroduced in Congress |
| 1992 | Colorado voters approve antigay Amendment 2, considering gay rights "special rights" and refusing to protect against orientation-based discrimination |
| | Transgender Nation is founded |
| | Oregon voters defeat antigay Measure 9, which asked for all levels of government, including public education, to discourage gay and lesbian behaviors, calling them "perverse" and "abnormal" |
| | *In the Life,* a gay and lesbian TV show, premiers |
| 1993 | "Don't Ask, Don't Tell" policy passed, prohibiting military personnel from discriminating against or harassing closeted homosexual or bisexual service members/applicants while barring openly gay, lesbian, or bisexual persons from military service |

Hate Crimes Sentencing Enhancement Act passed, requiring increased sentencing for crimes wherein a victim is selected due to their "actual or perceived race, color, religion, national origin, ethnicity, gender, disability, or sexual orientation" (28 U.S.C. 994)

Intersex Society of North America is founded

*Philadelphia* (film) opens in theatres, one of the first mainstream Hollywood films to discuss HIV/AIDS and homophobia

"Camp Trans" sets up outside Michigan Womyn's Music Festival protesting transwomen's exclusion from the festival

1994  Antigay measures in Idaho (Prop 1) and Oregon (Prop 13) defeated in elections, both would have forbid state and local governments from passing antidiscrimination ordinances

1995  Antigay initiative in Maine defeated, would have forbid state and local governments from passing antidiscrimination ordinances

1996  Employment Non-Discrimination Act (ENDA) defeated in a 49-50 Senate vote; would prohibit discrimination against employees on the basis of sexual orientation by civilian, nonreligious employers with at least 15 employees; has been reintroduced in every Congress since, but has not yet passed

*Romer v. Evans:* Supreme Court declares Colorado's antigay Amendment 2 unconstitutional

*Baehr v. Miike* (formerly *Baehr v. Lewin*): Hawaii Supreme Court rules in favor of same-sex marriage

Defense of Marriage Act (DOMA) passed, defining marriage as a legal union between one man and one woman on the federal level; under this, no state has to recognize a same-sex marriage considered "legal" by another state; bars same-sex partners from receiving federal spousal benefits

1997  APA passes a resolution questioning the effectiveness of "conversion therapy" for lesbians and gays

1998  Executive order bans antigay discrimination in federal government

Hawaii constitutional amendment passes, banning same-sex marriage

Maine's gay rights law repealed by voters, no longer protecting gay men and lesbians from discrimination

Matthew Shepard, a gay student at the University of Wyoming dies from an antigay beating, bringing international attention to hate crime legislation in America

1999  *Boys Don't Cry* (film) premiers; Hilary Swank wins Best Actress Academy Award for her portrayal of Brandon Teena, a trans man from Nebraska who was raped and murdered in 1993

Gay and Lesbian Pride Month is declared by President Clinton (June)

2000    Vermont legislature approves civil unions for same-sex couples

*Boy Scouts of America v. Dale:* Supreme Court rules that Boy Scouts can exclude gay people

2003    *Goodridge v. Massachusetts Department of Public Health:* Massachusetts Supreme Court declares same-sex marriage constitutional

*Lawrence v. Texas:* Supreme Court overturns *Bowers v. Hardwick*, making all state-level antisodomy laws unconstitutional

2004    Antigay marriage amendments pass in eleven states

Massachusetts becomes the first state to offer same-sex marriage licenses

Challenging California law, San Francisco Mayor Gavin Newsom directs the city-county clerk to issue marriage licenses to same-sex couples; city authorities perform fifteen same-sex weddings and issue an additional dozen licenses to gay and lesbian couples

2005    *Brokeback Mountain* (film) opens, depicting gay cowboys and winning three Academy Awards, including Best Director and Best Adapted Screenplay (from Annie Proulx's short story); becomes one of the highest-grossing romance films of all time

FDA bans gay men from being sperm donors despite all donated sperm being screened for STIs

2006    Anti-gay Federal Marriage Amendment fails in Congress

2007    ENDA passes the House of Representatives, but still has not yet passed Congress

2008    Connecticut is the second state to legalize same-sex marriage

Proposition 8 passes in California, bans same-sex marriage

2009    ENDA, now including gender identity, reintroduced in Congress

Matthew Shepard and James Byrd, Jr. Hate Crimes Prevention Act is signed by President Obama, expanding 1969 hate crime legislation to include crimes motivated by actual or perceived gender identity, sexual orientation, or disability; first federal law to extend protections to transgender people

Iowa, New Hampshire, and Vermont legalize same-sex marriage

Military Readiness Enhancement Act, aimed at repealing the military's "Don't Ask, Don't Tell" policy, introduced in Congress

2011    "Don't Ask, Don't Tell" is repealed; gay, lesbian, and bisexual individuals can serve openly in the military

New York legalizes same-sex marriage

Tennessee Senate passes bill mandating that no public elementary or middle school can discuss any sexual orientation other than heterosexuality

California law (Welfare and Institutions Code Section 8050) requiring state health officials to seek a "cure" for homosexuality is repealed

Secretary of State Hillary Clinton gives Human Rights Day address in Geneva; focuses entirely on the importance of support for LGBT equality, protections, assistance for activists, calling for the world to recognize that "gay rights are human rights"

President Obama directs all agencies engaged abroad to ensure that U.S. diplomacy and foreign assistance promote and protect the human rights of LGBT persons. Prioritizes fighting the criminalization of LGBT status or conduct, and supporting the protection of LGBT refugees and asylum seekers

2012 The U.S. Court of Appeals for the Ninth Circuit rules in *Perry v. Schwarzenegger* that California's Proposition 8 (which restricts marriage to mixed-sex couples) is unconstitutional

North Carolina bans same-sex marriages, civil unions, and domestic partnerships

The U.S. FIrst Circuit Court of Appeals strikes down Section 3 of DOMA as unconstitutional

Washington state Governor Chris Gregoire signs same-sex marriage into state law

Tammy Baldwin becomes the first openly gay person to be elected to the Senate

Maine, Maryland and Washington approve same-sex marriage by public vote referendum

# BIBLIOGRAPHY

*The author does not endorse the opinions or all of the facts suggested by these materials.*

PUT THIS ON THE {MAP}. "ABOUT PUT THIS ON THE {MAP}." Accessed January 21, 2011. http://www.putthisonthemap.org/about.

"ACLU Files Lawsuit Challenging Illegal Sex Segregation in Louisiana Public School." American Civil Liberties Union. September 9, 2000. Accessed March 4, 2012. http://www.aclu.org/womens-rights/aclu-files-lawsuit-challenging-illegal-sex-segregation-louisiana-public-school.

Abelove, Henry, Michèle Aina Barale, and David M. Halperin, eds. *The Lesbian and Gay Studies Reader.* New York: Routledge, 1993.

Adovasio, J. M., Olga Soffer, and Jake Page. *The Invisible Sex.* New York: HarperCollins, 2007.

Anzaldúa, Gloria. "La Conciencia de la Mestiza: Towards a New Consciousness." In Gloria Anzaldúa. *Borderlands/La Frontera: The New Mestiza.* San Francisco: Aunt Lute Books, 1999. Accessed February 6, 2012. http://www.oaklandleaf.org/sources/anzaldua.pdf.

"Alice Paul." Alice Paul Institute. Accessed January 31, 2012. http://www.alicepaul.org.

Allen, L. S., and R. A. Gorski. "Sexual Orientation and the Size of the Anterior Commissure in the Human Brain." *Proceedings of the National Academy of Sciences of the United States of America, Vol. 89 (August)* (1992), 7,199–7,202. As referenced in Rebecca M. Jordan-Young, *Brain Storm: The Flaws in the Science of Sex Differences.* Cambridge, MA, and London: Harvard University Press, 2010, 50.

Allen, David W., and Diane E. Wall. "Role Orientations and Women State Supreme Court Justices." *Judicature Vol. 77* (1993): 156–165. As referenced in Massie, T., S Johnson, and Sara Margaret Gubala. "Of Gender and Race in the Decisions of Judges on The United States Courts of Appeals." Paper presented at the 2002 Midwest Political Science Association Annual Meeting, Chicago, IL. Accessed March 20, 2012. http://www.cas.sc.edu/poli/psrw/MassieJohnsonGubala.pdf.

Armstrong, Walter. "Brutality in Blue." *Amnesty International* magazine. March 27, 2007. Accessed March 26, 2012. http://www.amnestyusa.org/node/87367.

Altman, Dennis. *Homosexual Oppression and Liberation:* Sydney: Angus and Robertson, 1972 [1971], 94, quoted in Annemarie Jagose. *Queer Theory: An Introduction.* Melbourne: Melbourne University Press, 1996, 41.

American Psychiatric Association. *Diagnostic and Statistical Manual of Mental Disorders: DSM-IV-TR.* Washington, D.C.: American Psychiatric Association, 2000.

American Psychiatric Association. *DSM-5 Development.* "Gender Dysphoria." Accessed February 29, 2012. http://www.dsm5.org/ProposedRevision/Pages/GenderDysphoria.aspx.

Anthony, Susan B. "Social Purity" [1875]. In Estelle B. Freedman, ed. *The Essential Feminist Reader*. Trade paperback ed. New York: The Modern Library, 2007, 86–91. As in Harper, Ida Husted. *The Life and Work of Susan B. Anthony: Including Public Addresses, Her Own Letters and Many From Her Contemporaries During Fifty Years, Vol. 2*. Indianapolis: Bowen-Merrill Company, 1898, 1004–1012.

APA Task Force on Gender Identity and Gender Variance. *Report of the Task Force on Gender Identity and Gender Variance*. Washington, D.C.: American Psychological Association, 2008.

Arnold, A. P. and S. M. Breedlove. "Organizational and activational effects of sex steroids on brain and behaviors: A reanalyisis." *Hormones and Behavior, Vol. 19* (1985), 469–498, referenced in Anne Fausto-Sterling. *Sexing the Body*. New York: Basic Books, 2000, 232.

Aronsen, Gavin. "Map: Transgender Employment Rights Make Headway." *Mother Jones*. April 22, 2011. Accessed February 9, 2012. http://motherjones.com/mojo/2011/04/transgender-lgbt-employment-map.

"Attorney General Eric Holder Announces Revisions to the Uniform Crime Report's Definition of Rape." U.S. Department of Justice. January 6, 2012. Accessed February 2, 2012. http://www.fbi.gov/news/pressrel/press-releases/attorney- general-eric-holder-announces-revisions-to-the-uniform-crime-reports-definition-of-rape.

Bagemihl, Bruce. *Biological Exuberance: Animal Homosexuality and Natural Diversity*. New York: St. Martin's Press, 1999.

Bailey, Michael, and Richard C. Pillard. "A Genetic Study of Male Sexual Orientation." *Archives General Psychiatry, Vol. 48* (1991), 1,089–1,096.

Bancroft, John. "Alfred Kinsey's work 50 years later." New Introduction to *Sexual Behavior in the Human Male* by Alfred Kinsey, et al. Bloomington, IN: Indiana University Press, 1998. Accessed January 18, 2012. The Kinsey Institute. http://www.iub.edu/~kinsey/about/images/Intro%20to%20Female%20vol.pdf

Barthes, Roland. *Mythologies*. Translated by Annette Lavers. New York: Hill and Wang, 1978 [Fr. 1957]. As referenced in Annemarie Jagose. *Queer Theory: An Introduction*. Melbourne: Melbourne University Press, 1996, 78.

Barnett, Rosalind, and Caryl Rivers. *Same Difference: How Gender Myths Are Hurting Our Relationships, Our Children, and Our Jobs*. New York: Basic Books, 2004.

Beauvoir, Simone de. *The Second Sex*. Translated by Constance Borde and Sheila Malovany-Chevallier. New York: Alfred A. Knopf, 2010 [Fr 1949].

Beauvoir, Simone de. "The Second Sex." In Estelle B. Freedman, ed. *The Essential Feminist Reader*. Trade paperback ed. New York: The Modern Library, 2007, 252–262. Originally published as Simone de Beauvoir. *The Second Sex*. H. M. Parshley, trans., ed. New York: Alfred A. Knopf, 1978, xiii–xxiv, xxvi–xxix.

"The Bechdel Test for Women in Movies." *Feminist Frequency.* Accessed February 22, 2012. http://www.feministfrequency.com/2009/12/the-bechdel-test-for-women-in-movies/

Beck, Koa. "Teachers Call Trangender Girl's Identity A 'Distraction.'" *Mommyish,* November 17, 2011. Accessed March 29, 2012. http://mommyish.com/stuff/treachers-school-transgender-child-identitiy-parienting-216/.

Beech, Hannah. "Where the 'Ladyboys' Are." *Time,* July 7, 2008. Accessed February 29, 2012. http://www.time.com/time/world/article/0,8599,1820633,00.html.

Begley, Sharon. "Gray Matters." *Newsweek,* March 27, 1995, 48–54. Referenced in Anne Fausto-Sterling. *Sexing the Body.* New York: Basic Books, 2000, 117.

Begley, Sharon. "Gray Matters." *Newsweek,* March 27 1995: 48–54. As quoted in Phyllis Burke. *Gender Shock: Exploding the Myths of Male & Female.* New York, Anchor Books, 1996, 192.

Belge, Kathy. "What are the legal benefits of marriage?" In Christina Fisanick, ed. *Feminism.* Farmington Hills: Greenhaven Press, 2008, 231. Originally published on http://lesbianlife.about.com, 2007.

Belge, Kathy and Marke Bieschke. *Queer: The Ultimate LGBT Guide for Teens.* San Francisco: Zest Books, 2011.

Benería, Lourdes. "Reproduction, production and the sexual division of labour." *Cambridge Journal of Economics, Vol. 3* (1979), 203–225.

Benjamin, Harry. "Transsexualism and Transvestitism as Psycho-Somatic and Somato-Psychic Syndromes." In *The Transgender Studies Reader,* edited by Susan Stryker and Stephen Whittle. New York: Routledge, 2006, 45–52. Originally published in *American Journal of Psychotherapy, Vol. 8* (1954), 219–239.

Berg, Barbara J. *Sexism in America: Alive, Well, and Ruining Our Future.* Chicago: Lawrence Hill Books, 2009.

Bérubé, Allan. *Coming Out Under Fire: The History of Gay Men and Women in World War II.* New York: Free Press, 1990.

Billings, Dwight B., and Thomas Urban. "The Socio-Medical Construction of Transsexualism: An Interpretation and Critique." *Social Problems Vol. 29* (1982), 266–276.

"S.909— Matthew Shepard Hate Crimes Prevention Act (Introduced in Senate - IS)." Bill Text 111th Congress (2009–2010) S.909.IS. The Library of Congress. Thomas. April 28, 2009. Accessed March 26, 2012. http://thomas.loc.gov/cgi-bin/query/z?c111:S.909:.

Bleier, Ruth. "Sex differences research: Science or belief?" In Ruth Bleier, ed., *Feminist Approaches to Science.* New York: Pergamon Press, 147–164. As referenced in Cordelia Fine. *Delusions of Gender.* New York: W. W. Norton & Company, Inc., 2010, 106.

Blanchard, Ray and Richard A. Lippa. "Birth Order, Sibling Sex Ratio, Handedness, and Sexual Orientation of Male and Female Participants in a BBC Internet Research Project." *Archives of Sexual Behavior, Vol. 36 (2)*(2007), 163–176. DOI: 10.1007/s10508-006-9159-7.

Bogaert, Anthony F. "Biological versus nonbiological order brothers and men's sexual orientation." *Proceedings of the National Academy of Sciences, Vol. 103 (28)* (2006), 10,771–10,774. DOI:10.1073/pnas.0511152103.

Bogaert, Anthony F. "Interaction of older brothers and sex-typing in the prediction of sexual orientation in men." *Archives of Sexual Behavior, Vol. 32 (2)*(2003), 129–134. PubMed: 12710827.

Bornstein, Kate. *Gender Outlaw: On Men, Women and the Rest of Us.* New York: Vintage Books, 1994.

Boswell, John. *Same-Sex Unions in Pre-Modern Europe.* New York: Random House, 1995.

Boushey, Heather, Jessica Arons, and Lauren Smith. "Families Can't Afford the Gender Wage Gap." *Center for American Progress,* April 20, 2010. Accessed February 23, 2012. http://www.americanprogress.org/issues/2010/04/equal_pay.html

"*Bowers v. Hardwick.*" Cornell Law. Accessed November, 19, 2011. http://www.law.cornell.edu.

"Boys to Men: Entertainment Media Messages About Masculinity." Children Now, September 1999. And "Boys to Men: Conference Report: Media Messages About Masculinity." Sixth Annual Children and the Media Conference, 1999. Accessed February 22, 2012. http://www.childrennow.org/uploads/documents/boys_to_men_1999.pdf.

Bray, Alan. *Homosexuality in Renaissance England.* London: Gay Men's Press, 1988 [1982]. As referenced in Annemarie Jagose. *Queer Theory: An Introduction.* Melbourne: Melbourne University Press, 1996.

Brizendine, Louann, M.D. *The Female Brain.* New York: Morgan Road Books, 2006.

Brownmiller, Susan. *Against Our Will: Men, Women and Rape.* In Estelle B. Freedman, ed. *The Essential Feminist Reader.* Trade paperback ed. New York: The Modern Library, 2007, 312–317. Originally published as Susan Brownmiller. *Against Our Will: Men, Women and Rape.* New York: Simon and Schuster, 1975, 14–15, 209, 309–310, 312–313, 39, 396–397, 404.

Brownmiller, Susan. *In Our Time: Memoir of a Revolution.* New York: The Dial Press, 1999.

Bullough, Vern. "When Did the Gay Rights Movement Begin?" History News Network of George Mason University. April 17, 2005. Accessed March 26, 2012. http://hnn.us/articles/11316.html.

Burke, Phyllis. *Gender Shock: Exploding the Myths of Male & Female.* New York: Anchor Books, 1996.

Butler, Judith. *Gender Trouble: Feminism and the Subversion of Identity.* Second ed. New York: Routledge, 1999 [1990].

Buck, Claire. *H.D. & Freud: Bisexuality and a Feminine Discourse.* New York: St. Martin's Press, Inc., 1991.

Byne, W., M. S. Lasco, E. Kemether, A. Shinwari, M. A. Edgar, S. Morgello, L. B. Jones, and S. Tobet. "The interstitial nuclei of the human anterior hypothalamus: an investigation of sexual variation in volume and cell size, number and density." *Brain Research, Vol. 856 (1–2)* (2000), 254–258. As referenced in Jordan-Young, Rebecca M. *Brain Storm: The Flaws in the Science of Sex Differences.* Cambridge, MA, and London: Harvard University Press, 2010, 50.

Cahill, Sean. "Bisexuality: Dispelling the myths." National Gay and Lesbian Task Force. Accessed March 23, 2012. http://thetaskforce.org/downloads/reports/BisexualityDispellingtheMyths.pdf.

Canaday, Margot. *The Straight State: Sexuality and Citizenship in Twentieth-Century America.* Princeton, NJ: Princeton University Press, 2011 [2009].

"CEDAW." United Nations. Division for the Advancement of Women. Department of Economic and Social Affairs. Accessed December 29, 2011. http://www.un.org/womenwatch/daw/cedaw/.

Chapman, Emma, Simon Baron-Cohen, Bonnie Auyeung, Rebecca Knickmeyer, Kevin Taylor, and Gerald Hackett. "Fetal testosterone and empathy: Evidence from the Empathy Quotient (EQ) and the 'Reading the Mind in the Eyes' test." *Social Neuroscience, Vol. 1(2)* (2006), 135–148.

Chatard, A., S. Guimond, and L. Selimbegovic. "'How good are you in math?' The effect of gender stereotypes on students' recollection of their school marks." *Journal of Experimental Social Psychology, Vol. 43(6)* (2007), 1,017–1,024. As referenced in Cordelia Fine. *Delusions of Gender.* New York: W. W. Norton & Company, Inc., 2010, 8.

"Chromosomes." National Human Genome Research Institute. Accessed January 17, 2012. http://www.genome.gov/26524120.

Chung, Cecilia. "Transgender People, HIV and the Law." September 10, 2011. Accessed March 1, 2012. http://ceciliachung.com/2011/09/10/transgender_hiv_law/.

Clark-Elliott, Barb. Personal interview. August 29, 2011.

Clatterbaugh, Kenneth. *Contemporary Perspectives on Masculinity: Men, Women, and Politics in Modern Society.* Boulder, CO: Westview Press, Inc., 1990.

Clearfield, M. W., and N. M. Nelson. "Sex differences in mothers' speech and play behavior with 6-, 9-, and 14-month-old infants." *Sex Roles, Vol. 54 (1/2)* (2006), 127–137. As referenced in Cordelia Fine. *Delusions of Gender.* New York: W. W. Norton & Company, Inc., 2010, 198.

Cleveland, Stephanie. "Pornography is harmful to women." In Christina Fisanick, ed. *Feminism*. Farmington Hills: Greenhaven Press, 2008, 67–76.

Coalition Against Trafficking in Women—Asia Pacific. "Women do not have the right to be prostitutes." In Christina Fisanick, ed. *Feminism*. Farmington Hills: Greenhaven Press, 2008, 99–109.

Cochran, Bryan N., Angela J. Stewart, Joshua A. Ginzler, and Ana Mari Cauce. "Challenges faced by homeless sexual minorities: Comparison of gay, lesbian, bisexual, and transgender homeless adolescents with their heterosexual counterparts." *American Journal of Public Health, Vol. 92(5)*(2002), 773–777. As referenced by Sarah Mountz. "Revolving Doors: LGBTQ Youth at the Interface of the Child Welfare and Juvenile Justice Systems." *LGBTQ Policy Journal at the Harvard Kennedy School: 2011 Edition*. Accessed March 29, 2012. http://isites.harvard.edu/icb/icb.do?keyword=k78405&pageid=icb.page414421.

"congenital disorder." *Encyclopædia Britannica Online*. Encyclopædia Britannica Inc., 2012. Accessed March 24, 2012. http://www.britannica.com/EBchecked/topic/132266/congenital-disorder.

Corbett, Ken. *Boyhoods: Rethinking Masculinities*. New Haven, CT, and London: Yale University Press, 2009.

"Coretta Scott King." Academy of Achievement: A Museum of Living History. Accessed February 6, 2012. http://www.achievement.org/autodoc/page/kin1bio-1.

Craft, Christopher. "'Kiss Me With Those Red Lips': Gender and Inversion in Bram Stoker's *Dracula*" in Elaine Showalter, ed. *Speaking of Gender*. New York: Routledge, Chapman and Hall, 1989, 216–242, as referenced in Annemarie Jagose. *Queer Theory: An Introduction*. Melbourne: Melbourne University Press, 1996, 17.

D'Emilio, John. *Sexual Politics, Sexual Communities: The Making of a Homosexual Minority in the United States, 1940–1970*. Chicago: University of Chicago Press, 1983: 3, 5–8, 65, 233, as referenced in Annemarie Jagose. *Queer Theory: An Introduction*. Melbourne: Melbourne University Press, 1996, 12–13, 25, 29, 33.

Darwin, Charles. *The Descent of Man and Selection in Relation to Sex*. New York: D. Appleton and Company, 1871, 301. As quoted in Estelle B. Freedman. *No Turning Back: The History of Feminism and the Future of Women*. New York: Ballantine Books, 2002, 38.

Datnow, A., L. Hubbard, and E. Woody. "Is single-gender schooling viable in the public sector? Lessons from California's pilot program." Ford Foundation executive summary, May 20, 2001. As referenced in Rosalind and Rivers Barnett, and Caryl Rivers. *Same Difference: How Gender Myths Are Hurting Our Relationships, Our Children, and Our Jobs*. New York: Basic Books, 2004, 242.

Däumer, Elizabeth D. "Queer Ethics; or, The Challenge of Bisexuality to Lesbian Ethics." *Hypatia, Vol. 7(4)*(1992), 91–105. As quoted and referenced in Annemarie Jagose. *Queer Theory: An Introduction*. Melbourne: Melbourne University Press, 1996, 69–70.

"Decline in newsroom jobs slows." American Society of News Editors, 2010. Accessed February 22, 2012. http://asne.org/article_view/articleid/763/decline-in-newsroom-jobs-slows.aspx

Demir, Ebru and Barry J. Dickson. "*fruitless* Splicing Specifies Male Courtship Behavior in *Drosophila.*" *Cell, Vol. 121 (5)*(2005), 785–794.

*Diagnosing Difference.* Dir. Annalise Ophelian. Floating Ophelia Productions LLC, 2009.

Diamantopoulou, A. Speech at the conference *Violence against women: zero tolerance* Lisbon, May 4, 2000: http://www.eurowrc.org/.

Dines, Gail. *Pornland: How Porn Has Hijacked Our Sexuality.* Boston: Beacon Press, 2010.

Donovan, W., N. Taylor, and L. Leavitt. "Maternal sensory sensitivity and response bias in detecting change in infant facial expressions: Maternal self-efficacy and infant gender labeling." *Infant Behavior and Development, Vol. 30 (3)*(2007), 436–452. As referenced in Cordelia Fine. *Delusions of Gender.* New York: W. W. Norton & Company, Inc., 2010, 198.

"Don't Ask, Don't Tell, Don't Pursue." Robert Crown Law Library. Stanford Law School. Accessed January 8, 2012. http://dont.stanford.edu/doclist.html.

Dority, Barbara. "Pornography is not harmful to women." In Christina Fisanick, ed. *Feminism.* Farmington Hills: Greenhaven Press, 2008, 77–87.

Drum, Kevin. "Pentagon: DADT Repeal Not a Problem." *Mother Jones.* November 30, 2010. Accessed March 26, 2012. http://motherjones.com/kevin-drum/2010/11/pentagon-dadt-repeal-not-problem.

Eaklor, Vicki L. *Queer America: A People's GLBT History of the United States.* New York: The New Press, 2008.

Ekdahl, Jana. Personal interview. July 8, 2011.

Ekins, Richard and Dave King. *The Transgender Phenomenon.* Thousand Oaks: SAGE Publications Ltd., 2006.

Eisenberg, M. E., and M. D. Resnick. "Suicidality among gay, lesbian and bisexual youth: The role of protective factors." *Journal of Adolescent Health, Vol. 39(5)* (2006), 662–668.

Eisenberg, Nancy and Randy Lennon. "Sex differences in empathy and related capacities." *Psychological Bulletin, Vol. 94(1)*(1983), 100–131. As referenced in Cordelia Fine. *Delusions of Gender.* New York: W. W. Norton & Company, Inc., 2010, 16.

"Embryology." *The American Heritage Dictionary of the English Language, 4th edition.* New York: Houghton Mifflin, 2009, [2000].

"Employment Non-Discrimination Act." ACLU. Accessed Jan. 11, 2012. http://www.aclu.org/hiv-aids_lgbt-rights/employment-non-discrimination-act.

Epstein, C. F. *Deceptive Distinctions: Sex, Gender, and the Social Order.* New Haven, Yale University Press; New York: Russell Sage Foundation, 1988, as referenced in Rosalind Barnett, and Caryl Rivers. *Same Difference: How Gender Myths Are Hurting Our Relationships, Our Children, and Our Jobs.* New York: Basic Books, 2004, 240.

"eugenics." *Concise Oxford English Dictionary.* New York: Oxford University Press, 2008.

"Exploring Borderlands: Authors: Gloria Anzaldúa." American Passages: *A Literary Survey.* Accessed February 6, 2012. http://www.learner.org/amerpass/unit02/authors-1.html.

"Facts for Families: Teen Suicide." No. 10 (2008). American Academy of Child & Adolescent Psychiatry. Accessed March 13, 2012. http://www.aacap.org/galleries/FactsForFamilies/10_teen_suicide.pdf.

Faderman, Lillian. *Surpassing the Love of Men: Romantic Friendship and Love Between Women from the Renaissance to the Present.* London: The Women's Press, 1985.

Faderman, Lillian. *Odd Girls and Twilight Lovers: A History of Lesbian Life in Twentieth-Century America.* New York: Penguin Group, 1991.

Anne Fausto-Sterling. *Myths of Gender, Biological Themes About Women and Men,* 2nd ed. New York: Basic Books, 1992 [1985].

Anne Fausto-Sterling. *Sexing the Body: gender Politics and the Construction of Sexuality.* New York: Basic Books, 2000.

"female." Oxford Dictionaries. April 2010. Oxford University Press. Accessed January 14, 2012. http://oxforddictionaries.com/definition/female.

Ferber, Marianne A.; Brigid O'Farrell, and Allen LaRue. *Work and Family: Policies for a Changing Work Force.* National Research Council (U.S.). Committee on Women's Employment and Related Social Issues. Panel on Employer Policies and Working Families. Washington, D.C.: National Academy Press, 1991.

Cordelia Fine. *Delusions of Gender: How Our Minds, Society, and Nerosexism Create Difference.* New York: W. W. Norton & Company, Inc., 2010.

Fisanick, Christina, ed. *Feminism.* Farmington Hills: Greenhaven Press, 2008.

Foreman, J. "Brainpower's sliding scale." *Boston Globe,* May 16, 1994, 25, 29. referenced in Anne Fausto-Sterling. *Sexing the Body.* New York: Basic Books, 2000, 116.

Foucault, Michel. *The History of Sexuality, Vol. 1: An Introduction* [1978], trans. Robert Hurley, Harmondsworth: Penguin, 1981 [Fr 1976].

Fox, R. "Bisexual Identities." In A. D'Augelli, and C. Patterson, Eds. *Lesbian, Gay, and Bisexual Identities Over the Lifespan: Psychological Perspectives.* New York: Oxford University Press, 1995, 73. As referenced by Sean Cahill. "Bisexuality: dispelling the myths." National Gay and Lesbian Task Force, 2.

Francis, Andrew M. "Family and sexual orientation: the family-demographic correlates of homosexuality in men and women." *Journal of Sex Research, Vol. 45* (2008), 371–377.

Friedan, Betty. "The Feminine Mystique." In Estelle B. Freedman, ed. *The Essential Feminist Reader.* Trade paperback ed. New York: The Modern Library, 2007, 270–282. Originally published as Betty Friedan. *The Feminine Mystique.* New York: W. W. Norton & Company, 1963, 15–25, 29–32, 338, 342, 344, 370, 377–78).

Estelle B. Freedman. *No Turning Back: The History of Feminism and the Future of Women.* New York: Ballantine Books, 2002.

Estelle B. Freedman, ed. *The Essential Feminist Reader.* Trade paperback ed. New York: The Modern Library, 2007.

Freeman, N. K. "Preschoolers' perceptions of gender appropriate toys and their parents' beliefs about genderized behaviors; Miscommunication, mixed messages, or hidden truths?" *Early Childhood Education Journal, Vol. 34(5)* (2007), 357–366. As referenced in Cordelia Fine. *Delusions of Gender.* New York: W.W. Norton & Company, Inc., 2010, 202.

Freud, Sigmund. *Three Essays on the Theory of Sexuality* (reprint, 7th ed.) [1975]. Translated by James Strachey. New York: Basic Books, 1962 [First English edition 1910, German 1905].

Frye, Marilyn. *The Politics of Reality: Essays in Feminist Theory.* New York: The Crossing Press, 1983), 129, 130, 132, 140. As referenced in Annemarie Jagose. *Queer Theory: An Introduction.* Melbourne: Melbourne University Press, 1996, 51–53.

Furth, Charlotte. "Androgynous Males and Deficient Females: Biology and Gender Boundaries in Sixteenth- and Seventeenth-Century China." In Henry Abelove, Michèle Aina Barale, and David M. Halperin, eds. *The Lesbian and Gay Studies Reader.* New York: Routledge, 1993, 479–497.

Garber, Eric. "A Spectacle in Color: The Lesbian and Gay Subculture of Jazz Age Harlem." *Hidden From History.* Eds. Martin Bauml Duberman, Martha Vicinus, and George Chauncey, Jr. New York: NAL Books, 1989, 318–331.

Gaudio, "Male Lesbians and Other Queer Notions in Hausa." In Steven O. Murray, and Will Roscoe, eds. *Boy-Wives and Female Husbands: Studies of African Homosexualities.* New York: Palgrave Macmillan, 1998, 124. As quoted in Wallace, "Discovering Homosexuality," in Robert Aldrich, ed. *Gay Life and Culture: A World History.* London: Thames & Hudson, Ltd., 2006, 249–270.

"Gay marriage 'improves health.'" BBC News Health. December 15, 2011. Accessed March 26, 2012. http://www.bbc.co.uk/news/health-16203621.

Geidner, Chris. "Acting Globally: Administration lays out commitment to support LGBT equality worldwide." December 8, 2011. Accessed Jan. 9, 2012. http://www.metroweekly.com/news/?ak=6845.

"Gendered Advertising Remixer." Designed by Jonathan McIntosh. Accessed April 1, 2012. http://www.genderremixer.com/.

"The Gender Gap: Women Are Still Missing as Sources for Journalists." Pew Research Center's Project for Excellence in Journalism. May 23, 2005. Journalism.org. http://www.journalism.org/node/141. As cited on International Women's Media Foundation. "Stats and Studies." Both accessed February 22, 2012. http://iwmf.org/archive/articletype/articleview/articleid/456/stats-and-studies.aspx.

"Gender Stereotypes: An Analysis of Popular Films and TV." Geena Davis Institute on Gender in the Media. Annenberg School for Communication. 2008. http://www.thegeenadavisinstitute.org/research/. Accessed February 22, 2012 via NOW.org. National Organization for Women. "Women in Media Fact Sheet." http://www.now.org/issues/media/women_in_media_facts.html.

"Genetic factors and hormones that determine gender." Human Embryology Organogenesis. Online course in embryology for medicine students. Universities of Fribourg, Lausanne and Bern (Switzerland). Embryology.ch. Accessed January 17, 2012. http://www.embryology.ch/anglais/ugenital/molec02.html.

Gillham, Nicholas Wright. *Genes, Chromosomes, and Disease: From Simple Traits, to Complex Traits, to Personalized Medicine*. Upper Saddle River: FT Press, 2011.

Gilmore, John H., et al. "Regional gray matter growth, sexual dimorphism, and cerebral asymmetry in the neonatal brain." *Journal of Neuroscience, Vol. 27(6)* (2007), 1,255–1,260. As referenced in Cordelia Fine. *Delusions of Gender*. New York: W. W. Norton & Company, Inc., 2010, 106.

Glavinic, Tonei. "Research Shows Lack of Support for Transgender and Gender-Nonconforming Youth in U.S. School Systems." *Student Pulse: Online Academic Student Journal, Vol. 2(1)* (2010).

"Global Media Monitoring Project 2010." Who Makes The News? Accessed February 22, 2012. http://www.whomakesthenews.org/images/stories/website/gmmp_reports/2010/gmmp_2010_prelim_key_en.pdf. As cited on Media Report to Women "Industry Statistics." http://www.mediareporttowomen.com/statistics.htm.

Gokova, Jonah. "Challenging Men to Reject Gender Stereotypes." *Sex Health Exchange (2)*(1998), 1–3. As quoted in Estelle B. Freedman, ed. *The Essential Feminist Reader*. Trade paperback ed. New York: The Modern Library, 2007, 422–423.

Gotanda, Neil. "A Critique of 'Our Constitution is Colorblind.'" In *Critical Race Theory: The Key Writings That Formed the Movement*. Kimberle Crenshaw, Neil Gotanda, and Gary Peller. Thomas, Kendall, ed. New York: The New Press, 1995. As referenced in Dean Spade. "Mutilating Gender." [In Stryker, Susan and Stephen Whittle, eds. *The Transgender Studies Reader*. New York: Routledge, 2006, 322.]

Grant, Jaime M., Lisa A. Mottet, Justin Tanis, Jack Harrison, Jody L. Herman, and Mara Keisling. "Injustice at Every Turn: A Report of the National Transgender Discrimination Survey." Washington: National Center for Transgender Equality and National Gay and Lesbian Task Force, 2011. [Also corresponding data sets, with permission.]

Green, Jamison. *Becoming a Visible Man.* Nashville, TN: Vanderbilt University Press, 2004.

Griffiths, A. J. F., J. H. Miller, D. T. Suzuki, et al. "Sex chromosomes and sex-linked inheritance." *An Introduction to Genetic Analysis,* 7th ed. New York: W. H. Freeman, 2000. Accessed January 17, 2012. Bookshelf. U.S. National Library of Medicine. http://www.ncbi.nlm.nih.gov/books/NBK22079/.

Grimké, Sarah M. "Letters on the Equality of the Sexes and the Condition of Woman." In Miriam Schneir, ed. *Feminism: The Essential Historical Writings.* New York: Vintage Books, 1994, 35–48. Originally published as Sarah M. Grimké. *Letters on the Equality of the Sexes and the Condition of Woman.* Boston, 1838. Reprinted by Burt Franklin (New York, 1970).

Grosz, Elizabeth. "Experimental Desire: Rethinking Queer Subjectivity." In Joan Copjec, ed. *Supposing the Subject.* London: Verso, 1994, 133–157. As quoted in Annemarie Jagose. *Queer Theory: An Introduction.* Melbourne: Melbourne University Press, 1996, 89.

Grow, Sammy. Personal interview. May 22, 2011.

Haeberle, Erwin J. *The Birth of Sexology: A Brief History in Documents.* World Association for Sexology. University of Michigan, 1983.

Halperin, David. "Homosexuality: A Cultural Construct. An Exchange with Richard Schneider." In *One Hundred Years of Homosexuality and Other Essays on Greek Love.* New York: Routledge, 1991, 41–53.

Halperin, David. *Saint Foucault: Towards a Gay Hagiography.* New York: Oxford University Press, 1995, 62. As quoted in Annemarie Jagose. *Queer Theory: An Introduction.* Melbourne: Melbourne University Press, 1996, 96.

Hamer, Dean H.; S. Hu, V. L. Magnuson, H. Hu, and A. M. Pattatucci. "A linkage between DNA markers on the X chromosome and male sexual orientation." *Science, Vol. 261 (5119)* (1993), 321–327. PubMed: 8332896.

Hamer, Dean H. "Genetics and Male Sexual Orientation." *Science, Vol. 285 (5429)* (1999), 803. DOI: 10.1126/science.285.5429.803a.

Hamzelou, Jessica. "Transsexual differences caught on brain scan." *New Scientist.* (January 26, 2011). Accessed July 5, 2011. http://www.newscientist.com/article/dn20032-transsexual-differences-caught-on-brain-scan.html.

Hanna, Kathleen. "Riot Grrrl Manifesto." Originally published in Kathleen Hanna. *Bikini Kill.* Olympia, WA 1992 No. 2.

"Hate Crime Statistics." FBI. Accessed February 9, 2012. http://www.fbi.gov/about-us/cjis/ucr/ucr#cius_hatecrime.

Herek, Gregory. "Lesbians and Gay Men in the U.S. Military: Historial Background 'Don't Ask, Don't Tell Revisited.'" Accessed January 8, 2012. http://psychology.ucdavis.edu/rainbow/html/military_history.html.

"Heteronormative." "Words You Might See Here." Reteaching Gender and Sexuality. Accessed March 6, 2012. http://www.reteachinggenderandsexuality.org/engage/.

Hillman, Thea. *Intersex (For Lack of a Better Word).* San Francisco: Manic D Press, Inc., 2008.

Melissa Hines. *Brain Gender.* Oxford and New York: Oxford University Press, 2004.

Hirschfeld, Magnus. *The Transvestites: The Erotic Drive to Cross-Dress.* In Susan Stryker, and Stephen Whittle. *The Transgender Studies Reader.* New York: Routledge, 2006, 28–39. From Magnus Hirschfeld. *The Transvestites: The Erotic Drive to Cross-Dress.* Translated by Michael A. Lombardi-Nash, PhD. Amherst, NY: Prometheus Books, 1991, 147–148, 158–159, 179–183, 198–199, 202–203, 211, 215–236 [1910].

"HIV in the United States: At A Glance." National Center for HIV/AIDS, Viral Hepatitis, STD, and TB Prevention. March 2012. Accessed March 27, 2012. http://www.cdc.gov/hiv/resources/factsheets/PDF/HIV_at_a_glance.pdf.

Holland, Jack. *Misogyny: The World's Oldest Prejudice.* New York: Carroll & Graf Publishers, 2006.

"Homicide and Domestic Violence Facts: When Men Murder Women." National Coalition Against Domestic Violence. NCADV Violence Policy Center Annual Report, 2004. Accessed March 19, 2012. http://www.ncdsv.org/images/NCADV_HomicideDVFacts.pdf.

hooks, bell. *Feminist Theory: From Margin to Center,* 2nd ed. Cambridge: South End Press, 2000. [1984].

"How many chromosomes do humans have?" National Human Genome Research Institute. Accessed January 17, 2012. http://www.genome.gov/26524120.

"H.R.3396— Defense of Marriage Act." Library of Congress. Thomas. Accessed February 9, 2012. http://thomas.loc.gov/cgi-bin/query/z?c104:H.R.3396.ENR:.

Hurley, Jennifer A., ed. *Feminism: Opposing Viewpoints.* San Diego: Greenhaven Press, Inc., 2001.

Hyde, Janet Shibley. "Men and Women: No Big Difference." *American Psychologist,* September 2005. APA Online. http://www.psychologymatters.org/nodifference.html. As referenced in Barbara J. Berg, *Sexism in America: Alive, Well, and Ruining Our Future.* Chicago: Lawrence Hill Books, 2009, 174–175.

Annemarie Jagose. *Queer Theory: An Introduction.* Melbourne: Melbourne University Press, 1996.

James, Joy and T. Denean Sharpley-Whiting, eds. *The Black Feminist Reader.* Malden: Blackwell Publishers Ltd, 2000.

Jeffreys, Sheila. *The Lesbian Heresy: A Feminist Perspective on the Lesbian Sexual Revolution.* Melbourne: Spinifex Press, 1993. As referenced in Annemarie Jagose. *Queer Theory: An Introduction.* Melbourne: Melbourne University Press, 1996, 51.

Johnson, David K. *The Lavender Scare: The Cold War Persecution of Gays and Lesbians in the Federal Government.* Chicago: University of Chicago Press, 2004.

Johnson, Scott. Personal interview. February 15, 2012.

Jones, Michael. "A History of HIV/AIDS and Its Effect on LGBT Communities." Change.org. October 5, 2008. Accessed March 27, 2012. http://news.change.org/stories/a-history-of-hiv-aids-and-its-effect-on-lgbt-communities.

Jordan-Young, Rebecca M. *Brain Storm: The Flaws in the Science of Sex Differences.* Cambridge, MA and London: Harvard University Press, 2010.

Kaiser, A., S. Haller, S. Schmitz, and C. Nitsch. "On sex/gender related similarities and differences in fMRI language research." *Brain Research Reviews, Vol. 61(2)* (2009), 443–453. As referenced in Jordan-Young, Rebecca M. *Brain Storm: The Flaws in the Science of Sex Differences.* Cambridge, MA, and London: Harvard University Press, 2010, 51.

Kaufman, Michael and Michael Kimmel. *The Guy's Guide to Feminism.* Berkeley: Seal Press, 2011.

Katz, Jonathan. *Gay American History: Lesbians & Gay Men in the U.S.A.,* New York: Thomas Cromwell, 1976.

Keisling, Mara and Lisa Mottet. "Cutting-Edge Issues in Transgender Rights." Presentation at Gender Odyssey Conference, Seattle, WA, August 6, 2011.

Kimmel, Michael S. *The Gendered Society,* (2nd ed.) New York and Oxford: Oxford University Press, 2004.

King, Hanna. Personal interview. May 18, 2011.

Kitamoto, Toshihiro. "Conditional disruption of synaptic transmission induces male–male courtship behavior in *Drosophila*." *Proceedings of the National Academy of Sciences, Vol. 99 (20)* (2002): 13,232–13,237. DOI:10.1073/pnas.202489099.

Klinger, Kimberly. "Women have the right to be prostitutes." In Christina Fisanick, ed. *Feminism.* Farmington Hills: Greenhaven Press, 2008, 88–98.

Knickmeyer, Rebecca; Simon Baron-Cohen, Peter Raggatt, and Kevin Taylor. "Foetal testosterone, social relationships, and restricted interests in children." *Journal of Child Psychology & Psychiatry, Vol. 46(2)* (2005), 198–210.

Kolata, G. "Math genius may have hormonal basis." *Science, Vol. 222(4630)* (1983), 1,312. As referenced in Cordelia Fine. *Delusions of Gender.* New York: W. W. Norton & Company, Inc., 2010, 106.

Krafft-Ebing, Richard von. *Psychopathia Sexualis with Special Reference to Contrary Sexual Instinct: A Medico-Legal Study.* In Susan Stryker, and Stephen Whittle. *The Transgender Studies Reader.* New York: Routledge, 2006, 22–27 [1877].

Kruijver, Frank P. M.; Jiang-Ning Zhou, Chris W. Pool, Michel A. Hofman, Louis J. G. Gooren, and Dick F. Swaab. "Male-to-female transsexuals have female neuron numbers in the limbic nucleus." *The Journal of Clinical Endocrinology & Metabolism, Vol. 85(5)* (2000). Retrieved July 5, 2011 from http://jcem.endojournals.org/cgi/content/full/85/5/2034.

Lancaster, Roger N. *The Trouble With Nature: Sex in Science and Popular Culture.* Berkeley and Los Angeles, CA: University of California Press, 2003.

Lauzen, Martha. *Boxed In.* Center for the Study of Women in Television and Film, San Diego State University. Accessed February 22, 2012. http://womenintvfilm. sdsu.edu/research.html. As cited on Media Report to Women "Industry Statistics." http://www.mediareporttowomen.com/statistics.htm

Lauzen, Martha. *Celluloid Ceiling.* Center for the Study of Women in Television and Film, San Diego State University. http://womenintvfilm.sdsu.edu/research.html. As cited on Media Report to Women "Industry Statistics." Accessed February 22, 2012. http://www.mediareporttowomen.com/statistics.htm.

*"Lawrence v. Texas,* 539 U.S. 558 (2003)." *Justia.* Accessed November 19, 2011.

http://supreme.justia.com/us/539/558/case.html.

Lee, Valerie E., Robert G. Croninger, Eleanor Linn, and Xianglei Chen. "The culture of sexual harassment in secondary schools," *American Educational Research Journal Vol. 33* (1993), 383–418, As referenced in Rosalind Barnett, and Caryl Rivers. *Same Difference: How Gender Myths Are Hurting Our Relationships, Our Children, and Our Jobs.* New York: Basic Books, 2004, 243.

Lerner, Gerda. *The Creation of Patriarchy.* New York: Oxford University Press, 1986 as referenced in Estelle B. Freedman. *No Turning Back: The History of Feminism and the Future of Women.* New York: Ballantine Books, 2002, 23–24.

LeVay, Simon. "A Difference in Hypothalamic Structure Between Heterosexual and Homosexual Men." *Science, Vol. 253 (5023)* (1991), 1,034–1,037. PubMed: 1887219.

Levy, G. D., and R. A. Haaf, "Detection of gender-related categories by 10-month-old infants." *Infant Behavior & Development, 17(4)* (1994), 457–459. As referenced in Cordelia Fine. *Delusions of Gender.* New York: W. W. Norton & Company, Inc., 2010, 211.

Lewes, Kenneth. *The Psychoanalytic Theory of Male Homosexuality.* New York: Simon & Schuster, 1988.

Lillie, F.R. "The theory of the free-martin." *Science 43* (1917): 39-53, as referred to in Anne Fausto-Sterling. *Sexing the Body.* New York, Basic Books, 2000, 163.

Logel, Christine; Emma C. Iserman, Paul G. Davies, Diane M. Quinn, and Steven J. Spencer, "The perils of double consciousness: The role of thought suppression in stereotype threat." *Journal of Experimental Social Psychology, Vol. 45(2)* (2008), 299–312. As referenced in Cordelia Fine. *Delusions of Gender.* New York: W. W. Norton & Company, Inc., 2010, 33.

Lohrasbi, Emery. Personal interview. April 29, 2011.

"Loux". Personal interview. May 17, 2011.

Lutchmaya, Svetlana, Simon Baron-Cohen, and Peter Raggatt. "Foetal testosterone and eye contact in 12-month-old human infants." *Infant Behavior and Development, Vol. 25* (2001), 327–335.

MacKinnon, Catherine A. "Feminism, Marxism, Method, and the State: An Agenda for Theory." *Signs, Vol. 7 (3)* (1982), 515–44, as quoted and referenced in Eve Kosofsky Sedgwick. *Between Men: English Literature and Male Homosexual Desire.* New York: Columbia University Press, 1992.

Majd, Katayoon, Jody Marksamer, and Carolyn Reyes. "Hidden Injustice: Lesbian, Gay, Bisexual, and Transgender Youth in Juvenile Courts." 2009. Equity Project. As referenced by Sarah Mountz. "Revolving Doors: LGBTQ Youth at the Interface of the Child Welfare and Juvenile Justice Systems." *LGBTQ Policy Journal at the Harvard Kennedy School: 2011 Edition.* Accessed March 29, 2012. http://isites.harvard.edu/icb/icb.do?keyword=k78405&pageid=icb.page414421.

"male." Oxford Dictionaries. April 2010. Oxford University Press. Accessed January 14, 2012. http://oxforddictionaries.com/definition/male.

"Margaret Chase Smith Biography." Margaret Chase Smith Library. Last Modified January 2012. Accessed February 6, 2012. http://www.mcslibrary.org/bio/biog.htm.

Marie Stopes International. Accessed February 2, 2012. http://www.mariestopes.org.uk/.

"Martha Wright Griffiths." National Women's History Project. Women's History Month; 2007 Honorees. Accessed February 6, 2012. http://nwhp.org/whm/griffiths_bio.php.

Martin, Elaine. "The Representative Role of Women Judges." *Judicature, Vol. 77* (1993a),

166–173. As referenced in T. Massie, S. Johnson, and Sara Margaret Gubala. "Of Gender and Race in the Decisions of Judges on The United States Courts of Appeals." Paper presented at the 2002 Midwest Political Science Association Annual Meeting, Chicago, IL. Accessed March 20, 2012. http://www.cas.sc.edu/poli/psrw/MassieJohnsonGubala.pdf.

Matzner, Andrew. "Prince, Virginia Charles." *glbtq: An Encyclopedia of Gay, Lesbian, Bisexual, Transgender, and Queer Culture.* Chicago: qlbtq, Inc., 2004. http://www.glbtq.com/social-sciences/prince_vc.html.

"Maxine Hong Kingston." Women's History. *Contemporary Authors Online,* Gale, 2009. Reproduced in *Biography Resource Center.* Farmington Hills, MI.: Gale, 2009. Accessed February 6, 2012. http://www.gale.cengage.com/free_resources/whm/bio/kingston_m.htm.

McFadden, Dennis and Edward G. Pasanen. "Comparison of the auditory systems of heterosexuals and homosexuals: Click-evoked otoacoustic emissions." *Proceedings of the National Academy of Sciences, Vol. 95 (5)* (1998), 2,709–2,713, referenced by "Born Gay." Accessed December 30, 2011. ProCon.org.

McQuiston, John T. "Christine Jorgensen, 62, Is Dead; Was First to Have a Sex Change." *The New York Times.* May 4, 1989. Accessed February 8, 2012. http://www.nytimes.com/1989/05/04/obituaries/christine-jorgensen-62-is-dead-was-first-to-have-a-sex-change.html.

Mead, Margaret. *Coming of Age in Samoa.* New York: William Morrow Paperbacks, 2001 [1928].

Mead, Margaret. *Sex and Temperament: In Three Primitive Societies.* New York: Harper Perennial, 2001. [1935].

Menefee-Libey, Sam. "For Transgender Americans, Don't Ask, Don't Tell Repeal Not Enough." Campus Progress. Center for American Progress. September 20, 2011. Accessed March 29, 2012. http://campusprogress.org/articles/for_transgender_americans_dont_ask_dont_tell_repeal_not_enough/.

"Metrosexual." Merriam-Webster Online Dictionary. Accessed March 20, 2012. http://www.merriam-webster.com/dictionary/metrosexual.

Meyerowitz, Joanne. *Holding Their Own: Working Women Apart from Family in Chicago, 1880–1930,* PhD. dissertation, Stanford University, 1983, 1. As referenced in Lillian Faderman. *Odd Girls and Twilight Lovers: A History of Lesbian Life in Twentieth-Century America.* New York: Penguin Group, 1991, 38.

Mill, John Stuart. "The Subjection of Women." In *Feminism: The Essential Historical Writings,* edited by Miriam Schneir. New York: Vintage Books, 1994 [1972]. Originally published as John Stuart Mill. *The Subjection of Women.* London, 1869. Reprinted by M.I.T. Press, Cambridge, MA, 1970.

*Miss Representation.* Dir. Jennifer Siebel Newsom. Girls' Club Entertainment, 2011.

Moè, Angelica. "Are males always better than females in mental rotation? Exploring a gender belief explanation." *Learning and Individual Differences, Vol. 19(1)* (2008), 21–27. As referenced in Cordelia Fine. *Delusions of Gender.* New York: W. W. Norton & Company, Inc., 2010, 28–29.

Mogul, Joey L., Ritchie, Andrea J., and Kay Whitlock. *Queer (In)justice: The Criminalization of LGBT People in the United States.* Boston: Beacon Press, 2011.

Mondschein, Emily R., Karen E. Adolph, and Catherine S. Tamis-LeMonda. "Gender Bias in Mothers' Expectations about Infant Crawling." *Journal of Experimental Child Psychology, Vol. 77(4)* (2000), 304–316. As referenced in Cordelia Fine. *Delusions of Gender.* New York: W. W. Norton & Company, Inc., 2010, 199.

Moore, Celia L.; Hui Dou, and Janice M. Juraska. "Maternal stimulation affects the number of motor neurons in a sexually dimorphic nucleus of the lumbar spinal cord." *Brain Research, Vol. 572(1-2)* (1992), 52–56. Referenced in Cordelia Fine. *Delusions of Gender.* New York: W. W. Norton & Company, Inc., 2010, 104-105.

Moore, D. S., and S. P. Johnson. "Mental rotation in human infants: A sex difference." *Psychological Science. Vol. 19(11)* (2008), 1,063–1,066. As referenced in Cordelia Fine. *Delusions of Gender.* New York: W. W. Norton & Company, Inc., 2010, 27.

Murray, Steven O. and Will Roscoe, eds. *Boy-Wives and Female Husbands: Studies of African Homosexualities.* New York: Palgrave Macmillan, 1998.

"Nancy Pelosi: Biography/About." Congresswoman Nancy Pelosi. DemocraticLeader.gov. Accessed February 6, 2012. http://pelosi.house.gov/about/biography.shtml.

Nash, Alison and Giordana Grossi. "Picking Barbie's brain: Inherent sex differences in scientific ability?" *Journal of Interdisciplinary Feminist Thought, Vol. 2(1)* (2007), Article 5. As referenced in Cordelia Fine. *Delusions of Gender.* New York: W. W. Norton & Company, Inc., 2010, 106.

Nash, A. and R. Krawczyk. "Boys' and girls' rooms revisited: The contents of boys' and girls' rooms in the 1990s." Paper presented at the Conference on Human Development, Pittsburgh, PA, 2007. As referenced in Cordelia Fine. *Delusions of Gender.* New York: W. W. Norton & Company, Inc., 2010, 198.

"National Crime Victimization Survey." U.S. Department of Justice. 2006–2010. As quoted in "How often does sexual assault occur?" Rape Abuse & Incest National Network. Accessed March 19, 2012. http://www.rainn.org/get-information/statistics/frequency-of-sexual-assault.

National Defense Research Institute. *Sexual Orientation and U.S. Military Personnel Policy: Options and Assessment.* Santa Monica, CA: Rand, 1993.

National Organization for Disorders of the Corpus Callosum. "What is the corpus callosum?" Accessed January, 16, 2012. https://www.nodcc.org.

n.b. *Asexy Life: On Asexuality and Challenging Heteronormativity.* Lansing, KS: Microcosm Publishing, initial publication date unknown [zine].

Nestle, Joan. "'I Lift My Face to The Hill': The Life of Mabel Hampton as Told by a White Woman" (1992). In *Queer Ideas: The David R. Kessler Lectures in Lesbian and Gay Studies.* New York: The Feminist Press at the City University of New York, 2003.

Nestle, Joan, Clare Howell, and Riki Wilchins, eds. *GenderQueer: Voices From Beyond the Sexual Binary.* Los Angeles and New York: alyson books, 2002.

Newton, Esther. "My Butch Career: A Memoir" (1996). In *Queer Ideas: The David R. Kessler Lectures in Lesbian and Gay Studies.* New York: The Feminist Press at the City University of New York, 2003.

Nguyen, Hannah-Hanh and Ann Marie Ryan. "Does Stereotype Threat Affect Test Performance of Minorities and Women? A Meta-Analysis of Experimental Evidence." *Journal of Applied Psychology, Vol. 93(6)* (2008): 1314-1334.

"Obama: DOMA Unconstitutional, DOJ Should Stop Defending In Court."AP/Huffington Post. Last Modified May 25, 2011. Accessed February 9, 2012. http://www.huffingtonpost.com/2011/02/23/obama-doma-unconstitutional_n_827134.html.

"Obama signs repeal of 'don't ask, don't tell' policy." CNN. December 22, 2010. Accessed January 8, 2012. http://articles.cnn.com/2010-12-22/politics dadt.repeal_1_repeal-openly-gay-men-president-barack-obama?_s= PM:POLITICS.

"On the Draft Convention on Political Rights of Women." National Coordinating Committee for UDHR50. Franklin and Eleanor Roosevelt Institute. Last Revised: August 5, 1998. Accessed February 1, 2012. http://www.udhr.org/history/124.htm.

"Out of The Picture 2007: Minority & Female TV Station Ownership in the United States." *Free Press.* October 2007. http://www.stopbigmedia.com/files/out_of_the_picture.pdf and "Off the Dial: Female and Minority Radio Station Ownership in the United States." *Free Press.* June 2007. http://www.stopbigmedia.com/files/off_the_dial.pdf Both accessed February 22, 2012 NOW.org. National Organization for Women. "Women in Media Fact Sheet." http://www.now.org/issues/media/women_in_media_facts.html.

Paoletti, Jo B. "The gendering of infants' and toddlers' clothing in America." In L. Martinez, and L. L. Ames, eds. *The Material Culture of Gender: The Gender of Material Culture.* Hanover, NH and London: University Press of New England, 1997: 27-35. As referenced in Cordelia Fine. *Delusions of Gender.* New York: W. W. Norton & Company, Inc., 2010, 207-209.

Pinker, Steven. *The Blank Slate.* New York: Penguin, 2003 [2002].

Poasa, K. H., R. Blanchard, and K. J. Zucker. "Birth order in transgendered males from Polynesia: a quantitative study of Samoan fa'afāfine."*Journal of Sex & Marital Therapy, Vol. 3 (1)*(2004), 13–23.

"Prevalence, Incidence, and Consequences of Violence Against Women Survey." National Institute of Justice and Centers for Disease Control and Prevention. 1998. As quoted in "Who are the Victims?" Rape, Abuse and Incest National Network. Accessed March 19, 2012. http://www.rainn.org/get-information/statistics/sexual-assault-victims.

ProCon.org. "Historical Timeline." Accessed December 20, 2011. http://borngay.procon.org/view.resource.php?resourceID=000028.

Prosser, Jay. *Second Skins: The Body Narratives of Transsexuality.* New York: Columbia University Press, 1998.

Rahman, Qazi, Veena Kumari, and Glenn D. Wilson. "Sexual orientation-related differences in prepulse inhibition of the human startle response." *Behavioral Neuroscience, Vol. 117(5)*(2003), 1,096–1,102. DOI: 10.1037/0735-7044.117.5.1096.

"Resolution on Sexual Orientation and Marriage." American Psychological Association.

Accessed November 19, 2011. http://www.apa.org/about/governance/council/policy/gay-marriage.pdf.

Rhode, Deborah L. *Speaking of Sex: The Denial of Gender Inequality.* Cambridge, MA: Harvard University Press, 1997, 19. As quoted in Cordelia Fine. *Delusions of Gender.* New York: W. W. Norton & Company, Inc., 2010, 216.

Rich, Adrienne. "Notes Toward a Politics of Location." In Estelle B. Freedman, ed. *The Essential Feminist Reader.* Trade paperback ed. New York: The Modern Library, 2007, 368–384. As published in *Blood, Bread, and Poetry: Selected Prose 1979–1985.* (New York: W.W. Norton & Company, 1986, 210–231.

Rich, Adrienne. "Compulsory Heterosexuality and Lesbian Existence." In Miriam Schneir, ed. *Feminism: The Essential Historical Writings.* New York: Vintage Books, 1994, 165. As quoted in Annemarie Jagose. *Queer Theory: An Introduction.* Melbourne: Melbourne University Press, 1996, 53.

Richtel, Matt. "For Pornographers, Internet's Virtues Turn to Vices." The New York Times, June 6, 2007. Web. Nov. 17, 2009. Accessed February 6, 2012. http://www.nytimes.com/2007/06/02/technology/02porn.html.

"*Roe v. Wade* (No. 70-18) 314 F.Supp. 1217, affirmed in part and reversed in part." Legal Information Institute. Cornell University Law School. Accessed February 2, 2012. http://www.law.cornell.edu/supct/html/historics/ USSC_CR_0410_0113_ZS.html.

Roosevelt, Anna C. "Gender in Human Evolution: Sociobiology Revisited and Revised." In *In Pursuit of Gender: Worldwide Archaeological Approaches.* Eds. S. M. Nelson, and M. Rosen-Ayalon. Lanham, MD: Rowman and Littlefield Publishers, 2002, 355–376.

Roughgarden, Joan. *Evolution's Rainbow: Diversity, Gender, and Sexuality in Nature and People.* Berkeley and Los Angeles: University of California Press, 2004.

Rush, Ramona R., Carol E. Oukrop, and Pamela J. Creedon, eds. *Seeking Equity for Women in Journalism and Mass Communication Education.* Mahwah, NJ: Lawrence Erlbaum Associates, Inc., 2004.

Rust, P. "Two Many and Not Enough: The Meanings of Bisexual Identities." *Journal of Bisexuality, Vol. 31* (2001), 58. As referenced in Sean Cahill, "Bisexuality: Dispelling the myths." National Gay and Lesbian Task Force, 1.

Safren, S. A. and R. G. Heimberg. "Depression, hopelessness, suicidality, and related factors in sexual minority and heterosexual adolescents." *Journal of Consulting and Clinical Psychology, Vol. 67(6)* (1999); 859–866.

Savic, Ivanka, Hans Berglund, and Per Lindström. "Brain response to putative pheromones in homosexual men." *Proceedings of the National Academy of Sciences, Vol. 102 (20)* (2005), 7,356–7,361. DOI:10.1073/pnas.0407998102.

Schackelford, T., D. Buss, and V. Weekes-Shackelford. "Wife killings in the context of a lovers' triangle." *Basic and Applied Social Psychology, Vol. 25(2)* (2003), 137–143.

Schilt, Kristen and Laurel Westbrook. "Doing Gender, Doing Heteronormativity: 'Gender Normals', Transgender People, and the Social Maintenance of Heterosexuality." *Gender & Society Vol. 23 (4)* (2009), 440–464.

Schneir, Miriam, ed. *Feminism: The Essential Historical Writings.* New York: Vintage Books, 1994 [1972].

"Secondary Sex Characteristics." Magnus Hirschfeld Archive for Sexology. Accessed January 13, 2012. http://www2.hu-berlin.de/sexology/ATLAS_EN/html/ secondary_characteristics.html.

Sedgwick, Eve Kosofsky. *Between Men: English Literature and Male Homosexual Desire*. New York: Columbia University Press, 1992 [1985].

Sedgwick, Eve Kosofsky. *Epistemology of the Closet*. Berkeley: University of California Press, 1990.

Sedgwick, Eve Kosofsky. *Tendencies*. Durham: Duke University Press, 1993, 9. As referenced in Annemarie Jagose. *Queer Theory: An Introduction*. Melbourne: Melbourne University Press, 1996, 99.

"Shifting the Paradigm of Intersex Treatment." Intersex Society of North America. Accessed January 17, 2012. http://www.isna.org/compare.

Shore, Rima and Barbara Shore. "Reducing the Teen Death Rate." KIDS COUNT Indicator Brief. The Annie E. Casey Foundation. July 2009. Accessed March 13, 2012. http://www.aboutpinellaskids.org/system/medias/152/original/ReducingTeenDeaths.pdf.

Silk, Joan B. "Primatoloigcal Perspectives on Gender Hierarchies." In *Sex and Gender Hierarchies*, ed. Barbara Diane Miller. Cambridge, England: Cambridge University Press, 1993, 212–235.

Smith, Barbara. "African American Lesbian and Gay History: An Exploration" (1994). In *Queer Ideas: The David R. Kessler Lectures in Lesbian and Gay Studies*. New York: The Feminist Press at the City University of New York, 2003.

Smith, J. C. and Brian Hogan, David Ormerod, ed. *Smith and Hogan Criminal Law: Cases and Materials*, 10th Edition. New York: Oxford University Press, 2009.

Soares, Rachel; Jan Combopiano, Allyson Regis, Yelena Shur, and Rosita Wong. "2010 Catalyst Census: Fortune 500 Women Executive Officers and Top Earners," Accessed February 4, 2012. http://www.catalyst.org/publication/459/2010-catalyst-census-fortune-500-women-executive-officers-and-top-earners.

Spade, Dean. "Building Trans Movements for Justice: Dismantling Racism, Ending Poverty, and Building a World We Want to Live In." Key Note Speech presented at Gender Odyssey Conference, Seattle, WA, August 6, 2011.

Spade, Dean. "Mutilating Gender." In Susan Stryker, and Stephen Whittle. *The Transgender Studies Reader*. New York: Routledge, 2006, 315–331.

Spain, Daphne. *Gendered Spaces*. Chapel Hill, NC and London: The University of North Carolina Press, 1992.

Stanton, Elizabeth Cady. "Declaration of Sentiments." In Estelle B. Freedman, ed. *The Essential Feminist Reader*. Trade paperback ed. New York: The Modern Library, 2007, 58–62. As in *History of Woman Suffrage: Vol. 1, 1,848-1,861*. Elizabeth Cady Stanton, Susan B. Anthony, and Matilda Joslyn Gage, eds. New York: Fowler & Wells, 1881, 70–73.

*State of World Population 2000: Lives Together, Worlds Apart: Men and Women in a Time of Change*. New York: United Nations, 2000. As quoted in *Handbook on effective police responses to violence against women*. United Nations Office on Drugs and Crime. New York: United Nations, 2010.

Stone, Lucy. "Disappointment Is the Lot of Woman." In Schneir, Miriam, ed. *Feminism: The Essential Historical Writings.* New York: Vintage Books, 1994, 106–109 [1972]. As in *History of Woman Suffrage, Vol. 1, 1,848-1,861.* Elizabeth Cady Stanton, Susan B. Anthony, and Matilda Joslyn Gage, eds. (New York: Fowler & Wells, 1881, 165–167.

Stone, Sandy. "The 'Empire' Strikes Back: A Posttranssexual Manifesto." In *Body Guards: The Cultural Politics of Gender Ambiguity.* Ed. Julia Epstein, and Kristina Straub. New York: Routledge, 1991, 280–304. As referenced in Susan Stryker. "(De)Subjugated Knowledges: An Introduction to Transgender Studies." In Susan Stryker, and Stephen Whittle. *The Transgender Studies Reader.* New York: Routledge, 2006, 1-17.

"Stonewalled: Police Abuse and Misconduct Against Lesbian, Gay, Bisexual and Transgender People in the U.S." Amnesty International. September 21, 2005. Accessed March 26, 2012. http://www.amnesty.org/en/library/asset/AMR51/122/2005/en/2200113d-d4bd-11dd-8a23-d58a49c0d652/amr511222005en.pdf.

Sax, Leonard. *Why Gender Matters.* New York: Doubleday, 2005.

"Study: Men with older brothers more likely to be gay." *The Associated Press. USA Today.* June 26, 2006. Accessed January 18, 2012. http://www.usatoday.com/news/nation/2006-06-26-brothers_x.htm

Stryker, Susan. "(De)Subjugated Knowledges: An Introduction to Transgender Studies." In Susan Stryker and Stephen Whittle. *The Transgender Studies Reader.* New York: Routledge, 2006, 1–17.

Stryker, Susan and Stephen Whittle. *The Transgender Studies Reader.* New York: Routledge, 2006.

Substance Abuse and Mental Health Services Administration (SAMHSA), the Center for Mental Health Services (CMHS), offices of the U.S. Department of Health and Human Services. As referenced by "Eating Disorders 101 Guide." The Renfrew Center Foundation for Eating Disorders. Accessed February 22, 2012. www.renfrew.org.

"Survivors of Prostitution and Trafficking Manifesto." Survivors of Prostitution and Trafficking Conference. "Who Represents Women in Prostitution." European Parliament. Oct. 17, 2005. In Christina Fisanick, ed. *Feminism.* Farmington Hills: Greenhaven Press, 2008, 102–107.

"Talking Points about Employment Protections." *Get Busy. Get Equal.* ACLU. Accessed March 29, 2012. http://gbge.aclu.org/discrimination/talking-points-about-employment-protections.

Taormino, Tristan. *Opening Up: A Guide to Creating and Sustaining Open Relationships.* San Francisco: Cleis Press, 2008.

Tavris, Carol. *The Mismeasure of Woman.* New York: Simon & Schuster, 1992.

Theriot, Nancy M. *Mothers & Daughters in Nineteenth-Century America: The Biosocial Construction of Femininity.* Lexington, KY: The University Press of Kentucky, 1996.

Thompson, Denise. *Flaws in the Social Fabric: Homosexuals and Society in Sydney.* Sydney: George Allen & Unwin, 1985.

Thorne, Barrie. *Gender Play: Boys and Girls in School.* Piscataway, NJ: Rutgers University Press, 1994. As referenced in Rosalind Barnett, and Caryl Rivers. *Same Difference: How Gender Myths Are Hurting Our Relationships, Our Children, and Our Jobs.* New York: Basic Books, 2004, 220–224.

"Title IX, Education Amendments of 1972." United States Department of Labor. Accessed March 4, 2012. http://www.dol.gov/oasam/regs/statutes/titleix.htm.

"Title 10 of the United States Code." Cornell Law. Accessed December 22, 2011. http://www.law.cornell.edu/uscode/10/654.html#b.

Trans Murder Monitoring Project. Transrespect Versus Transphobia Worldwide. Transgender Europe. March 2012 Update. Accessed March 30, 2012. http://www.transrespect-transphobia.org/en_US/tvt-project/tmm-results/march-2012.htm.

Traub, Valerie. "The Psychomorphology of the Clitoris." *GLQ: A Journal of Lesbian and Gay Studies, Vol. 2 (1-2)* (1995), 81–113.

Truth, Sojourner. (1851). Speech presented at the Ohio Woman's Rights Convention. In Estelle B. Freedman, ed. *The Essential Feminist Reader.* Trade paperback ed. New York: The Modern Library, 2007, 64. As in *The Anti-Slavery Bugle* Salem, Ohio, June 21, 1851; reprinted in C. Peter Ripley, ed. *The Black Abolitionist Papers, Vol. 4: The United States 1847–1858.* Chapel Hill: University of North Carolina Press, 1991, 81–83.

"Two Spirits: A Map of Gender-Diverse Cultures." *(I)ndependent Lens,* PBS. Accessed January 13, 2012. http://www.pbs.org/independentlens/two-spirits/map.html.

Udry, J. Richard. "The Nature of Gender." *Demography, Vol. 31 (4)* (1994), 561–573. Accessed January, 16, 2012. http://www.jstor.org/pss/2061790.

"Universal Declaration of Human Rights." National Coordinating Committee for UDHR50. Franklin and Eleanor Roosevelt Institute. Last Revised: August 5, 1998. Accessed February 1, 2012. http://www.udhr.org/history/Biographies/bioer.htm

Van Leeuwen, James M. et al. "Lesbian, gay, and bisexual homeless youth: An eight-city public health perspective." *Child Welfare, Vol. 85(2)* (2006): 151–170. As referenced by Sarah Mountz. "Revolving Doors: LGBTQ Youth at the Interface of the Child Welfare and Juvenile Justice Systems." *LGBTQ Policy Journal at the Harvard Kennedy School: 2011 Edition.* Accessed March 29, 2012. http://isites.harvard.edu/icb/icb.do?keyword=k78405&pageid=icb.page414421.

Walker, Rebecca. "Becoming the Third Wave." In Estelle B. Freedman, ed. *The Essential Feminist Reader.* Trade paperback ed. New York: The Modern Library, 2007, 398–401. Originally published in *Ms.,* Jan.-Feb. 1992, 39–41.

Wallace, Lee. "Discovering Homosexuality: Cross-Cultural Comparison and the History of Sexuality." In Robert Aldrich, ed. *Gay Life and Culture: A World History.* London: Thames & Hudson Ltd., 2006, 249–270.

In Stryker, Susan and Stephen Whittle, eds. *The Transgender Studies Reader.* New York: Routledge, 2006

Weeks, Jeffrey. *Coming Out: Homosexual Politics in Britain from the Nineteenth Century to the Present.* London: Quartet Books, 1977, 2, 203. As quoted in Annemarie Jagose. *Queer Theory: An Introduction.* Melbourne: Melbourne University Press, 1996, 15–16, 45.

Weisberg, Ryan. Personal interview. January 17, 2012.

"What are zines?" *Zine World: A Reader's Guide to the Underground Press.* Accessed March 29, 2012. http://www.undergroundpress.org/faq/.

"What color for your baby?" *Parents, Vol. 14(3)* (1939), 98. Quoted in Jo B. Paoletti. "The gendering of infants' and toddlers' clothing in America." In L. Martinez, L. L. Ames, eds. *The Material Culture of Gender: The Gender of Material Culture.* Hanover, NH, and London: University Press of New England, 1997, 27-35. As referenced in Cordelia Fine. *Delusions of Gender.* New York: W. W. Norton & Company, Inc., 2010, 208.

"What is DNA?" Genetics Home Reference. U.S. National Library of Medicine. Accessed January 17, 2012. http://ghr.nlm.nih.gov/handbook/basics/dna.

"What is an endocrinologist?" The Hormone Foundation. Accessed March 14, 2012. http://www.hormone.org/Public/endocrinologist.cfm.

"What is heteronormativity?" Gender and Education Association. March 26, 2011. Accessed March 3, 2012. http://www.genderandeducation.com/issues/what-is-heteronormativity/.

"What is intersex?" Intersex Society of North America. Accessed January 17, 2012. http://www.isna.org/faq/what_is_intersex.

"When Gender and Gender Identity are Not the Same." *The Rights Stuff Newsletter,* November 2006. Accessed January 11, 2012. http://www.humanrights.state.mn.us/education/articles/rs06_4gender_protections.html.

White, Edmund. "The Personal is Political: Queer Fiction and Criticism" (1993). In *Queer Ideas: The David R. Kessler Lectures in Lesbian and Gay Studies.* New York: The Feminist Press at the City University of New York, 2003.

Wijngaard, Marianne van den. *Reinventing the Sexes: The Biomedical Construction of Femininity and Masculinity.* Bloomington, IN: Indiana University Press, 1997 [Amsterdam, 1991].

Wikan, Unni. "The Omani Xanith: A Third Gender Role?" *Man, Vol. 13, No. 3* (1978), 473–475.

Wilber, Shannan, Carolyn Reyes, and Jody Marksamer. "The Model Standards Project: Creating Inclusive Systems for LGBT Youth in Out-of-Home Care." *Child Welfare, Vol. 85(2)* (2006), 133–149. As referenced by Sarah Mountz. "Revolving Doors: LGBTQ Youth at the Interface of the Child Welfare and Juvenile Justice Systems." *LGBTQ Policy Journal at the Harvard Kennedy School: 2011 Edition.* Accessed March 29, 2012. http://isites.harvard.edu/icb/icb.do?keyword=k78405&pageid=icb.page414421.

Williams, Joan C. *Reshaping the Work-Family Debate: Why Men and Class Matter.* Cambridge, MA, and London: Harvard University Press, 2010.

Wittig, Monique. "One Is Not Born a Woman." In Estelle B. Freedman, ed. *The Essential Feminist Reader.* Trade paperback ed. New York: The Modern Library, 2007, 360–366. Originally published in *Feminist Issues, Vol. 1, No. 2* (1981), 47–50, 52–53.

Wolf, Naomi. *The Beauty Myth: How Images of Beauty Are Used Against Women.* New York: Anchor, 1992.

Wollstonecraft, Mary. *A Vindication of the Rights of Women: With Strictures on Political and Moral Subjects,* 3rd ed. London: J. Johnson, No. 72, St. Paul's Church Yard, 1796.

"Women in Elective Office 2011," Center for American Women and Politics. Rutgers, the State University of New Jersey. Accessed February 4, 2012. http://www.cawp.rutgers.edu/fast_facts/levels_of_office/documents/elective.pdf.

*Women in the Labor Force: A Databook.* U.S. Department of Labor. U.S. Bureau of Labor Statistics. December 2011, updated February 9, 2012. Accessed February 23, 2012. http://www.bls.gov/cps/wlf-databook-2011.pdf

The World Professional Health Association for Transgender Health. *Standards of Care for the Health of Transsexual, Transgender, and Gender Nonconforming People,* 7th Version (2011). www.wpath.org.

Young, R. M. and E. Balaban. "Psychoneuroindocrinology." *Nature, Vol. 443* (2006), 634. As referenced in Cordelia Fine. *Delusions of Gender.* New York: W. W. Norton & Company, Inc., 2010, 157–158.

Zihlman, Adrienne L. "Sex Differences and Gender Hierarchies Among Primates: An Evolutionary Perspective." In *Sex and Gender Hierarchies.* Ed. Barbara Diane Miller. Cambridge, England: Cambridge University Press, 1993, 32–56.

Zupanc, Günther K. H. *Behavioral Neurobiology: An Integrative Approach.* New York: Oxford University Press, 2010.

# ACKNOWLEDGEMENTS

My first thanks go to the many scholars and activists whose work I draw heavily upon in this book, especially: Annemarie Jagose, Anne Fausto-Sterling, Cordelia Fine, Estelle B. Freedman, Susan Stryker, Dean Spade, Judith Butler, Rebecca M. Jordan-Young and Lillian Faderman.

Secondly, to Jeffrey Lewis for believing in this project and in the necessity of interweaving social justice work with all artistic endeavors. A huge, special thank you to Dawn Reshen, whose idea it was that I write this book. Thank you for understanding how important it is that academics not be the only voices heard on these subjects. To my editor, Merrilee Warholak, and everyone at For Beginners. To Frank Weimann and Elyse Tanzillo, whose assistance in my literary career has been so great as to render most of my opportunities in their debt. To Chris Estey and Dave Halsell, for helping the book find a voice in a daunting marketplace. Belisa Vranich, for friendship and for saying all the right things.

Thank you to those who read early drafts and offered feedback: Sid Jordan, Noah Collins, Ingrid Dahl, and Emily Wittenhagen. Eva Jakubowicz, for assistance in transcribing interviews. To everyone who allowed me to interview them for this book. Special thanks to Scott Johnson, Hanna Shimona Kipnis King, Emery Lohrasbi, Ryan Weisberg, Jana Ekdahl, Sammy Grow and Loux. Barb Clark-Elliott and everyone at PFLAG. Aidan Key at Gender Odyssey. Jack Harrison, Justin Tanis, and both the National Gay and Lesbian Taskforce and the National Center for Trans Equality, for access to data sets. Jessica Mack, for current reproductive health information. Jon Horn, for art and synergy. Thank you to everyone at Reteaching Gender and Sexuality for the access and insights you offered me. Thank you to everyone at The Vera Project: You are my inspiration in every effort I make for a better world. Special thanks to Alison Kreitzberg, Theo Shure, Rani Ban, Sequoia O'Connell, Ryan Rood, Monica Martinez, Chris Reath, Kate Becker, Eric Carnell, Alix Kolar, Johnathan Smith, and Jeffery McNulty for constantly reminding me that my allyship matters.

Thank you to my family: My incredible parents, Robert and Diane Garbacik; my beloved brother, Jesse; Don and Linda Fucci; Bob and Eleanor Chezako; Kate Wing, Tom and Adam Gee. Thank you to all of my friends, both in Seattle and back east, for not giving up on me when I disappear into my work. Extra special thanks to Laura Borrelli, my platonic soul mate. Thank you for fiscal support in the completion of this book: Henry Joseph, Garrett Wenig, Jeffery McNulty, Andrew Parker, Paige Weinheimer, Tristan Carosino, Andrea Kao, Kristina Goetz, Sean Walker, Jon Horn, Kira Cox, Jocelyn Johnson, Morgan Hargraves, Patrick Kettner, David Dawes, Alex Billig, Don and Linda Fucci, Kim Berardi, Carole Powell-Gerber, Marc Mazique, Adam Phillabaum, and Jenny Wu.

Above all else, thank you to Joshua Powell for tireless support, encouragement, love, devotion, honesty, and always bringing out the best version of me. There is absolutely no way I could have done this without you.

# THE FOR BEGINNERS® SERIES

| | |
|---|---|
| AFRICAN HISTORY FOR BEGINNERS: | ISBN 978-1-934389-18-8 |
| ANARCHISM FOR BEGINNERS: | ISBN 978-1-934389-32-4 |
| ARABS & ISRAEL FOR BEGINNERS: | ISBN 978-1-934389-16-4 |
| ART THEORY FOR BEGINNERS: | ISBN 978-1-934389-47-8 |
| ASTRONOMY FOR BEGINNERS: | ISBN 978-1-934389-25-6 |
| AYN RAND FOR BEGINNERS: | ISBN 978-1-934389-37-9 |
| BARACK OBAMA FOR BEGINNERS, AN ESSENTIAL GUIDE: | ISBN 978-1-934389-44-7 |
| BLACK HISTORY FOR BEGINNERS: | ISBN 978-1-934389-19-5 |
| THE BLACK HOLOCAUST FOR BEGINNERS: | ISBN 978-1-934389-03-4 |
| BLACK WOMEN FOR BEGINNERS: | ISBN 978-1-934389-20-1 |
| CHOMSKY FOR BEGINNERS: | ISBN 978-1-934389-17-1 |
| DADA & SURREALISM FOR BEGINNERS: | ISBN 978-1-934389-00-3 |
| DANTE FOR BEGINNERS: | ISBN 978-1-934389-67-6 |
| DECONSTRUCTION FOR BEGINNERS: | ISBN 978-1-934389-26-3 |
| DEMOCRACY FOR BEGINNERS: | ISBN 978-1-934389-36-2 |
| DERRIDA FOR BEGINNERS: | ISBN 978-1-934389-11-9 |
| EASTERN PHILOSOPHY FOR BEGINNERS: | ISBN 978-1-934389-07-2 |
| EXISTENTIALISM FOR BEGINNERS: | ISBN 978-1-934389-21-8 |
| FDR AND THE NEW DEAL FOR BEGINNERS: | ISBN 978-1-934389-50-8 |
| FOUCAULT FOR BEGINNERS: | ISBN 978-1-934389-12-6 |
| GLOBAL WARMING FOR BEGINNERS: | ISBN 978-1-934389-27-0 |
| HEIDEGGER FOR BEGINNERS: | ISBN 978-1-934389-13-3 |
| ISLAM FOR BEGINNERS: | ISBN 978-1-934389-01-0 |
| JANE AUSTEN FOR BEGINNERS: | ISBN 978-1-934389-61-4 |
| JUNG FOR BEGINNERS: | ISBN 978-1-934389-76-8 |
| KIERKEGAARD FOR BEGINNERS: | ISBN 978-1-934389-14-0 |
| LACAN FOR BEGINNERS: | ISBN 978-1-934389-39-3 |
| LINGUISTICS FOR BEGINNERS: | ISBN 978-1-934389-28-7 |
| MALCOLM X FOR BEGINNERS: | ISBN 978-1-934389-04-1 |
| MARX'S *DAS KAPITAL* FOR BEGINNERS: | ISBN 978-1-934389-59-1 |
| MCLUHAN FOR BEGINNERS: | ISBN 978-1-934389-75-1 |
| NIETZSCHE FOR BEGINNERS: | ISBN 978-1-934389-05-8 |
| PHILOSOPHY FOR BEGINNERS: | ISBN 978-1-934389-02-7 |
| PLATO FOR BEGINNERS: | ISBN 978-1-934389-08-9 |
| POETRY FOR BEGINNERS: | ISBN 978-1-934389-46-1 |
| POSTMODERNISM FOR BEGINNERS: | ISBN 978-1-934389-09-6 |
| RELATIVITY & QUANTUM PHYSICS FOR BEGINNERS: | ISBN 978-1-934389-42-3 |
| SARTRE FOR BEGINNERS: | ISBN 978-1-934389-15-7 |
| SHAKESPEARE FOR BEGINNERS: | ISBN 978-1-934389-29-4 |
| STRUCTURALISM & POSTSTRUCTURALISM FOR BEGINNERS: | ISBN 978-1-934389-10-2 |
| WOMEN'S HISTORY FOR BEGINNERS: | ISBN 978-1-934389-60-7 |
| UNIONS FOR BEGINNERS: | ISBN 978-1-934389-77-5 |
| U.S. CONSTITUTION FOR BEGINNERS: | ISBN 978-1-934389-62-1 |
| ZEN FOR BEGINNERS: | ISBN 978-1-934389-06-5 |
| ZINN FOR BEGINNERS: | ISBN 978-1-934389-40-9 |